'*Informative and well-judged . . . There is so much that is inspirational in this book*'
NICHOLAS LEZARD, *Guardian*

'*You haven't walked the streets of London unless you've understood the secret history of revolt and rebellion hidden all around you. Rosenberg takes you there as no other writer has done*'
PAUL MASON

David Rosenberg's subtle, wide-ranging Rebel Footprints *connects place to place and era to era . . . A book of detail and passion*
DANNY DORLING,
author of *Inequality and the 1%*

This brilliant book is a fitting testimonial to the collective struggles of Londoners of every colour and creed
FRANCES O'GRADY,
General Secretary of the TUC

Anyone who wants to know how the individual human spirit can assert itself, whether in the city or the suburbs, could do no better than turn to Rebel Footprints
JACQUELINE BANNERJEE,
Times Literary Supplement

Rosenberg brings his London stories and their characters alive
DAVE HILL, *Guardian*

REBEL
FOOTPRINTS

REBEL
FOOTPRINTS

*A Guide to Uncovering
London's Radical History*

SECOND EDITION

David Rosenberg

Foreword by Ash Sarkar

This edition published 2019 by Pluto Press
First published 2015 by Pluto Press
345 Archway Road, London N6 5AA

www.plutobooks.com

British Library Cataloguing in Publication Data
A catalogue record for this book is available from the British Library

ISBN 978 0 7453 3856 9 Hardback
ISBN 978 0 7453 3855 2 Paperback
ISBN 978 1 7868 0414 3 PDF eBook
ISBN 978 1 7868 0416 7 Kindle eBook
ISBN 978 1 7868 0415 0 EPUB eBook

This book is printed on paper suitable for recycling and made from fully
managed and sustained forest sources. Logging, pulping and manufacturing
processes are expected to conform to the environmental standards of the
country of origin.

10 9 8 7 6 5 4 3 2

Illustrations: Chris Browne
Typesetting: Melanie Patrick

For Julia, Jacob and Reuben,
and in memory of a ground-breaking London historian,
Bill Fishman (1921–2014)

CONTENTS

ACKNOWLEDGEMENTS

I would like to thank the staff at Pluto Press, who have been consistently encouraging and helpful. Thanks to the staff of the libraries and archives who have provided access to historical materials and assistance with images: Bishopsgate Institute (special thanks to Stefan Dickers); British Library Newspaper Archive; East End Women's Museum; Hull History Centre; Humanist Library, Conway Hall; Labour History Archive at the People's History Museum; LSE Reading Room; Marx Memorial Library; Modern Records Centre, Warwick University; Southwark Local History Library; Tower Hamlets Local History Library; TUC Library Collections; Wandsworth Heritage Service; Women's Library at LSE; and the Working Class Movement Library. Thanks to City Lit students who road-tested several walks and gave invaluable feedback. Special thanks to Chris Browne at Pluto Press for mapping the walks so imaginatively and helping with photos. Thanks also to musician, activist and fellow West Ham fan, Billy Bragg, for his foreword to the first edition, and to writer, broadcaster and activist Ash Sarkar for her foreword to this second edition. Finally I would like to thank Julia Bard for expert editorial advice and personal encouragement and support.

FOREWORD

Which is the biggest gang in London? In the years following the 2011 riots after the killing of Mark Duggan, territories have become ever more fragmented and fractious. Postcode wars are getting smaller. But perhaps it's time to cede the honour to the Metropolitan Police. Despite our CCTV-saturated streets, not a single officer has been successfully convicted in a criminal court for any of the 180-plus deaths at their hands since the millennium. The majority of the victims were in custody, but 22 were shot and 44 died during pursuit.

Now, though, even the Metropolitan Police find that their domain is under threat from interlopers. You'll see them around Camden, Greenwich, Newham, Tower Hamlets. The footsoldiers of gentrification trussed up in stab-proof vests and hi-vis, clunky walkie-talkies clipped to the waist. These private security workers are to police what hoverflies are to wasps; responding to noise complaints and displacing rough sleepers on behalf of whatever housing association or corporation it is they work for.

But their power rests on more than imitation. London is in the middle of a wave of urban enclosures – except this time, there aren't any fences to let you know when you're on private land. The only way you'll know is when a security worker orders you to stop doing something like filming, drinking, or lying down on the wrong bit of grass. Corporations are winning a turf war that most of the city doesn't even know it's fighting.

As David Rosenberg explores in this book, London has always been a city of thieves. Not just muggers and cutpurses but, as pointed out in a new chapter, also the wardens of Fleet Prison, who would charge prisoners for food, lodging and the privilege of being unshackled. The jailer's racket of the eighteenth century has enjoyed a second-life in the modern day, as G4S, Serco and Sodexo lap up lucrative contracts to incarcerate one of the biggest prison populations of any country in Europe.

A second new chapter includes a social commentator's disparaging quote about the nineteenth-century slums in Bethnal Green and Shoreditch: 'Industry is the exception, robbery is the rule.' With rents for a one-bedroom flat costing around £2,000 a month on Boundary Street in 2018, the landlord class have certainly kept the spirit of 'Old Nichol' alive.

But as *Rebel Footprints* reminds the reader at each turn, London isn't just the product of scams and exploitation, but of collective struggle too. Our city belongs to the tailors and bakers, the matchwomen, rioters and rent strikers – and perhaps if we draw inspiration from these repertoires of organising and insurrection, it could belong to us too. This book isn't a mere guided tour of London's curios. It's the basis of a radical project in its own right. It's a call to walk the streets, and learn their histories, so that we might just one day run this city.

Ash Sarkar

INTRODUCTION

REBELLIOUS CITY

London from the 1830s to the 1930s

[A]gainst those who laud the present state of society, with its unjustly rich and its unjustly poor, with its palaces and its slums, its millionaires and its paupers, be it ours to proclaim that there is a higher ideal in life than that of being first in the race for wealth . . . Be it ours to declare that health, comfort, leisure, culture, plenty for every individual are far more desirable than the breathless struggle for existence, furious trampling down of the weak by the strong, huge fortunes accumulated out of the toil of others, to be handed down to those who had done nothing to earn them.

Annie Besant

The writer and activist Annie Besant wrote these extraordinary lines in 1885,[1] when she was living in the comfort of London's West End but becoming increasingly immersed, albeit transiently, in the struggles for better lives led by impoverished Eastenders. She depicts a city mired in conflict between the powerful and the marginalised, the exploiters and the exploited, and the brazen

---

[1] 'The Evolution of Society', published in *Our Corner*, September 1885.

sense of entitlement by those who were ravaging the lives of an underclass. Her description reads just as hauntingly today as the struggles for a more equal city that marked the decades after the Second World War have given rise to a widening gap between London's rich and poor. The wealthy classes are rampantly recolonising significant pockets of inner London, expanding the number of gated communities, installing exclusive boutiques, gyms, restaurants and luxury outlets, while pushing long-standing residents towards the city limits, where new pound shops open weekly.

But Besant was writing, speaking and acting in the middle of a remarkable era of campaigning and protest, in which significant numbers of London's citizens of all ages showed that they refused to accept injustice. Five decades earlier, on 13 May 1833, around 3,000 people gathered for a political rally in London's Coldbath Fields – an open space lying in the shadow of London's largest prison, the Middlesex House of Correction, which occupied the plot of land between Farringdon Road and Gray's Inn Road where Mount Pleasant Postal Sorting Office stood throughout the twentieth century. Until 1850 the prison housed men, women and children – some as young as six years old – usually serving short-term sentences. Its capacity rose from 600 in 1825 to 1,150 by 1832. Its inmates were typically described through their economic roles, 'beggars, tramps, thieves and debtors', though the prison occasionally held political radicals too. In 1820 it had temporarily housed the 'Cato Street conspirators', who had been accused of plotting to murder the Prime Minister and his entire Cabinet. Five of the conspirators were later executed at Newgate Prison.

After 1850 the Middlesex House of Correction accommodated

only male offenders over the age of 17. It became notorious for its widespread use of solitary confinement, its adoption of the 'silent system', which forbade conversation between prisoners, its use of leg-irons restricting prisoners' movements, its paltry bread and water diets, and its rigorous application of 'hard labour'. Some of these tasks were unproductive, making them especially humiliating for the prisoners. The poets Coleridge and Southey coined a verse:

> As he went through Cold-Bath Fields, he saw
> a solitary cell;
> And the Devil was pleased, for it gave him a hint
> for improving his prisons in hell.[2]

Barely a stone's throw away stood another prison: Clerkenwell Bridewell House of Detention. Less than a mile further east was Whitecross Debtors' Prison.

Harsh and demeaning as the treatment was in these institutions – and Coldbath Fields certainly evoked the most fear – the rally in May 1833 was not about the treatment of prisoners or even about prisons at all. It was protesting about more mundane matters: rising prices, low pay and increasing unemployment, all compounded by the complete lack of political representation for the people suffering economic hardship. The much-vaunted 'Great' Reform Act of 1832, passed by a Whig government, had got rid of some of the rotten boroughs, such as Amersham, represented by two MPs from one large, landowning family – the Drakes – voted in by a tiny electorate since the 1600s. The Act

---

2 'The Devil's Thoughts', 1835 version published in Walter Thornbury, *Old and New London*, Vol. 2, London: Cassell and Co, 1879.

also created new constituencies in the larger cities that had grown up in the Industrial Revolution but the electorate was still tiny. Around one in six adult males now had the vote, all of them men of property. Birmingham, Leeds and Manchester gained their first MPs, but, in general, the newly emerging urban centres were still poorly represented.

The organisation that mobilised London's discontented people at that moment was the grandly named National Union of the Working Classes (NUWC). Its constitution proclaimed three key principles:

- to secure for every workingman the full value of his labour;
- to protect workingmen against the tyranny of masters and manufacturers;
- to bring about parliamentary reform (including suffrage for all adult males).

The government was in no mood to tolerate openly rebellious behaviour from the 'lower orders'. The Home Secretary, Lord Melbourne, declared the gathering at Coldbath Fields illegal. The NUWC, convinced that its protest was justified, went ahead with the rally anyway. However, their numbers were soon more than matched by those of the police, who kettled the demonstrators. When the protesters were completely penned in, the police attacked them in order to break up the rally.

It was just four years since Sir Robert Peel's Act of Parliament had established the Metropolitan Police. The novice force had hardly any experience of handling demonstrations, though they would soon get more practice than they might have wished for.

On that day the demonstrators fought back and three policemen were stabbed. Sergeant Brooks and PC Redwood later recovered from their knife wounds. PC Robert Culley stumbled into a nearby inn, announced that he wasn't feeling well, then collapsed and died.

An inquest was held with a jury comprising 17 men, most of them bakers from the nearby Gray's Inn district. The coroner set out the case and sent the jury to deliberate. He directed them to record a verdict of 'wilful murder'. They discussed the evidence for 30 minutes, then announced that they had a verdict on which 16 of the 17 jurors were agreed. PC Culley's death, they declared, was not wilful murder but a case of 'justifiable homicide'. Describing the police behaviour as 'ferocious, brutal and unprovoked', their foreman reported: 'We are firmly of the opinion that if they [the police] had acted with moderation the deceased would not have been stabbed.'

The coroner might have seen this verdict as perverse, but it was popular among ordinary people. So popular that cheering crowds carried the jurors through the local streets that night in a torch-lit procession. Their rebellious stand, defending the right to protest, won support beyond the working poor. Moneyed supporters laid on special treats for the jurors: a boat trip along the Thames to Twickenham and a free theatre visit to see *A Roland for an Oliver*. Each juror also received a medallion inscribed 'in honour of the men who nobly withstood the dictation of a coroner'.

This single incident reveals so much about London in the early 1830s. Economic divisions were widely acknowledged, though use of the term 'working classes' – plural – indicated that there was still a long way to travel before those exploited in different sectors would perceive their more profound commonality. Oppositional forces, though, had begun to use the tools of mobilisation and protest – leaflets, placards and posters – and could mobilise beyond an immediate locality. Public protest was on the agenda and activists acquainted themselves with suitable outdoor venues. They were not cowed by the threats of politicians, backed by an emergent police force ready to use violent means to quell protest, and courts freely dishing out severe sentences.

In the decades that followed, London was a great centre of agitation and protest. The class-conscious Chartist movement placed the struggle for political rights firmly on the map, unimpressed by a 'Great Reform Act' that failed to live up to its title, offering crumbs to elements of a rising urban bourgeoisie. It adopted its People's Charter at the Crown and Anchor pub on the Strand, and launched the first mass struggles for democratic rights in London. Assorted groups organised and campaigned for political and economic goals, and fought for rights they believed they were absolutely entitled to claim. Certain locations became especially associated with great protest rallies and platforms for free speech by political agitators: Trafalgar Square, Hyde Park (Speakers' Corner) and Parliament Square in central London; Kennington Common and Southwark Park in south London;[3] and Clerkenwell Green and Victoria Park, north of the river heading east. As more and more areas gave birth to their own significant individuals and campaigning organisations, these groups established local pitches from which to share their concerns and demands with their public. Politics moved from the austere, forbidding surroundings of the House of Commons in Westminster to street corners, squares and public spaces.

---

3 In 1854 the government enclosed Kennington Common, converted it into a park and banned political meetings.

The fear stalking London's elites in the late 1840s brought troops into the capital to guard strategic buildings, while Queen Victoria was spirited away from potential harm. In the 1860s, protesters, demanding political reform, unceremoniously removed the railings enclosing Hyde Park, London's most elegant green space. The 1880s saw bloody battles for free speech in Trafalgar Square and an explosion of industrial struggles, spontaneously ignited by atrociously paid women workers in London's original and largest manufacturing area – the East End. During the 1900s and 1910s, women's economic struggles in London were temporarily overshadowed by political battles. Rebellious women were imprisoned for smashing shop windows along London's showpiece thoroughfare of Oxford Street, attacking government property and randomly setting fire to pillar boxes – the modern equivalent of a cyberattack, given their crucial contents – as they forced politicians to notice and respond to their agenda for change. Even behind bars women protesters found ways to continue to challenge the authorities through hunger strikes and doing damage to their cells. In the 1920s, two London prisons – Brixton and Holloway – temporarily hosted elected councillors who refused to accede to demands on them, which they considered an injustice and an outrage to the people who had democratically elected them.

Fifty years *after* Besant's blast at inequality, the people of the East End and of Bermondsey built barricades on the streets to thwart the ambitions of Oswald Mosley, a true son of the aristocracy, who had focused his attention especially on the capital city. He had mesmerised segments of all classes within London, including significant numbers of workers, and built a paramilitary movement, spreading hatred and promoting dictatorship.

But rebellion has not always taken such sensational forms. Other dissenters adopted peaceful means to challenge and subvert the orthodoxies of the age, expose hypocrisies and pose questions and demands using the power of the written word. They published radical newspapers, wrote provocative pamphlets and generated mass petitions that simultaneously shook the powerful and gave heart and inspiration to those struggling for change.

This book tells stories of defiance: how Londoners responded to their circumstances, especially between the 1830s and the 1930s. It takes the reader into the heart of several localities where campaigning groups were born and developed; where they declared their agendas, captured the imagination of their wider public, mobilised for actions, took on powerful forces and suffered great setbacks, but also won important victories.

Who were these Londoners? In 1831 London was a city of 1.7 million people; a century later, the population of inner London alone had reached 5 million, with another 3 million in the growing suburbs of outer London. The development of the railways from the 1850s and 1860s displaced several very poor communities, without any compensation, but also enabled a massive expansion of factories and workshops. This drew new communities to the capital and, in turn, provided a basis for large numbers of workers to come together to fight collectively for better pay and conditions within their workplaces. The trade union movement expanded, especially among men in skilled work. An all-London Trades Council was formed in 1860, and towards the end of the nineteenth century local trades councils emerged, enabling workers across industries to support each other's struggles. By the 1890s a 'new unionism' was adding swathes of low-skilled and unskilled workers to a bigger and more combative trade union movement in London.

When Annie Besant was writing, one out of three Londoners had been born outside of the metropolis. Some had travelled to the capital from other towns and villages within Britain; others arrived as international migrants seeking opportunities for economic advancement. In many cases they also sought greater freedom, security and refuge from persecution and oppression. London had long been a city of migrants, but their numbers increased dramatically towards the end of the nineteenth century and in the early part of the twentieth century.

The influx and settlement of these people coincided with an upsurge of rebellious political movements. But this was not just a coincidence. Although new migrants were reluctant to put themselves in a position of confrontation with the authorities here, they were also determined that their children should have freer and more prosperous lives than they had had. They arrived with a finely tuned sense of the necessity to fight for their rights, and with a determination not to let those rights slip away once they had grasped them. Many new Londoners threw themselves into struggles for better lives and played an outstanding role in London's rebellious campaigns. This book features in particular the individual and collective contributions of migrants of African-Caribbean, Indian, Jewish and Irish heritage.

Rebellious Londoners spoke several different mother tongues but had a common campaigning language. They learned from each other's struggles and derived strength from each other's efforts and victories. Many participants had their eyes open to the wider world and were confirmed internationalists. Some among them found creative ways to give solidarity to their counterparts in other countries and publicise their causes here, but their efforts were primarily focused on democracy, freedom and equality in the city where they lived and worked.

Grassroots Movements

This book is about grassroots movements for change. To the extent that it celebrates outstanding and iconoclastic individuals, it highlights those who based their hopes for change on a collective movement. Some of these individuals are more well known, such as the docks strike leader Ben Tillett, suffragette Emmeline Pankhurst, secularist and anti-war campaigner Bertrand Russell, writer and activist Eleanor Marx, and Labour politician George Lansbury. But readers will also meet individuals with whom they may be less familiar, such as the Chartist leader William Cuffay, whose father was born into slavery in the Caribbean (Chapter 2), the sweatshop worker and anarchist campaigner Milly Witkop (Chapter 4), Rosa May Billinghurst, a suffragette who undertook courageous acts of civil disobedience from her wheelchair (Chapter 8), the veteran East End brushmaker Mrs Savoy, who made a powerful impact on the Prime Minister, Herbert Asquith, when they met in June 1914 (Chapter 9), and Charlie Goodman, whose anti-fascist activism took him from the charge room at Leman Street police station on the day of the Battle of Cable Street, over the Pyrenees to Spain where he joined the British Battalion, Fifteenth International Brigade (Chapter 11).

The word 'rebel' derives from the Latin *rebellis*, which signified a fresh declaration of war (*bellum*) after a defeat. Many of the rebels celebrated through this book were true to this spirit. They were resilient people, undaunted by temporary setbacks, who believed they would ultimately triumph. All of them challenged the status quo, some from the most marginalised and embattled starting points, others more comfortably ensconced within the mainstream, but their common attributes were their fervent refusal to let injustices go unchallenged, their belief that change was possible, and their determination to see their battles through to a conclusion. The book explores these people's lives to find out what motivated and inspired them to act. It illuminates the methods they adopted and, with the aid of specially commissioned maps and suggested routes for each chapter, invites you to walk in their footsteps.

In keeping with its 'history from below' approach, this book particularly celebrates those movements that have been less conspicuous in mainstream narratives. Much has been written about the Chartist movement, but less about its predecessors, such as the London Corresponding Society and the National Union of the Working Classes, whose ideas and activities are outlined in the Introduction and first two chapters. The Women's Freedom League, whose motto was 'Dare to be Free', fought for the vote but also for equal opportunities, equal rights and equal justice for women. History records them as being less 'militant' than Emmeline Pankhurst's Women's Social and Political Union but, as Chapter 8 argues, they were more politically radical. The Battle of Cable Street in October 1936 was an extraordinary event that dealt a severe blow to Oswald Mosley's fascist movement. But it was one battle in a long war, and the complementary actions of the people of Bermondsey, who took to the streets and built their own barricades exactly a year after the Cable Street conflagration, are described in Chapter 11.

The book ends on the eve of the Second World War, by which time the rebel Londoners and their counterparts nationwide, who had mobilised, marched, petitioned, demonstrated and endured imprisonment, had chalked up several significant gains. Fascism had been defeated domestically and within years would be defeated internationally; trade unions were an accepted part of society; the Labour Party was a mass party seeking redistribution of wealth, whose members were drawn largely from the working class; there was free universal education, and higher educational opportunities were about to expand. With very few exceptions, all female and male adults could vote, basic freedoms were guaranteed, and organisations such as the National Council for Civil Liberties (now Liberty) were monitoring and challenging breaches of civil rights. A freely speaking national press was widely read and, although ownership of newspapers was still largely concentrated in the hands of Conservative political and economic elites, newspapers such as the *Daily Worker*, the *Daily Herald* and the *News Chronicle* flourished and provided accessible and affordable alternatives. The post-war Labour administration brought in further radical reform, reflecting a broad consensus in society, demanding greater fairness, democracy and equality of opportunity.

This war, in which, for the second time in three decades, ordinary workers had proportionally made the greatest sacrifice, was a watershed for Britain and especially for its capital city, which suffered so much damage during the Blitz. Thousands of homes were destroyed and communities dislocated. Slum clearance and renovation of the city's infrastructure, which had been taking place all too slowly from the end of the nineteenth century, suddenly presented itself as an urgent necessity. The economic divisions in British society and in its capital city remained conspicuous, but the rebels and protesters taking to

London's streets in the 1950s, and in the decades immediately beyond, could generally undertake their activities from a more comfortable and stable starting point. Protests in London became focused on a more diverse and eclectic, though no less urgent, set of issues – for example, the environment, lesbian and gay rights, women's equality, antiracism, disability equality, nuclear disarmament, the Vietnam War, apartheid in South Africa, trade justice – all of which are much more difficult to locate specifically within the London context as opposed to the national or global context.

Areas Covered

Most of the events described in this book took place within inner London boroughs and central London areas. London grew unevenly as a city. The financial centre developed first, while its legal and political institutions emerged to the west of the financial district. Industry in London was founded towards the east. The development of the East India and West India docks there brought a host of related industries into existence. Gradually the urbanisation combined with industrial development that occurred in the east was replicated across the capital. But this meant that the demands of rebellious movements for change were first fought out and often took their most dramatic forms in east London, so five of the chapters and the walks that accompany them are in different parts of the East End.

Several areas south of the river underwent rapid urbanisation and industrialisation later than east London, towards the end of the nineteenth century and the beginning of the twentieth century. The two southern districts that developed particularly strong radical movements, motivated and energised by extraordinary individuals, were Battersea and Bermondsey, and they are the south London areas represented in the walks.

The most central location represented is Westminster. In contrast with the east London and south London districts, this was not at the heart of a local community struggle, but rather the focus of a broader movement – the suffragettes – spread over several areas, that concentrated its rallies and public protests on visible centres and symbols of political power, which were plentiful in Westminster.

Although the complete period the book covers ranges, with this edition's new material, from the 1790s to the end of the 1930s, most chapters with their corresponding walks relate to narrower slices of time. The Bermondsey chapter, for example, covers the 1890s to the 1930s. The Bloomsbury chapter is the exception to the pattern. This area was a hothouse for the development of radical ideas throughout the period the book covers and that is reflected in a wide-ranging walk. Two other important locations that the book will lead you through are Fleet Street and Clerkenwell. They are the focus of the first two chapters. Our story begins there.

Using the Book: Text and Maps

This second edition of *Rebel Footprints* includes two brand new chapters, complete with their maps and annotated walks. All the other chapters have been revised to remove any inaccuracies that have been found, and to insert additional information gathered since the first edition. The chapters follow a roughly chronological pattern, although several are more thematic. Each chapter conveys accounts of rebellious individuals, movements, incidents and campaigns that occurred principally within that specific locality. The walks stop at key points mentioned in the chapter, and indicate physical remnants that recall this history, but also add other intriguing fragments of historical information. Each chapter, together with its accompanying walk, can be used in a 'stand-alone' manner, although it is worth reading the whole of the relevant chapter first in order to get the most out of the walk. And if you do the walks in the order in which they appear in the book, the way in which different individuals and movements inspired and related to each other will become more apparent.

The skyline of our city today is rapidly changing as tall glass-covered office blocks and luxury flats are built at breathtaking speed. The traces of a rebellious history are being erased before our eyes. This book attempts to resist that process. It cannot put back the bricks and mortar of the original buildings where momentous decisions were made or powerful words spoken, but it can help to preserve our collective memory of these struggles for better lives for people in the capital.

Londoners today are never short of issues to protest about. And as we continue to march through the streets of our capital city, holding placards and banners, singing, blowing whistles, chanting slogans and voicing our demands, we are walking on well-trodden ground. But we are also elevated, as we stand on the shoulders of those rebels who came before us, who refused to accept the status quo, and who set out on the paths of protest.

This book honours and celebrates these rebels who dreamt of a better life for all. It aims to ensure that their ideals continue to live in the hearts and minds of those who campaign for justice and equality in our metropolis today.

William Cobbett accuses his army officers of ill-treatment and fraud

1

WRITERS AND RIOTERS IN THE FLEET STREET PRECINCT

The year is 1381. Armed and angry mobs from Kent and Essex converge at Blackheath, south of the Thames, before they cross London Bridge and engage in several days of targeted riots that became known as the 'Peasants' Revolt'. The Savoy Palace, on the site of today's luxurious Savoy Hotel on London's Strand, is one of the rebels' chief targets. Built by Simon de Montfort in 1245, this palace passed through the hands of various 'nobles', into those of John of Gaunt, not only the richest man in England, but effectively the most powerful: he determines the policies made in name by his teenage nephew, King Richard II. Gaunt introduces a flat-rate Poll Tax hated by the poor, upon whom it falls most heavily, intended to pay for military adventures to which ordinary people have not consented. The peasants fight back collectively. Margaret Thatcher failed to recall this stark history lesson in 1990 when she introduced a similarly unpopular Poll Tax. As the mob reaches London, John of Gaunt wisely stays in Scotland. He is threatened with beheading by the rebels if he returns to his London home.

An angry riot by the poor in 1377 over a poll tax introduced that year was suppressed, but the 1381 revolt is far greater in scale.

The rebels burn the Savoy Palace to the ground, destroying rather than looting its treasures. Their leader, Wat Tyler, expounds the principles and purpose of the protest: an attack on wealth and unaccountable power. He threatens a death sentence for any participant taking this opportunity to profit personally.

On their journey to London Tyler's rebels rampage through prisons, freeing the prisoners before burning these oppressive institutions to the ground. At Maidstone Prison they free the radical preacher John Ball, who had declared that: 'Things will never go well in England – nor shall they ever – until all things be held in common, and the lords are no greater masters than ourselves.'

A few hundred yards east of the Savoy Hotel stands a street with meandering side alleys, many of whose occupants inherited Tyler's spirit of revolt. Between the sixteenth and eighteenth centuries the antagonisms between its richer and poorer inhabitants frequently spilled on to Fleet Street, but by the nineteenth century that spirit was expressed more by the pen than the sword. It was home to radical writers and pamphleteers, whose works were bought and sold, passed around, read aloud, and clandestinely distributed in times of repression.[1] Sharing John Ball's vision of a fairer, more equal society, their authors wrote incendiary words to challenge those who exercised power only for the benefit of elites; they exposed injustices, provided information, gave confidence to campaigners, and incited rebellion among the disenfranchised and neglected. Like John Ball, they were willing to be imprisoned for making a stand.

That tradition of radical pamphleteering was already well

---

[1]   Omasius Gorgut, *Strange Confused Tumults of the Minde: Wanderings in the Past, Present and Future of Radical Pamphleteering*, London: Past Tense, 2014.

established by the 1830s, which is when this book's main chunk of history begins. This chapter tells the story of these earlier writers and publishers of the Fleet Street precinct, who laid the ground for the grassroots movements that followed in their wake, and are described in subsequent chapters.

An economic migrant from Alsace, Wynkyn de Worde, established a printing press near the eastern end of Fleet Street in the early 1500s. The street became the country's pre-eminent home for printing and publishing. London's first daily newspaper, the *Daily Courant*, was published here from 1702. By the early 1800s, its central area, and the courts and alleys running from it, contained printing presses and bookshops circulating a range of radical publications. These included *Pig's Meat*, published by Thomas Spence, a radical teacher from Newcastle, who moved to London in 1792; the satirical *Black Dwarf*, published by Yorkshire-born Thomas Jonathan Wooler; and *The Republican*, by Devon-born Richard Carlile. These same courts and alleys housed the offices of organisations seeking to bring about fundamental social change.

For many decades, though, this same street also provided a home for national newspapers that were firm upholders of the capitalist status quo and bastions of right-wing reaction. In the early 1930s, when the *Daily Mail* published articles enthusiastically welcoming Hitler's takeover of Germany and extolling Oswald Mosley's ideas for 'a Greater Britain', with headlines such as 'Youth Triumphant'[2] and 'Hurrah for the Blackshirts' respectively, its offices and printing works were in Northcliffe House, just south of Fleet Street. For many years the

---

2 'Youth Triumphant' was written from 'Somewhere in Naziland' on 10 July 1933. 'Hurrah for the Blackshirts' appeared on 15 January 1934.

Daily Mail lived across the road from the Victoria House Printing Company, which published the *Daily Herald*, a newspaper that began its life as a strike bulletin for printing workers campaigning for a 48-hour week in January 1911. The *Herald* launched itself formally as an unofficial and rebellious Labour daily with capital of £300, and was later owned by the Trade Union Congress. When the *Daily Mail* left the Fleet Street precinct for west London, its owner, Lord Rothermere, took the boardroom with him and relocated it in its new premises.

Just beyond Fleet Street's far end, on the eastern bank of the River Fleet,[3] a prison was built in 1187. It was deliberately burnt down during the Peasants' Revolt of 1381, unintentionally destroyed on the third day of the Fire of London in September 1666, and then burnt down again during the Gordon Riots of 1781. These riots initially comprised a popular protest against the relaxation of anti-Catholic discrimination, but morphed into a more general attack by the poorer classes on targets they identified with their wretchedness and oppression, such as the prisons filled by hopeless debtors. Two inmates of Fleet Prison in the seventeenth and early eighteenth centuries – John Lilburne and Samuel Byrom – wrote some of the earliest radical tracts relating to this precinct. Their work inspired many radical pamphleteers later associated with Fleet Street.

John Lilburne was known to his followers as 'Freeborn John' for promoting the concept that people possessed 'inalienable rights' from birth, irrespective of any 'rights' grudgingly granted by the state. During the English Civil War, Freeborn John prominently supported the egalitarian and anti-establishment

---

3   One of London's hidden rivers, which now runs under Farringdon Road.

movement whose members were disparaged by their opponents as 'Levellers'.[4]

On 18 April 1638, Lilburne was flogged on his bare back as he was dragged from Fleet Prison along Fleet Street, his hands tied to the rear of an ox cart, to a pillory at Westminster. After facing the fury of a mob there, he was returned to his cell. He began writing an account of his punishment in Fleet Prison that same year, which he called *The Work of the Beast*. He had been jailed for falling foul of repressive censorship laws by publishing pamphlets making incendiary attacks on the power and authority of the bishops. At the turn of the seventeenth century, Queen Elizabeth had delegated to the Court of High Commission 'the licensing and monitoring of pamphlets, plays and ballets to ensure that "nothing therein should be either heretical, seditious or unseemly for Christian ears"'.[5] There were public burnings of pamphlets seen as subversive.

Modern-day human rights campaigners are challenging the increasing privatisation of prisons as state-run institutions for punishment and rehabilitation. Companies enjoy lucrative contracts for running prison services privately, and many corporations employ cheap prison labour. There are historical precedents. For example, in 1725, Samuel Byrom, son of the poet John Byrom, was incarcerated for debts he hadn't repaid. In a 1729 petition to his old schoolfriend, the Duke of Dorset (Lionel Cranfield Sackville), Byrom wrote a blistering critique of Fleet Prison's profit-making activities, enacted under the

---

4   For opposing property rights and promoting fair distribution of wealth they were called 'Levellers'. They positively embraced this name. In similar fashion, the Women's Social and Political Union, whose first offices were in Clements Inn, close to Fleet Street, embraced the name 'suffragettes' coined by their opponents (see Chapter 8).

5   Gorgut, *Strange Confused Tumults*.

notorious wardenship of Thomas Bambridge, who came into the post the previous year. Byrom described how prisoners had to pay for food and lodging, with additional fees for turning keys or for taking irons off. Fleet Prison had the highest prison fees in England. Byrom wrote:

> What barbarity can be greater than for gaolers (without any provocation) to load prisoners with irons, and thrust them into dungeons, and manacle them, and deny their friends to visit them, and force them to pay excessive fines for their chamber-rent, their victuals and drinks; to open their letters and seize the charity that is sent to them . . . by all the ways that the worst of tyrants can invent? Such cruelty reduces the prisoners to despair . . . many choose to shoot, hang or throw themselves out of the window, than to be insulted, beaten and imposed upon by the gaolers.[6]

In the book's preface he displayed his own penchant for poetry:

> Whoever reads this Book, in it will find,
> Reasons to move the Sov'reignty to be kind,
> And free the Prisoners from a troubled Mind
> That Gaolers may no more our Bodies grind.[7]

Fleet Street in the early 1700s had a striking visual appearance,

---

6   Samuel Byrom, *An Irrefragable Argument Fully Proving that to Discharge Great Debts is less Injury, and More Reasonable than to Discharge Small Debts*, London, 1729.

7   *Ibid.*

described in George Walter Thornbury's *Old and New London*. It was, he writes:

> . . . rendered picturesque, not only by its many gable-ended houses adorned with quaint carvings and plaster stamped in patterns, but also by the countless signs, gay with gilding and painted with strange devices, which hung above the shop-fronts . . . Lions blue and red, falcons, and dragons of all colours, alternated with heads of John the Baptist, flying pigs, and hogs in armour. On a windy day these huge masses of painted timber creaked and waved overhead, to the terror of nervous pedestrians.[8]

Thornbury recounts that on 2 December 1718 a signboard opposite Bride Lane, Fleet Street, 'suddenly gave way, fell, and brought the house down with it, killing four persons, one of whom was the Queen's jeweller'. It was not until 40 years later that King George II ordered the signboards in Fleet Street to be placed flat against the walls of the houses.

Thornbury describes a street full of taverns and coffee houses. These were populated by journalists and pamphleteers, exchanging stories and gossip which would often end up as news copy. The corporate newspaper giants have relocated to new fortresses in Wapping after the bruising battles between Margaret Thatcher's government and the print unions in the 1980s, but several of Fleet Street's taverns remain. Others, though, have changed their usage. The Devil Tavern, at 2 Fleet Street, was acquired by Child's Bank which had established itself next door

---

8   Walter Thornbury, *Old and New London*, London, 1878.

in the 1660s. The tavern once housed the Apollo Club, presided over by the playwright, poet and literary critic Ben Jonson, or as Thornbury described him, 'that grim but jovial despot'.

With so many taverns in one street, publicans vied to attract customers by offering bizarre attractions. According to Thornbury, 'between the "Queen's Head" and "Crooked Billet" . . . two strange, wonderful, and remarkable monstrous creatures – an old she-dromedary, seven feet high and ten feet long, lately arrived from Mongolia, and her young one' were exhibited. He continued: 'At the "Rummer" in Three Kings' Court, was to be seen an Essex woman . . . not nineteen years old, though seven feet high . . . at the "Globe" was shown Matthew Buckinger, a German dwarf, born in 1674 . . . twenty-nine inches high.'[9]

In between the taverns, more mundane business was conducted. At 161 Fleet Street, Thomas Hardy, who had moved to London from Larbert in Scotland at the age of 22 with just 18 pence in his pocket, made and sold boots and shoes. Hardy's father, a merchant seaman, died when Thomas was eight years old. He learnt shoemaking from his maternal grandfather, but had very little education beyond his training in this work-skill. Outside of working hours, though, he traded in radical ideas, heavily influenced by the French Revolution, the writings on civil liberty by the moral philosopher and dissenting minister Richard Price, and ideas spread by middle-class and working-class dissenters he found locally.[10] Hardy helped to form a short-lived but very important grassroots movement to advocate for these ideas collectively.

---

9   Thornbury, *Old and New London*.

10 Richard Price wrote *Observations on the Nature of Civil Liberty* in 1776. He was a minister at Newington Green Meeting House, and was acquainted with and influential upon Mary Wollstonecraft.

The number of Londoners of different classes voicing radical ideas in the wake of the French Revolution was rapidly growing. Thomas Paine and Mary Wollstonecraft had both published substantial volumes – *Rights of Man* (the first part in 1791, the second a year later) and *A Vindication of the Rights of Woman* (1792), respectively – providing a solid theoretical base for such views. Paine described the 'wretched condition of man' under the 'corrupt systems of monarchy and aristocracy', and called for a 'general revolution in the principle and construction of Governments', to bring about a form of representative democracy.[11] Wollstonecraft described the existing system of representation as 'a convenient handle for despotism', and declared that 'women ought to have representatives, instead of being arbitrarily governed without having any direct share allowed them in the deliberations of government'.[12]

The establishment was unnerved by political ideas that might weaken its grip on power, and was ready to act against any organised expression of radicalism. In repressive times it made sense to activists to partially obscure their assault on the political status quo by giving their fledgling organisations innocuous sounding names. Hardy was one of four individuals who launched the London Corresponding Society (LCS). Its initial platform made two demands that 45 years later became part of the six-point people's charter for democratic rights that would herald a mass movement for democracy: the LCS called for universal (male) suffrage and annual parliaments.

The Bell Tavern on Exeter Street, off the Strand, at which the LCS had its inaugural meeting, was a stone's throw from the

---

11 Thomas Paine, *Rights of Man, Part 2*, London, 1792.

12 In chapter 9 of Mary Wollstonecraft, *A Vindication of the Rights of Woman*, London, 1792.

Crown and Anchor Tavern on the other side of the Strand (closer to Fleet Street), where the London Working Men's Association effectively launched the Chartist movement. Both movements identified the working class as the class that had most to gain from a democratic political challenge and would be most enthusiastic about participating in their ranks. Hardy had experienced business troubles himself, which he saw not simply as personal difficulties but as a symptom of wider economic relations in a society governed by and for the complacent rich. In 1792 he wrote about, 'the low and miserable conditions the people of this nation were reduced to by the avaricious extortions of the haughty, voluptuous and luxurious class of beings who wanted us to possess no more knowledge than to believe that all things were created for the use of that small group of worthless individuals'. He was determined that this organisation would be open to, 'journeymen tradesmen of all denominations . . . a class of men who deserve better treatment than they generally meet with from those who are fed, and clothed, and enriched by their labour, industry, or ingenuity'.[13]

The society initially grew slowly. Hardy recorded that at the LCS's third meeting, 'nine more were added, which made the number of the society amount to twenty five and the sum in the treasury, four shillings and one penny. A mighty sum!'[14] One early recruit was the freed slave Olaudah Equiano, kidnapped from his home in Benin and sold into slavery at the age of 11. He worked in Barbados, Virginia and Montserrat before arriving in London as a free man aged 26. In the late 1780s he helped another freed

---

13 Mary Thale (ed.), *Selections from the Papers of the London Corresponding Society*, Cambridge: Cambridge University Press, 1983, p. 8.

14 *Ibid.*, p. 7.

slave, Ottobah Cugoano, to write his memoirs, and then followed suit with his own, which were translated into several languages. Equiano toured Britain and Ireland, reading from his work. Once he had joined the LCS, he combined readings out of London with making contacts for the LCS in several towns. At its height the society had more than 3,000 paid-up members, with sister branches in several towns outside London, including Sheffield, Manchester, Stockport and Norwich. Whenever a group of the society grew beyond 30 members, they would split to make a new 'division' of the society. This was to ensure democratic participation. Many of the LCS's 90 divisions met twice a week.

The society's motto was 'Unite, persevere and be free', and LCS made explicit connections between the fight against slavery and the struggle for democracy. Hardy affirmed that 'the rights of man are not confined to this small island but are extended to the whole human race, black, white, high or low, rich or poor'.[15] A fellow LCS leader, John Thelwall, argued that in order to 'dispense justice to our distant colonies we must root out from the centre the corruption by which that cruelty and injustice is countenanced and defended.'[16] Mobilising for large indoor and outdoor meetings, the LCS submitted a petition to parliament with 6,000 signatures supporting its core demands in May 1793.

It organised especially among artisans – a relatively autonomous section of the working class whose ability to earn a living was unlikely to be affected by their political opinions. One less typical member was the surgeon, geologist and palaeontologist

---

15 *A Complete Collection of State Trials*, Thomas Bayly Howell, Thomas Jones Howell, London: T. C. Hansard, 1794, p. 302.

16 Peter Fryer, *Staying Power: The History of Black People in Britain*, London: Pluto Press, 1984, p. 212.

James Parkinson, from Shoreditch, whose medical research first identified a condition that was later named after him. He wrote a series of radical pamphlets French Revolution, some under his own name, others under the pseudonym Old Hubert.

Another member with an unusual background was Edward Despard, of Huguenot and Anglo-Irish ancestry. Towards the end of a distinguished army and naval career of nearly 20 years, during which he became a close associate of Horatio Nelson, he was elevated to the role of Superintendent of British Honduras and Belize. There he initiated a policy of treating freed slaves and white settlers equally, and married a black woman called Catharine. He was summoned back to London to answer charges that were made by the white settlers. Catharine and their son James accompanied him. He ran up considerable debts in responding to the charges and ended up languishing in a debtors' prison while events towards the end of his career were forensically investigated. He read Thomas Paine's *Rights of Man* while in prison. Catharine campaigned for his release. Shortly after he was freed he joined the LCS, and also Wolfe Tone's Society of United Irishmen.

Encouraged by government ministers, the right-wing press attacked the LCS as 'a motley crew of pickpockets, seditionists, modern reformers, housebreakers, and revolutionists'. Newspaper cartoonists ridiculed them in the press and incited violence against their leaders. Hardy's heavily pregnant wife escaped a baying mob by climbing awkwardly out of a back exit of their home when it was surrounded. Her child was stillborn.

On 26 October 1795 the LCS held its largest outdoor meeting in Copenhagen Fields, Islington. They had distributed several thousand handbills promoting the meeting and claimed that

150,000 people attended. The chair of the meeting, John Binns, spoke of threats and insults to the society's members and the cruel and unjust treatment they had received, but he urged 'every true and sincere friend of liberty' to 'boldly deliver his real sentiments'. He warned: 'When the citizens of Britain become careless and indifferent about the preservations of their rights, or the choice of their representatives . . . arbitrary power is essentially introduced, and the utter extinction of individual liberty and the establishment of general despotism are inevitable.' Binns declared that it was their purpose 'to convince ministers that when the voice of a united people goes forth it is their duty to attend to it . . . if they do not they are guilty of high treason against the people'.[17]

However, Parliament passed a seditious meetings Act, and Hardy plus several other leaders found themselves charged with high treason. The government suspended *habeas corpus* in 1794. Many reformers were incarcerated for several months without a trial date. At the Treason Trial of 1794, Hardy and his fellow defendants were eventually found not guilty. But after the trial, and the tragic circumstances in which his wife lost their sixth child, Hardy took more of a back seat, concentrating on his shoe business. Others within and beyond the society would pick up the baton, arguing for its ideas, despite the repression of the courts.

The society formally closed in 1799 in the wake of the Corresponding Societies Act which effectively made it illegal for the LCS to meet, although by then it was in decline and facing financial difficulties. The Act was one of thirteen pieces of legislation passed in the period 1792–9 aimed at restricting the society's activities. Edward Despard was rearrested in 1798

---

17 *Account of the Proceedings of a Meeting of the London Corresponding Society, Held in a Field near Copenhagen House, 26 October 1795*, London: Citizen Lee, p. 7.

on suspicion of involvement in the Irish Rebellion. He was held at several successive prisons, including Coldbath Fields in Clerkenwell, until he was released without charge in 1801. Catharine Despard continued to agitate on his behalf and campaigned more widely about prisoners' conditions.

Edward's freedom was short-lived. The following year, government informers fingered Despard and several others, who had attended a 40-strong meeting of at the Oakley Arms Tavern in Lambeth. They were charged with a conspiracy to seize the Tower of London and Bank of England, and assassinate the King. Catharine persuaded Horatio Nelson to provide a character witness for her husband. Edward and six others were convicted of high treason, and despite the jury appealing for mercy, they were executed at Horsemonger Lane Gaol in Southwark in front of a crowd estimated at 20,000 people. His fellow convicted conspirators were buried in one grave in St George's Field, Southwark, but Catharine succeeded in obtaining a burial for her husband at St Paul's Cathedral, albeit in an unmarked grave.

The name Despard would live on in London's radical history: Edward's grand-nephew Maximillian married Charlotte French, who took his surname. After her husband's death, when she was in her mid-forties, she began an extraordinary activist career.[18]

Between 1808 and 1810, more than a dozen radical journalists and pamphleteers faced trails in British Courts. However, a new wave of pamphleteers in and around Fleet Street asserted themselves towards the end of the next decade, especially Richard Carlile.

Carlile established himself as a seller of radical literature from various successive Fleet Street addresses (numbers 166, 183 and

---

18 See Chapters 7 and 8.

62) close to Hardy's shoe shop. He was the son of a shoemaker from Devon who abandoned Carlile's mother soon after she gave birth to her third child. As a child Carlile was fortunate to receive six years of free education from the Church. Free Church schools were few and far between at this time. He recalled an annual local ceremony from his childhood, organised by the church, at which they burnt an effigy of a man they claimed was 'evil'. That man was Thomas Paine. Perhaps the young Carlile was paying too much attention to the stories about this man, perhaps he paid too little, but by his twenties he was selling serialised publications from his Fleet Street premises penned by the self-same Thomas Paine.

During his training as a tin plate worker back in Devon, he had already been active in agitation concerning the rights of apprentices in the workplace. In London, Carlile was radicalised further at open-air meetings, especially those addressed by Henry Hunt, who lambasted the unrepresentative parliamentary system. Carlile began selling a range of radical publications, including Thomas Wooler's satirical *Black Dwarf*, after it had been banned. He also became the editor and publisher of his own radical paper – *The Republican* – after its previous publisher William Sherwin felt reluctant to continue, because of government harassment. Sherwin had changed *The Republican*'s name to *Sherwin's Political Register*. He was seeking an agent for the *Register*, who might shield him from prosecution. Carlile relished this risky opportunity. He took over Sherwin's shop in Fleet Street, and restored the publication's original name: *The Republican*.

Carlile first tasted prison life in autumn 1817. He was selling satirical parodies of the Lord's Prayer by William Hone, which Hone himself had withdrawn because he feared prosecution.

Both Hone and Carlile were prosecuted for blasphemous libel. Hone was acquitted. Carlile was on remand for four months, but his case never came to trial. While he was inside, his wife Jane reopened the shop.

In 1819, Hunt invited Carlile to join him on the platform at a mass pro-democracy meeting to be held at St Peter's Fields, Manchester. Local magistrates asked the yeomanry (cavalry) to break up the meeting. Eighteen protesters were killed in what became known as the 'Peterloo Massacre' – a reference to Waterloo. Carlile found himself in prison soon afterwards, not for anything he had said in Manchester, but for writing about it in *The Republican*. He was charged with seditious libel, convicted, and spent three years in Dorchester Jail.

His premises in Fleet Street were raided, but the publication continued courtesy of Jane. Carlile had asked his jailers for access to writing materials. His request was granted and he sent articles back to Jane. The circulation of *The Republican* increased while he was in prison. When Jane herself was convicted for material that was published, she joined him in prison, but his sister Mary took over as publisher. After Carlile was released from prison in 1825, he continued to publish newspapers and pamphlets, exploring controversial issues such as women's equality, birth control and child labour. Carlile was a declared atheist, and he endured a further prison sentence, for blasphemy, after he published Thomas Paine's *The Age of Reason*. In total Carlile spent 10 of his adult years in prison.

In the early 1830s he acquired the Rotunda building at the River Thames end of Blackfriars Road. It became a meeting place for a range of political radicals, and headquarters of the recently formed National Union of the Working Classes. It was in this building that William Benbow set out his plan for a general strike, or 'grand national holiday' as he put it, later distributed as an agitational pamphlet.

A fellow Fleet Street shopkeeper and local political figure called Robert Waithman rose to Carlile's defence when he was imprisoned after Peterloo. Waithman, a draper, developed a deep interest in politics as a result of the events of the French revolution. He spoke out against the sedition bills that attempted to cripple the London Corresponding Society. As a local councillor from 1795 for the City ward of Farringdon Without (which incorporated Fleet Street), he built a reputation as a powerful radical orator, frequently denouncing the Corporation of London and central government. In September 1809 he openly challenged the London Corporation's scheme to celebrate the King's jubilee: his drapery shop was attacked and its windows broken. Waithman expressed his commitment to the radical press not only by supporting Carlile but also by strongly opposing the Stamp Act of 1815, which raised taxes on newspapers to 4d a copy, and threatened to restrict the audience for such publications to those with higher incomes.[19] Waithman was an elected MP for the City of London from 1818 to 1820, and again from 1826 until his death in 1833, and he used his parliamentary platform to continue to fight to protect radical newspapers.

Bolt Court, an alley off Fleet Street's northern side, from which William Cobbett's *Political Register* was published, stood almost opposite Carlile's premises at 62 Fleet Street. The *Register* monitored and commented on debates in the House of Commons.

---

19 The tactics used against the Stamp Act are described further in Chapter 5.

Cobbett had a chequered history as a radical writer. When the *Political Register* was founded in 1802, Cobbett was regarded as a 'lover of King and constitution', favourable to the Tory Party but simultaneously 'a hater of injustice, dishonesty and hypocrisy.'[20] His reputation for exposing abuses 'in high places and low' was first established through his publication of *The Soldier's Friend*, a thorough and devastating critique of corrupt and degrading practices in the army, including ill-treatment and defrauding of soldiers, and a protest against low pay.

During eight years' service Cobbett frequently clashed with his officers. After he wrote his booklet he fled to France, fearing arrest and imprisonment. He travelled on to America, earning a living by teaching English to French immigrants. He established a reputation there as a maverick, controversial pamphleteer, writing under his pen name Peter Porcupine. He was feted and befriended by Tories when he returned from America, but they could not hold his allegiance.

When Cobbett revisited the theme of mistreatment in the army, exposing flogging after a mutiny, he was jailed for two years. Soon after he was released, he wrote an address to journeymen and labourers urging 'the people' to claim their share of political power. He supported and promoted the protests against the Stamp Act, and began publishing the *Political Register* in pamphlet form with a cover price of just 2d as a gesture of defiance. His audience grew to many thousands. The government suspended *habeas corpus* once more, threatening radical political writers with arrest.

Cobbett withdrew from the front line of battle and went back to America for two years. When he returned to Britain shortly

---

20 Ramsden Balmforth, *Social and Political Pioneers of the Nineteenth Century*, London: Swan, Sonnenschein & Co, 1900, p. 13.

after the Peterloo Massacre, he stayed close to other radicals who were frequently attacking the government, pushing agendas for parliamentary reform, a widening of democratic rights, and economic justice for the poor. Cobbett declared: 'I am above all for the good feeding and clothing of those who raise all the food and make all the clothing.'

Just a few years after Cobbett died, the Chartist Movement was born. From February to August 1839 the early Chartist movement had daily meetings at Dr Johnson's Tavern at 8 Bolt Court, close to the building in which Cobbett's *Political Register* had been published. Most of the individuals who came together within the London Working Men's Association which drew up the People's Charter – William Lovett, Henry Hetherington, John Cleave, James Watson, Henry Vincent and George Julian Harney – had encountered each other, and Cobbett, for the first time within the agitation for an unstamped press. That agitation came to a head in the 1830s, and during the main period of Chartist agitation of the 1830s and 1840s there were up to 12 different radical newspapers promoting the cause. One of the centres of Chartist agitation in London was Clerkenwell. Its social conditions and political atmosphere are described in Chapter 2.

CITY OF LONDON THAMESLINK

FARRINGDON STREET

ST BRIDE'S AVENUE

DORSET RISE

TUDOR STREET

THE MIRACLE OF FLEET STREET
The Story of The DAILY HERALD

GEORGE LANSBURY
Price 2/

RIVER THAMES

14
13
12
8 9
MAGPIE ALLEY
11
BOUVERIE STREET
BOLT COURT
7
10

FETTER LANE

FLEET STREET

CHANCERY LANE

6
MIDDLE TEMPLE LANE

5

CLEMENTS INN

4
ARUNDEL STREET
TEMPLE
VICTORIA EMBANKMENT

SURREY STREET

3
STRAND LANE

VOTES FOR WOMEN

ALDWYCH

STRAND

STRAND UNDERPASS

WATERLOO BRIDGE

SAVOY STREET

2
STRAND

100M

N

WELLINGTON STREET

EXETER STREET

1

WALK

Start outside the Savoy Hotel, corner of the Strand and Savoy Court, WC2R OEZ.

1. Savoy Hotel

This grand hotel stands on the site of the Savoy Palace, destroyed in the Peasants' Revolt of 1381, during days of protest against wealth and the hated Poll Tax. Cross the road and walk up Exeter Street. Continue under a grand archway.

2. Corner of Exeter Street and Wellington Street

The London Corresponding Society, which campaigned for universal (male) suffrage and annually elected parliaments through the 1790s, held its inaugural meeting at the Bell Tavern, which stood at 15 Exeter Street. Turn right into Wellington Street, cross to the southern side of the Strand, walk east past Somerset House and King's College, then turn into Surrey Street.

3. 'Roman Baths' Strand Lane/Surrey Street

Remnants of a cistern actually built in the early 1600s to service a fountain in nearby Somerset House, were advertised from the 1830s as a 'Roman remnant'! A sign to the 'Roman Bath' appears on the right just past the Norfolk Building. Reverse back to the Strand and head east until you reach the forecourt of St Clement Danes Church.

4. St Clement Danes

Designed by Christopher Wren, and opened in 1682, this church has particularly close links with the Air Force. The block of luxury flats on the corner of the Strand and Arundel Street stands on the site of the former Crown and Anchor Tavern, where the demands of the People's Charter were read to a huge gathering on 28 February 1837. The opposite side of the forecourt faces Clements Inn, where a later incarnation of the fight to extend democracy had its first offices: the Pethwick-Lawrences at 4 Clements Inn provided accommodation for the Women's Social and Political Union, later known as the 'Suffragettes'. The Tea Cup Inn, round the corner in Portugal Street, was a suffragette-friendly cafe that advertised regularly in the WSPU newspaper, *Votes for Women*. Walk round to the back of the church to a statue of Samuel ('Dr') Johnson, poet, essayist and lexicographer. He declared that 'patriotism is the last refuge of a scoundrel' and also opined that 'when a man is tired of London he is tired of life'. Continue up the Strand until you reach Temple Bar, indicated by a winged dragon on a curious structure in the middle of the road.

5. Temple Bar

This marks the boundary between the London's political and legal centre, Westminster, and its financial centre, the City of London. The bank at number 1 Fleet Street, on the road's southern side, incorporates the site of the Devil Tavern, home of poet and playwright Ben Jonson's Apollo Club, whose rules forbade itinerant fiddlers, the reciting of insipid poetry, and lovers who 'mope about unsociably in corners'. Fleet Street's many inns and taverns were well used by journalists and pamphleteers. Almost directly opposite 1 Fleet Street is Bell Yard. Martha Gurney ran a bookshop at 34 Bell Yard from 1772 to 1782 before joining forces with another bookseller, William Fox, at his shop on Holborn Hill. Timothy Whelan describes Gurney as 'London's leading female Dissenting printer/bookseller during the 1780s and '90s, printing and/or selling more than thirty radical pamphlets, fourteen of which vehemently attacked the slave trade.'[21] Continue along Fleet Street. Between the shops on the southern side, occasional large gates lead into the lawyers' chambers of the Inner Temple.

6. Middle Temple Lane

(The gates are open from 8 a.m. to 8 p.m. on weekdays.) These buildings are typical of those in the alleys at this end of Fleet Street's southern side. John Evelyn – a diarist who, like Samuel Pepys, recorded the events of the Fire of London – lived in Essex Court. The writer and essayist Charles Lamb was born in Crown Office Row in 1775. 'I am determined,' Lamb said, 'that my children shall be brought up in their father's religion, if they can find out what that is.' The novelist and satirical writer William Makepeace Thackeray, author of *Vanity Fair*, had chambers in the Middle Temple while briefly studying law. Return to Fleet Street and continue eastwards to the corner of Fleet Street and Bouverie Street. On the way, pause to view the building on the northern side, just past St Dunstan's Church, which retains the mosaics advertising several newspaper titles formerly published here.

---

21 Timothy Whelan, 'William Fox, Martha Gurney, and Radical Discourse of the 1790s', in *Eighteenth Century Studies*, Vol. 42, No. 3, Spring 2009.

7. Fleet Street/Bouverie Street

The middle section of Fleet Street was the home of radical writers and organisations. At different times Richard Carlile had premises at 55, 62 and 183 Fleet Street, selling pamphlets, serialised segments of Thomas Paine's writings and radical newspapers, including his own. Number 62 Fleet Street can be found just inside Bouverie Street. Cross over Fleet Street to the entrance into Bolt court. A few yards eastwards is 166 Fleet Street, where J. S. Johnston first printed Paine's *Rights of Man*, and 161 Fleet Street, where Thomas Hardy, the founder of the London Corresponding Society, made and sold shoes.

8. Bolt Court

Enter Bolt Court. William Cobbett's *Political Register* was published from number 11 in the 1830s, having earlier been published from 183 Fleet Street (where Richard Carlile had also traded). Next door at number 10, the *Beehive*, newspaper of the International Working Men's Association or 'First International', was published between 1861 and 1875. A rebellious group led by Karl Marx broke from it. Number 8 Bolt Court housed Dr Johnson's Tavern, where the Chartists met frequently in 1839, continuing discussions that had started in Birmingham. Britain's first Marxist organisation, the Social Democratic Federation, had an office at number 3 in the 1890s. Continue through Bolt Court and follow signs pointing you rightwards to a square with seating, a statue of Hodge (Dr Johnson's cat) and a fine view of Dr Johnson's house. Return to Fleet Street.

9. Fleet Street/Bolt Court

The relative absence of radical women in and around Fleet Street was partially redressed in the rooms above what is now McDonald's at 152 Fleet Street. It housed the offices of two publishing organisations in which the socialist suffragette Sylvia Pankhurst and two socialist women, Nellie Cohen and May O'Callaghan, played a central role. One office was dedicated to the newspaper *Workers' Dreadnought*, which began life in 1914 as the *Woman's Dreadnought*, the organ of the East London Federation of Suffragettes (ELFS). The ELFS are discussed in Chapter 9. Above it was the People's Russian Information Bureau, whose pamphlets between 1918 and 1920 offered a very different perspective on the Russian Revolution's achievements than could be found in Fleet Street's mainstream media. Sylvia Pankhurst recruited the gay, Jamaican-born writer, poet and revolutionary Claude Mackay to write for the *Workers' Dreadnought*, one of the first black journalists on Fleet Street. Cross over to Bouverie Street.

10. Bouverie Street/Fleet Street

The geographical extent of the rebellion against the *Beehive*, led by Karl Marx, was limited. Marx and his co-workers published the *Commonwealth* newspaper as the 'official' organ of the International Working Men's Association Central Council at 2 Bouverie Street. On the opposite corner of Fleet Street and Bouverie Street (63 Fleet Street) was Charles Bradlaugh's Freethought Publishing Company, which had moved there from nearby Stonecutter Street. Bradlaugh, the Liberal MP for Northampton from 1880 until his death in 1891, co-founded the

National Secular Society in the 1860s. The left-wing journalist Annie Besant worked with Bradlaugh and edited her newspaper *The Link* from here. In the mid-1880s Besant's powerful article in *The Link* in June 1888 helped to precipitate the strike by women workers at Bryant & May's match factory in Bow (see Chapter 3). Two years earlier Besant persuaded a reluctant Bradlaugh to provide office space for Charlotte Wilson, a Cambridge-educated anarchist, to launch the anarchist newspaper *Freedom* in 1886. The first 17 issues of *Freedom* were produced at Bradlaugh's premises before the paper moved to Ossulton Street in Somerstown, and later to Whitechapel. Continue down Bouverie Street, then turn left into Magpie Alley.

11. Magpie Alley

The history of printing and publishing in and around Fleet Street, going back to Wynkyn de Worde, is attractively displayed on the wall tiles. Take time to follow this rewarding display. Turn right at the end, passing a smaller display showing the printing process. Turn right again and stop at Tudor Street.

12. Tudor Street

Political opposites are well represented here. Northcliffe House at number 26 printed the right-wing *Daily Mail* here from 1907. Victoria House, diagonally right at number 25, with its three carved faces staring outwards, published the left-wing *Daily Herald*, which emerged in January 1911 as a continuation of *The World*, the daily strike bulletin of the London Society of Compositors, who were campaigning for a 48-hour week and had downed tools a few weeks earlier. The recently elected Labour MP George Lansbury played a key role in developing the paper.

The *Daily Mail* was launched by the Rothermere family in 1896, which was also the year that the fascist Sir Oswald Mosley was born. He and the *Daily Mail* would frequently be spoken of in the same breath, especially in the first six months of 1934, when the *Daily Mail*'s enthusiasm for Mosley's British Union of Fascists was at its height. Turn left along Tudor Street, then left again into Dorset Rise.

13. Dorset Rise

As you walk up Dorset Rise, on the left, just behind the site of the seventeenth-century Salisbury Court Playhouse (marked by a plaque), there is an obelisk dedicated to Robert Waithman, local linen draper and 'common councilman' in Farringdon, who stood up for the tradesmen against what he called 'the great interests', and had two spells as a rebellious MP between 1818 and 1833. A plaque here describes him as a 'friend of liberty in evil times'. Walk a short distance north and turn right into the alleyway, St Bride's Avenue. Turn left around St Bride's Church, with its remarkable steeple, on which the wedding cake was modelled. Stop at the first fork.

14. St Bride's Avenue/Fleet Street

On your right, with the number 88 painted in the black and red of anarcho-syndicalists, are the May Day Rooms, an archive of radical movements in Britain during the last 50 years, and an organising space for activists today. The May Day Rooms bring today's activists together with the archives of the struggles they are focused on, enabling those archives to live and breathe again in the campaigning work of contemporary radical movements.

Old Finsbury Town Hall, Rosebery Avenue.

2

TRAILBLAZERS FOR DEMOCRACY IN CLERKENWELL GREEN

When furious suffragettes aimed their first stones at Downing Street's windows in the summer of 1908, as part of their struggle for the vote, government ministers feigned shock and hurt, and asked naïvely what might have provoked such violent actions. From faraway New Zealand, where women won the vote in 1893, the *Wanganui Chronicle* reminded them of an earlier incident: 'In 1830 the Duke of Wellington declared the House of Commons did not need reform; but when an angry mob smashed his windows and let in a little more light, he saw the matter differently.'[1]

Not differently enough to make real change, though. The following year, Wellington's government fell to the Whigs, who promised a Great Reform Act and won a landslide victory. For the vast majority, long excluded from having any political voice, this election created a rare frisson of excitement. 1831 had been unusually wet and thundery, especially August: an omen, perhaps, of imminent political turbulence. But in the early months of 1832, many Londoners were exercised more by the right to live than the right to vote.

A few suspected cholera cases in January 1832, the first reported in Limehouse, east London, heralded a major outbreak

---

1   *Wanganui Chronicle*, 3 July 1908.

of the killer disease. It swept across the city's more overcrowded and insanitary areas, where the poorest workers eked out their living. Similar outbreaks in Berlin and Hamburg in 1831 claimed thousands of lives. In Paris cholera killed 9,000 residents in just one month. The government declared it 'proof of the judgement of God among us', though the symptoms resembled severe food poisoning. It announced a National Fast Day on 21 March to halt the spread of the disease.

Henry Hetherington's *Poor Man's Guardian* disagreed. Telling the poor to fast was 'superfluous', since they were 'lucky to be able to eat meat once a week let alone be able to forgo it'. This radical penny broadsheet was published at 13 Kingsgate Street, Holborn, in defiance of government-imposed stamp duty. With the paper's support, a newly formed organisation of skilled workers and small shopkeepers from London's poorer communities transformed rejection of this government proposal into a physical and political challenge to the authorities.

The National Union of the Working Classes (NUWC) organised on a branch basis with one spokesperson for every 30–40 members. It sought economic justice and political reform, demanding annual parliaments and full suffrage for adult males, as the London Corresponding Society (LCS) advocated in the 1790s, but also demanded voting by (secret) ballot and 'no property qualification for members of parliament'. The NUWC argued that 'until intelligent men from the productive and useful classes of society' were allowed to 'represent the interests of the working people, justice in legislation will never be rendered unto them'.

These were radical, not revolutionary, demands. However, in a period in which carpenters, shoemakers and tailors were forming unions and organising strikes, Robert Owen's cooperative and communitarian ideas were circulating, and a rising capitalist class was challenging the old landed and financial oligarchy, the ruling elites felt genuinely fearful.[2] They condemned the NUWC as 'destructive revolutionists, pickpockets and incendiaries, meditating an attack on every person of property and the uprooting of law and order'.[3]

The NUWC declared that the cholera outbreak had nothing to do with God, but was caused by 'want, wretchedness and insanitary conditions'. It dubbed the Fast Day a 'Farce Day', and encouraged its supporters to enjoy a 'Feast Day' instead, which, it argued, would benefit the poor far more. It called on its supporters to assemble on the 'Farce Day' at Finsbury Square, on the edge of the City's financial district, 'for the purpose of walking round the Metropolis in procession and enjoying the fresh air'.

Its leaders devised a scenic route through fashionable areas – the City, Fleet Street, the Strand, Piccadilly and Hyde Park – before returning through Oxford Street and Holborn, for a feast in the East End. The organisers wanted to show their disdain for the government's feeble 'explanation' in a militant but disciplined manner. Respecting legal advice, they asked supporters not to bring banners, flags or anything that might be construed as a weapon. By 12 o'clock on the day of the march, some 40,000 men and women had assembled in Finsbury Square and the surrounding streets.

---

2   Carpenters and shoemakers in London held strikes in 1825, tailors in 1830.

3   See George Howell's handwritten account, *A History of the Working Men's Association* (1901), held in the archives of the Bishopsgate Institute. The NUWC was formed by a group of activists within the British Association for Promoting Cooperative Knowledge.

The newly formed Metropolitan Police placed no such restrictions on its own accoutrements. It had little experience in policing demonstrations but knew how to present a show of force. At Temple, thick ranks of police armed with staves and cutlasses blocked the protesters' path. A cat-and-mouse game followed: marchers turned off the route into Chancery Lane, but were blocked again. They headed for Gray's Inn Road. The organisers sent runners ahead to check where police were massing. A major altercation took place on Tottenham Court Road, near Howland Street, where large numbers of police had hidden themselves in a side alley. A phalanx of police suddenly threw themselves into the march, swinging staves indiscriminately as they tried to split the front ranks from those following. Some protesters threw missiles using whatever materials they could gather. Until then, they had been entirely peaceful. The marchers rallied at North Crescent, opposite Goodge Street, where their leaders, fearing further disorder, advised them to return home and eat.

Three organisers of the protest – William Lovett and James Watson, both in their early thirties, and William Benbow, in his mid-forties – were arrested in the aftermath and committed for trial at Middlesex Sessions House in Clerkenwell. Prosecutors labelled them 'disaffected and ill-disposed persons', who, 'with force of arms . . . made a great riot, tumult and disturbance', causing 'terror and alarm' to the King's subjects for five hours.

Watson had moved to London from Malton, Yorkshire, in the early 1820s and was a radical publisher based in Finsbury, strongly influenced by Robert Owen's cooperative ideas.[4] He published Tom Paine, and the poets Byron and Shelley. Benbow

---

4   Finsbury, formerly a separate borough to the south of Islington, was incorporated into
    Islington in 1965.

was apprenticed as a shoemaker in Manchester. He became a non-conformist preacher and joined local radical circles. He had been held on remand in London for eight months during 1817 for political activities, and had no means to return north when he was released without trial. He immersed himself in London's radical publishing milieu, collaborating with the pamphleteer William Cobbett.[5] He was subsequently incarcerated in Coldbath Fields Prison, Clerkenwell, for 'seditious libel'.

In the early 1830s, Benbow ran a small coffee house used by radicals at 205 Fleet Street. He expounded his idea of a 'Grand National Holiday', at meetings hosted at the Rotunda in Black-friars, recently acquired by Richard Carlile.[6] Benbow published his plan in 1832 in a pamphlet entitled *The Grand National Holiday and Congress of the Productive Classes*. The 'holiday' – a one-month general strike – would generate an uprising and force political change. During this 'holiday' period, working-class representatives would draw up a constitution to 'place every human being on the same footing. Equal rights, equal enjoyments, equal toil, equal respect, equal share of production', and the ruling classes would be forced to negotiate this with them.

Lovett arrived in London from Newlyn, Cornwall, around the same time as Watson. He had a gentler introduction to political radicalism, joining a literary association in Soho and political discussion circles at the Mechanics Institute and at various coffee houses. He later opened his own coffee house on Greville Street, Clerkenwell, which had one room full of newspapers and books and the other 'fitted up as a

---

5   Cobbett's work is described in Chapter 1.

6   The Rotunda – a meeting place for radical freethinkers – was a London headquarters for the NUWC. Carlile's activities are described in Chapter 1.

conversation-room . . . to separate the talkers from the readers'. In the evenings, the conversation room hosted lectures, debates and classes. A society called Social Reformers met there regularly. Lovett actively promoted temperance. He petitioned Parliament in 1829 to open museums and galleries on Sundays as 'want of proper recreation and amusement' was a principal cause 'of drunkenness on that day'. Like Watson, he was strongly influenced by Owen's cooperative philosophy, and joined the British Association for Promoting Cooperative Knowledge.[7]

Watson, Benbow and Lovett represented themselves during their trial, eight weeks after the 'riot'. Witnesses testified that the procession was peaceful and orderly. One told the court that he heard police receive an order at Tottenham Court Road: 'Out with your truncheons . . . fall on them . . . show them no quarter.' The jury acquitted the defendants, to wild cheering both inside and outside the court, scenes that prefigured the response to PC Culley's inquest judgement after the NUWC's 1833 protest on Coldbath Fields, half a mile from the Sessions House.[8]

The Sessions House itself was located on Clerkenwell Green. Devoid of grass for centuries, this space became one of the three most prominent free speech venues in London – the others being Speakers' Corner at Hyde Park, and Trafalgar Square. Gissing captured its atmosphere: '[T]he voices of orators, swarmed with listeners, with disputants, with mockers . . . the roar of an enthusiastic total-abstainer blended with the shriek of a Radical politician.'[9]

---

7   W. Lovett, *Life and Struggles of William Lovett in His Pursuit of Bread, Knowledge, and Freedom*, New York: A. A. Knopf, 1920.

8   After the trial Lovett accused Benbow of acting provocatively on the 'Fast Day' procession.

9   G. Gissing, *The Nether World*, London: Smith, Elder & Co, 1889, 21.

Branch 1 of the Social Democratic Federation (SDF), Britain's first socialist party, was formed in Clerkenwell.[10] The party's leader, a wealthy Cambridge-educated businessman called Henry Mayers Hyndman, who, having read Marx, saw the world anew, claimed that he first divested himself of inherited class prejudices when he 'addressed a gathering . . . of rather debauched looking persons round the old pump at Clerkenwell Green'.

Clerkenwell Green gained a reputation as the 'home of community, commonality and solidarity' among reformers and rebels seeking change, and 'the headquarters of republicanism, revolution and ultra non-conformity' among those defending the status quo. The pardoned Tolpuddle Martyrs, exiled to Australia in 1834,[11] were welcomed back at a rally in Clerkenwell Green. The Green was a venue for rallies and an assembly point for marches of the Chartist movement, established that same decade.

Clerkenwell, an area of 'grovelling starving poverty', which boasted the highest murder rate in early Victorian London, became a pivotal locale for those challenging the authorities, fighting for democracy and championing the rights of London's emerging working classes, especially during the 1830s and 1840s. Thomas Beames, a preacher at St James's Church, Westminster, who published a powerful work on London's 'rookeries' in 1850, condemned the slums of St Giles and Seven Dials, and Old Pye Street for their 'squalid misery', 'extreme poverty' and 'abject distress', but ranked Clerkenwell's 'plague spots' second only to St Giles.[12] In Clerkenwell, wrote Beames, 'a most unsavoury black

---

10 Launched in 1881 as the Democratic Federation, its most active branches were in Clerkenwell, Battersea and east London.

11 See p. 147

12 Rookeries were densely populated areas of overcrowded, unhygienic, poorly ventilated, low-quality housing.

stream of some width, the open sewer of Field Ditch . . . [runs] impetuously between the walls of the houses'. By 'houses' he meant ramshackle buildings populated by 'trampers', 'beggars', 'persons of uncertain occupation', and 'the worst thieves and lowest prostitutes of London'.[13]

Beames's stark observations echoed those published earlier in the *Illustrated London News*. In Clerkenwell's lanes and alleys, wrote its reporter, Angus B. Reach, in 1847, 'broods the darkness of utter ignorance' where 'the lowest debauch, the coarsest enjoyment . . . the most unrestrained vice, roar and riot'. He lent further colour to his descriptions through a set of unflattering ethnic stereotypes:

> Jew receivers, with sharp leering eyes and tangled beards, lurk at corners . . . The burglar has his 'crib' in Clerkenwell – the pickpocket has his mart – the half-starved Italian minstrel herds there, crammed with his fellows into foul night cellars – the ragged Irish hodman vegetates in the filth of his 3-pair back. It is the locality of dirt, ignorance and vice.[14]

The short-lived NUWC, and its successor, the London Working Men's Association (LWMA), which drew up the iconic six-point People's Charter in 1837 (drafted principally by William Lovett), did not organise among Clerkenwell's most desperate poor. They built instead among more stable artisans and skilled workers who had formed unions and shown a willingness to

---

13   T. Beames, *The Rookeries of London*, London: Thomas Bosworth, 1850.

14   *Illustrated London News*, 22 May 1847

challenge their employers through industrial action. Builders, shoemakers and tailors all took industrial action during 1834, and the LWMA, which held organising meetings at 14 Tavistock Street, near Covent Garden, set up sub-committees to investigate the conditions among trades such as weavers, shoemakers, tailors and printers, to arm themselves with propaganda to campaign for better workplace conditions.[15] But those who suffered abject poverty formed the backdrop for political crusades over economic inequalities, which agitators wove together with campaigns to address the democratic deficit. The LWMA's first 'prospectus' stated that:

> No reflecting . . . mind can witness the scenes of misery
> . . . can read of the thousand wretched forms under which
> the demon of poverty tortures the millions, and at the
> same time reflect on the ample means wasted on folly and
> lavished on idleness . . . without resolving to enquire into
> the causes of the evils, and to devise . . . some means of
> . . . alleviating them.[16]

The LWMA connected industrial disputes with efforts to stimulate education, political discussion and agitation among working-class communities. Its unashamedly vanguardist approach attempted to unify an 'intelligent and influential portion of the working class', to challenge 'cruel laws that prevent circulation of thought'. This required a 'cheap and honest press' which would

---

15 Stonemasons struck in 1841 and 1842. Their strike started among workers rebuilding the Houses of Parliament after extensive fire damage and spread to those working in Trafalgar Square, erecting Nelson's Column.

16 Howell, *A History of the Working Men's Association*.

'collect statistics about wages . . . [and] promote education for the rising generation'. It demanded that 'all public buildings, museums, galleries of arts ought to be always open to the whole people free of charge'.

The People's Charter, adopted by 'Chartists' at the Crown and Anchor pub on the Strand, defiantly challenged political norms that entrenched power among a narrow elite. It restated four points drawn up earlier by the NUWC and LCS, and added 'equal constituencies' (number of electors), and 'payment of Members of Parliament', which would make it feasible for an elected worker to keep his family afloat. The response from the government and the more conservative newspapers veered from defensive to paranoid, yet the only point still not conceded today is the impractical demand for 'annual parliaments', intended to give electorates the power to dismiss MPs within a relatively short time if they were not performing. A minority of Chartists argued for three-yearly elections.

The government could not acquiesce to the Chartists' demands without risking some shift in the balance of power, but its paranoia about these demands reflected fear of 'the mob' engaging in civil disobedience. The LWMA had stated publicly that, 'those who are excluded from this share of political power are not justly included within the operation of the laws'.

After its London launch, Chartism spread its wings and flew north, gathering strength especially in the northern industrial centres of Lancashire, Yorkshire and the Midlands, where it focused on economic issues alongside democratic political demands. Although the Charter itself, with millions of signatures, would be taken to Parliament in London in huge processions in 1839, 1842 and 1848, most Chartists were recruited outside the capital. Feargus O'Connor published Chartism's most popular newspaper, the *Northern Star*, from Leeds, though it relocated to London in November 1844. Its intricate articles gave detailed analyses of economic and political events. But few workers would have received formal education. For those less literate, the *Star* conveyed political messages through poems. Between 1838 and 1852, the paper published nearly 1,500 poems from at least 390 Chartist poets.

In London, many Chartists were skilled craftsmen, often self-employed, and Chartism initially had some middle-class participation, but it became a predominantly working-class movement in the capital. The historian David Goodway identified 1841–2 as the Chartist movement's high point in London, with around 8,000 membership cards being issued there, compared with combined recruitment figures of 7,900 for three other significant Chartist areas, Leicester, Manchester and Sheffield, over the same period.[17] Within London, Chartists were most active north of the Thames in Finsbury/Clerkenwell, east London, the City and St Pancras and in Bermondsey, Camberwell and Walworth to the south.

Outside London, there were strong connections between Methodism and Chartism, but London's Chartists tended to be non-religious or actively anti-Christian, seeing the Church as one more institution defending an unjust status quo. Ideological influences on London Chartists were more likely to be anti-authoritarians like William Cobbett, or freethinkers such as Thomas Paine, whose birthday Chartists celebrated through annual suppers.

---

17 Leicester 3,100; Manchester 2,800; and Sheffield 2,000. David Goodway, *London Chartism 1838–1848*, Cambridge: Cambridge University Press, 1982.

Although Chartists broadly agreed on goals, there were deep divisions over strategy. 'Moral Force' Chartists were committed to peaceful persuasion and education through propaganda, but 'Physical Force' Chartists believed that economic and political elites would not relinquish power and privilege unless compelled to do so by people exerting their own collective power. In Newport, Wales, an armed uprising by Chartists was defeated in 1839.

Lovett, the Charter's principal author, Watson, a co-defendant in the 1832 'Farce Day' protest, and Hetherington, founder of the *Poor Man's Guardian*, were all moral force Chartists. So was John Cleave, another radical printer and publisher. He opened a print shop in Snow Hill near Clerkenwell, then moved to Shoe Lane, later opening a bookshop and a coffee house. Cleave urged Chartists to take a stand in favour of women's suffrage too and, in 1840, published a pamphlet called *Rights of Women*, which argued that:

> If a woman is qualified to be a queen over a great nation [she] ought not to be excluded from her share in the executive and legislative power of the country . . . If [a woman] be subject to pains and penalties [for] infringement of any laws . . . she ought to have a voice in making the laws she is bound to obey . . . women contribute to the wealth and resources of the kingdom. Debased is the man who would say women have no right to interfere in politics . . . they have as much right as a man.

Women struggled to have influence within the Chartist movement, but its City of London branch had prominent speakers mocked by the press as 'she-Chartists'. Susannah Inge and Mary Ann Walker toured Britain with Chartist leaders, and wrote for the *Northern Star*. Inge dealt confidently with internal critics of women taking on political roles. At a public meeting in 1842, when a male Chartist said women were not physically intended by nature to take part in politics, she replied that it took little physical force to vote! She also explained why women should be motivated to join the Chartist rebellion: 'Do not . . . leave such things for your husbands, fathers and brothers. You have . . . a deeper interest than you are aware of. If the country is misgoverned, and bad laws instituted, and good laws perverted, it is on you those laws fall heaviest.'[18]

Another London 'she-Chartist', Emma Matilda Miles, who spoke at a meeting at the National Charter Association hall at 55 Old Bailey, was described by the *Sunday Observer* not as an articulate advocate of Chartist politics but as a 'pretty looking young creature'. She argued the physical force case, insisting that Chartist demands would not be granted by justice, but must be 'extorted from the fears of their oppressors'.

Most Chartist orators were men, but women in London played important roles, holding collections for Chartist prisoners, making banners, organising meetings and tea parties, and developing a consumer boycott of shops that did not support the Chartists. The East London Female Patriotic Association, whose object was 'to assist our brethren in obtaining universal suffrage', shared premises with the East London Democratic Association (ELDA), a stronghold of physical force Chartism that had support particularly among Spitalfields silkweavers.

---

18 'Address to the Women of England', *Northern Star*, 2 July 1842, cited by Richard Brown's 'Looking at History' blog, 28 November 2007.

ELDA, founded by George Julian Harney, later broadened its geographical scope and shortened its name to London Democratic Association. Within London Chartism it challenged the more moderate LWMA. Harney was assisted by James Bronterre O'Brien, who had edited the *Poor Man's Guardian* for the moral force Chartist Hetherington, and later published another newspaper – *The Power of the Pence*, 'intended for those who know the look of a penny better than a pound'. O'Brien was an advocate of class struggle, arguing that disenfranchised workers without property produced all of society's wealth, but it was stolen from them by government and church, unproductive middlemen and aristocrats. After spending 18 months in prison in 1840–41, convicted for 'seditious libel', O'Brien shifted from his 'physical force' perspective, and in his latter years placed more emphasis on the Chartists' educational role than on militancy.

Other leading Chartists around the country faced more severe sentences – more than 100 were exiled to penal colonies in Australia. The revival of London Chartism in 1841 began in January with a large demonstration in support of three Chartist leaders who had been deported to Australia. As several leading Chartists in London were jailed for their writing and speeches, new leaders came forward. One was William Cuffay, a tailor less than five feet tall, born in Chatham in 1788, who rose to the interim presidency of the Chartists in London during their most active phase.

Cuffay's African grandfather was sold into slavery in St Kitts, where his father had been born a slave. The name Cuffay was a slave-owners variant of Kofi, the West African Ashanti name given to a male born on a Friday. Cuffay's father came to Britain after he was freed and married an English woman from Kent.

William Cuffay's first struggle was with his disabilities – he had a deformed spine and shinbones – but he became a tailor in his late teens and worked in tailoring throughout his life. He moved to London in 1819 and found work, mostly in Soho. In 1834 he participated in a failed tailors' strike for shorter hours and better pay. He was victimised for his role in the strike, and struggled to find regular employment afterwards. These difficulties, though, drew him into political activity, and he joined the Westminster Chartists. Linking the threads of his political and trade union work, he helped form the Metropolitan Tailors Charter Association. He spoke powerfully at a crowded meeting at the Owenite Social Institution in John Street near Tottenham Court Road in March 1842, urging tailors to support the Chartist petition, which would soon be submitted to Parliament. The first Chartist petition had nearly 1.3 million signatories; the one in May 1842 more than 3.2 million.

With Cuffay playing a leading role, *The Times* referred disparagingly to London's Chartists as 'the black man and his party'. Cuffay, though, was not the sole victim of this paper's racism. In due course *The Times* would describe the Chartists as 'tools in the hands of a gang of desperadoes . . . a ramification for the Irish conspiracy', claiming that 'The Repealers wish to make as great a hell of this island as they have made of their own.'

Several national and local Chartist leaders were Irish. In London there were radical Irish nationalist societies, whose members included active Chartists. Posters mobilising for the Kennington Common Demonstration on 10 April 1848, when the third national petition would be delivered to Parliament, advertised meeting points for 'the Chartists, the Trades, and the Irish Confederate and Repeal Bodies'. Their interests converged.

A large Irish contingent carried a banner of green silk with an orange fringe, a golden Irish harp and the words 'Let every man have his own country.'

Clerkenwell Green was the rallying point that day for the Chartists' City and Eastern Divisions. Other divisions gathered at Stepney Green, Russell Square and Peckham Fields. Mobilising posters attacked the press for vilifying the Chartists instead of acknowledging their just demands: 'We and our families are pining in misery, want and starvation! We demand a fair day's wages for a fair day's work! We are the slaves of capital – we demand protection to our labour. We are political serfs – we demand to be free.'

Revolutions had erupted in several European cities, and Britain's ruling classes were increasingly jittery about London. In the early 1820s, the French ambassador Chateaubriand had praised British institutions' stability to Lord Liverpool but Liverpool replied: 'One insurrection in London and all is lost.' A week before the April 1848 demonstration, London's Commissioner of Police declared the planned protest illegal. The government knew that the organisers would not comply. During that week a volunteer Special Constabulary, drawn principally from shopkeepers, lawyers and government clerks, was formed to bolster the police presence.[19] Armed police were placed outside the Foreign Office the night before, and armed protection organised for prisons, the General Post Office and the British Museum. The Queen was evacuated to the Isle of Wight, and her valuables, royal carriages and horses were removed. Three thousand troops were moved into the capital, expanding the central garrison to more than 7,000 soldiers. On the morning,

---

19 The origin of London Metropolitan Police's 'Specials'.

another 450 infantry and 37 marines were mobilised. Meanwhile, 4,000 police were positioned at the bridges, in Kennington, where the demonstration rally would gather, and in Westminster, where the petition would be brought.

With the bridges sealed and such a threatening armed presence in place, Chartist leader Feargus O'Connor met Police Commissioners and magistrates, and agreed to abandon plans to march as a body on Parliament from Kennington. He would ask the crowd to disperse after the rally and the petition would be delivered by a delegation in a hansom cab. Many Chartists felt that by crossing the bridges they had been led into a trap. They were willing to test whether the authorities would dare to prevent them marching back. Cuffay condemned O'Connor's 'cowardly' acquiescence.

The press derided the protest as a 'fiasco'. The Prime Minister, Viscount Palmerston, was more circumspect: 'The snake is scotched and not killed and we must continue on our guard.' His fears were well-founded. Throughout May and June there were fiery Chartist mass meetings, angry marches and mini-riots across the country. These included a running battle on the rooftops of Clerkenwell Green, a militant joint march with the Irish Democratic Federation from Finsbury Square to the West End on 31 May, and a pitched battle between Chartists and police in Bethnal Green in June. Many Chartist speakers were arrested and imprisoned for sedition. The fatal blow against London's Chartists was dealt in August, when police raids on secret Chartist meetings in pubs in Soho, Holborn and Southwark yielded loaded pistols, pikes, daggers, spearheads and swords. In St James Churchyard on Clerkenwell Close, 400 hidden ball cartridges were unearthed. Three prominent Chartists, including Cuffay, were sentenced to transportation for 'conspiring together to levy war against Her Majesty' and 15 others received sentences ranging from 18 months to two years. Most pleaded their innocence, and much of the evidence came from two police spies, Powell and Davis, who had infiltrated secret committees. The defendants claimed that Powell was 'constantly suggesting to his colleagues projects of conflagration and slaughter'. Witnesses said Powell had offered them daggers and firearms if they joined the Chartists. Cuffay protested that his trial was unfair. He was seeking neither pity nor mercy but to be tried by his peers, and without an atmosphere of press assassination: 'Everything has been done to raise a prejudice against me,' he said, 'and the press . . . have done all in their power to smother me with ridicule.' In reporting the charge against him, *The Times* had described Cuffay as 'half a nigger'.

He was transported to Tasmania for life, with a recommendation that he serve at least seven years, but was fully pardoned in 1856. However, he chose to stay in Tasmania, where his wife had joined him. He worked as a tailor and campaigned for workers' rights and democracy there until his death a workhouse infirmary in Hobart in 1870.

The revolutionary upheavals on the Continent brought several exiled revolutionaries to London as political refugees in the 1850s. Most settled in Soho, and some formed communist clubs and other radical associations here. One continental revolutionary who preceded them, collaborated with Chartists and operated within Clerkenwell, was Giuseppe Mazzini, founder of the Young Italy movement, which was struggling for a united democratic Italian republic. Arriving in 1837, he was perplexed by London's fog: 'We have had night at mid-day three or four times since our arrival . . . during which all the lamps are lit.

Imagine an immense cotton cap falling suddenly over the eyes of the town . . . passers-by resemble spectres, and one feels himself to be somewhat spectral.'[20]

Mazzini wanted to educate Italian migrant workers about Young Italy and recruit them to return home to fight; instead he helped them improve their practical situation in London. In November 1840 he founded *Unione degli Operai Italiani*, a workers' club and friendly society at 5 Hatton Garden, and introduced the members to ideas of 'association' – unionising.[21] He started an Italian newspaper, *Apostolato Popolare*, modelled on the Chartist press, with assistance from the Chartist printer, John Cleave.

In 1841, he established a Free Italian School at Hatton Garden, backed by Liberal benefactors, which later found bigger premises nearby at 5 Greville Street. The school sought to expand the cultural and educational horizons of adult migrant workers, but it soon had an additional function as Mazzini responded to the plight of Italian children working as street musicians. Poverty-stricken parents in Italy were coerced to sell children to *padroni* – labour trafficking gangs – who subsequently enslaved them. Several hundred Italian children gained a basic education at the school's evening classes. This opened up opportunities for them once they escaped the *padroni*'s clutches.

The democratic ideals that Mazzini and the Chartists shared were slow to come to fruition. But nearly two decades after London's Chartist movement had been smashed, new generations of reformers and rebels pressed for democratic change. The

---

20 Massimo Vangelista, 'Giuseppe Mazzini's Houses in London', http://byronico. com/2013/10/01/giuseppe-mazzinis-houses-in-london (accessed 19 January 2019).

21 It moved later to 101 Farringdon Road, then 10 Laystall Street.

Chartist movement had organised marches, rallies, petitions, economic boycotts and strikes, and even attempted armed uprisings. It failed to win its goals in its time, but set an agenda for radical change.

When Chartism was launched, around 15 per cent of men had the vote. The Reform Acts of 1867 and 1884 widened the franchise to roughly 60 per cent. In the agitation for change, a militant Reform League demonstration caused damage at Hyde Park in 1866. 'The beautiful flower beds with which the road is lined from Marble Arch to Hyde Park Corner were strewn with broken railings and masonry . . . having been trampled under the rough feet of a careless multitude.'[22] One letter-writer to the *London Evening Standard*, using the pseudonym 'Ferox', condemned rioters who 'yelled at the police and stoned them when their backs were turned', and described 'ladies who were ... pelted in their carriages at the Marble Arch'. He concluded that 'the working classes must not be permitted to come in their thousands to Hyde Park'.[23] When the suffragette movement, comprising women including those who would be described as 'ladies', filled Hyde Park in their struggles for democracy in 1908 and 1910, speakers proudly paid homage to those who had fought for democracy on the same turf decades before.

Back in Clerkenwell Green, where Chartists had protested and fought with the police, the London Patriotic Club, founded by the radical liberal, John Stuart Mill, began to meet at number 37a, once a school serving London's Welsh community. The Club spread propaganda supporting republicanism, trade unions, extending the vote, and equal rights for women. Unusually

---

22 *Manchester Guardian*, 26 July 1866.

23 *London Evening Standard*, 26 July 1866.

among London's radical 'workingmen's' clubs, it was open to women. Speakers included the Russian anarchist, Peter Kropotkin, and socialists such as Eleanor Marx and William Morris. By the 1890s many radical liberals redefined themselves as socialists, and Morris – artist, designer, poet, writer and activist, and a wealthy socialist – established a radical publishing house there, the Twentieth Century Press, in conjunction with the Social Democratic Federation. Much of the Marxist literature circulating around Britain in the 1890s and early 1900s emanated from this building in Clerkenwell Green.

Today it houses the Marx Memorial Library, acquired in 1933 by a committee seeking a fitting memorial for Karl Marx, 50 years after his death in the city where he had lived for more than three decades. In May that year, after Hitler's Nazi party took power in the land of Marx's birth, the Nazis publicly burnt Jewish and communist literature in Berlin's Bebelplatz. The committee had already planned to create a library of progressive literature, and felt more determined to do so following the Nazis' actions, but they had not found a suitable building. Marx's first address in Chelsea was beyond their means, and the homes he and his family lived in near Camden were not for sale. The rooms they had lodged in around Soho had deteriorated and were now unfit for human habitation, and could not house a library. On their way home from the committee meeting two leading figures from Battersea Communist Party, Clive and Noreen Branson (discussed in Chapter 7), passed through Clerkenwell Green. Aware of the Green's political significance in decades past they saw a substantial building in a very neglected state, whose upper floor was available to rent. Within days the decision was finalised, and weeks later the Bransons played a major role in finalising the purchase of the building. After a major facelift, the façade proudly displayed 'Marx House Library and Workers' School' in huge lettering, embodying Clerkwenwell Green's vibrant, rebellious history.

In 1967, those words disappeared. A further facelift restored its genteel Georgian appearance. This change guaranteed its Grade ll listed status, as several buildings on the Green were being redeveloped. But the echoes of generations of rebels who gathered there and fought for change continue to be heard every spring, when trade unionists, socialists, communists and young twenty-first-century radicals assemble on the cobbles in front of Marx Memorial Library for the annual May Day march to Trafalgar Square.

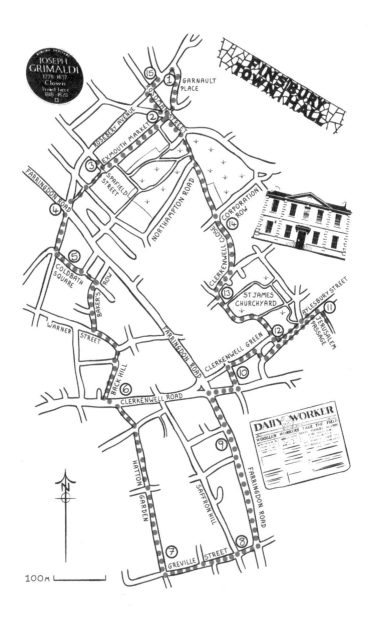

JOSEPH
GRIMALDI
1778-1837
Clown
lived here
1818-1828

GARNAULT
PLACE

FINSBURY
TOWN HALL

ROSEBERY AVENUE

EXMOUTH MARKET

SPAFIELD
STREET

FARRINGDON ROAD

NORTHAMPTON ROAD

CORPORATION
ROW

COLDBATH
SQUARE

BAKER'S ROW

CLERKENWELL CLOSE

ST JAMES
CHURCHYARD

AYLESBURY STREET

JERUSALEM PASSAGE

WARNER STREET

FARRINGDON ROAD

CLERKENWELL GREEN

BACK HILL

CLERKENWELL ROAD

DAILY WORKER
WOOLLEN WORKERS TAKE THE FIELD

HATTON GARDEN

SAFFRON HILL

FARRINGDON ROAD

N

100M

GREVILLE STREET

WALK

Start at Old Finsbury Town Hall, Rosebery Avenue, EC1R 4RP.

1. Rosebery Avenue

The Old Town Hall building was opened by Lord Rosebery in 1895 as the local vestry hall. It became the Town Hall when the Metropolitan Borough of Finsbury was created in 1900. In 1965 Finsbury was incorporated into Islington. In the 1830s the total population of Islington and Finsbury was approximately 137,000, with 100,000 of them in Finsbury. Its largest nineteenth-century industries were brewing, printing, and clock and watch manufacturing. Turn right into Garnault Place and cross Rosoman Street into Exmouth Market.

2. Exmouth Market

The food market established here in the 1890s had declined by the 1970s but has benefited from regeneration since the 1990s. Many international foods are sold there today. Halfway along this paved street a plaque commemorates Joseph Grimaldi, the son of Italian immigrants and the original 'Joey the Clown', who lived here. Grimaldi performed as a dancer at Sadler's Wells at three years of age. Italian migrants first settled in this area in the late eighteenth century. The nearby church was built in Italian-renaissance style in the 1880s. Turn into Spafield Street.

3. Spafield Street

Spa Fields stood to the south and east of this street. In November and December 1816, followers of Thomas Spence, a shoemaker and radical teacher from Newcastle who came to London in the 1790s and died in 1814, organised a series of meetings here attracting thousands of people. The authorities blamed Spenceans for bread riots that broke out in London in 1800–1. Police violently dispersed the meeting on 2 December 1816, arresting several leaders. They were charged with high treason, though the case eventually collapsed. Spence promoted egalitarianism, and supported land nationalisation and universal suffrage. He published a radical paper called *Pig's Meat*. Return to Exmouth Market. Cross over Farringdon Road.

4. Rosebery Avenue (west)
The Post Office's Mount Pleasant Sorting Office, opposite, was opened in 1889 on the site of the Middlesex House of Correction, also known as Coldbath Fields Prison. This, in turn, was built on the site of a former prison burnt down in the Gordon Riots of the 1780s. The National Union of the Working Classes demonstration, at which PC Culley was stabbed, took place on the fields behind the prison. Turn left into Coldbath Square.

5. Coldbath Square
The street name recalls the prison, as do the bars voluntarily placed on the windows of this more recent gated development. Continue along the paved pathway and turn right into Baker's Row. Several street names locally refer to bakers. The jury investigating PC Culley's death was composed mainly of bakers from the nearby Gray's Inn area. Turn left into Warner Street then right into Back Hill. This street was at the heart of the immigrant colony in Clerkenwell known as Little Italy. Italian

immigrants in this district worked mainly as knife grinders, lacemakers, street musicians, street food sellers and mosaic and terrazzo craft workers. Turn left into Clerkenwell Road.

6. Clerkenwell Road

St Peter's Italian Church was built in 1863. It became a major focus for London's Italian community, functioning also as a labour exchange after Sunday mass. An annual Italian parade (initiated in the 1880s), assembles near the church and along Back Hill on the first Sunday after 16 July. Cross Clerkenwell Road into Hatton Garden.

7. Hatton Garden

Hatton Garden has been the centre of London's jewellery trade for hundreds of years, and in the twentieth century was particularly associated with immigrant Hasidic Jews from central and eastern Europe. At number 5, a stone plaque commemorates the Italian revolutionary nationalist, Giuseppe Mazzini, who established his Free Italian School here. It moved later to Greville Street, opposite where Chartist William Lovett had his coffee house. Turn left into Greville Street. Stop on the corner of Saffron Hill.

8. Saffron Hill

'Near to the spot on which Snow Hill and Holborn Hill meet, there opens, a narrow and dismal alley leading to Saffron Hill', wrote Dickens in *Oliver Twist*. '[A] commercial colony of itself: the emporium of petty larceny.' Dickens located Fagin's den in that alley – Field Lane (now the southern section of Saffron Hill). Field Lane and Saffron Hill formed a significant part of the Clerkenwell rookery. Turn left into Farringdon Road.

9. Farringdon Road

Number 75, William Rust House, a former brushmakers' warehouse, is named after the first editor of the *Daily Worker*, the Communist Party paper launched in 1930. It was printed in this building for several decades from 1948. Rust took a post in Moscow in 1932 and was later the paper's correspondent in Spain during the Civil War, before returning to the editorship. He was in the post until his death in 1949 at the age of 45. When the first edition was printed in Farringdon Road, 20,000 supporters blocked the traffic and held a torch-lit procession, carrying William Rust to Clerkenwell Green where he auctioned two copies of the first edition for £45 each (the equivalent of more than £1,000 today). Turn right into Clerkenwell Road then left into the Green.

10. Clerkenwell Green

The Sessions House, built in 1779, where leaders of the National Union of the Working Classes were put on trial in 1832, is still standing. The red flag was hoisted for the first time in London at a rally here in 1871 in solidarity with the Paris Communards, who had seized control of their city for a brief two-month period. Eleanor Marx, active in the Socialist League, addressed a large rally of unemployed workers on Clerkenwell Green in October 1887, a few weeks before marching from here to Trafalgar Square on the fateful 'Bloody Sunday' demonstration (see Chapter 3). Marx Memorial Library is at number 37a. The library includes a room, which can be visited, that was rented by the Social Democratic Federation around the turn of the twentieth century. *Iskra* (*The Spark*), the Russian Revolutionary newspaper, was written and edited here by Lenin. His wife Krupskaya was secretary of the *Iskra* board. Harry Quelch of the SDF assisted Lenin with printing copies of *Iskra* which were smuggled back to Russia. Lenin, Krupskaya and several other exiled Russian revolutionaries lived within walking distance of Clerkenwell Green in Holford Square, Ampton Street and Sidmouth Street. Walk to Jerusalem Passage on the southeast side of the Green.

11. Jerusalem Passage

This leads towards the Priory of St John of Jerusalem – hence the name. For hundreds of years it was the headquarters of the crusading Knights Hospitaliers. The priory was burned down during the Peasants' Revolt in 1381. Its prior, Robert Hales, executed during the revolt, had been appointed Treasurer to Richard II and implemented the hated Poll Tax. A plaque on the corner with the Green celebrates the coal merchant Thomas Britton, a collector of rare books and music, who had a strong interest in chemistry and the occult. He held musical soirées above his shop here, attended by performers and composers including Handel. In the 1830s and 1840s, Chartists often met at coffee houses in Jerusalem Passage. Walk across the Green to the corner of Clerkenwell Close.

12. Clerkenwell Close

Lenin frequented the Crown Tavern on the corner of Clerkenwell Close. The original tavern incorporated the Red Star Coffee House, established in the 1870s, which served as the strike headquarters for local printing unions in the 1880s.

13. St James Churchyard

In this churchyard, 400 ball carriages were found, leading to the conviction of several Chartist leaders in the summer of 1848. Continue along Clerkenwell Close to the corner of Corporation Row.

14. Corporation Row

The former premises of Hugh Myddelton School, now converted into housing, had been the site of Clerkenwell House of Detention, between 1818 and 1890. The House of Detention had replaced an earlier prison here. In November 1867 it held two radical Irish nationalists: Richard O'Sullivan Burke and Joseph Casey. That month saw large demonstrations on Clerkenwell Green in support of Irish prisoners held in London and Manchester. Burke and Casey's associates in London's radical Irish circles plotted to free them by bombing the prison wall. The explosions literally backfired, destroying adjacent housing. Twelve people were killed and 40 wounded. In a letter to Engels, Marx described the event as 'a colossal stupidity . . . the London masses who have shown great sympathy towards Ireland will . . . be driven into the arms of a reactionary government. One cannot expect the London proletariat will let itself be blown into the air for the honour of Fenian emissaries.' Continue on to Rosoman Street. Turn right to the Old Town Hall.

15. Rosebery Avenue

Next to the entrance, a green plaque celebrates Dadabhai Naoroji, a mathematician, philosopher and one of the founders of the Indian National Congress, who influenced Mahatma Gandhi, and was Britain's first MP of colour. In 1892 he was elected as Liberal MP for Finsbury Central, which he won by three votes. His opponent demanded a recount, and his majority increased to five. Nevertheless, Naoroji was saddled with the nickname Dadabhai Narrow-Majority. In 1901 Naoroji published his seminal work *Poverty and un-British Rule in India*, which detailed the drain of wealth from the people of India to Britain under imperial control. He participated in the opening ceremony of India House in 1905, a student residence which became a hub for radical Indian nationalism. Naoroji and his private secretary, the revolutionary Bikhaji Cama, were frequent visitors there before Naoroji returned to India in 1908. Cama was due to return then too, but was asked to sign an agreement that she would cease her campaigning if she did. She refused and went into exile in Paris.

St James Churchyard, Clerkenwell Close, where weaponry was unearthed in 1848.

Confrontation at 'Bloody Sunday' demonstration in Trafalgar Square.

3

THE SPARK OF REBELLION
IN BOW

*A small deformed boy noticed by no one standing before him
. . . the face of an old man on the thin body of a child . . . a
cold shudder ran through Auban. It was the beginning of the
horror that had always turned him to ice when he returned
from the home of 'the disinherited,' the silent desolation of
the East End.*

J. H. Mackay, *The Anarchists*, 1891

It took the Liverpool-born son of a wealthy ship-owner and corn
merchant to uncover the depth of poverty in late nineteenth-
century London. Charles Booth had added glove manufacturing
and a leather and skins company to his inherited business
empire before he researched the victims of London's 'Victorian
prosperity'. Initially, Booth set out to refute the claims of another
wealthy businessman's son – Henry Hyndman, founder of the
Social Democratic Federation – who stated in the *Pall Mall
Gazette* that 25 per cent of Londoners lived in 'abject poverty'.

Slums were starting to be cleared. 'Philanthropic' housing
developments were expanding. Booth told Hyndman that he
'had greatly overstated the case'. But his own investigation of
the East End shook him: 35 per cent of east Londoners lived on

or below the 'poverty line' and a third of these were 'chronically distressed'.[1] Several thousand east Londoners slept rough or scrambled for places in shelters and lodging houses, mainly established by religious charities.

Many other Eastenders only kept a roof over their head by entering the workhouse. In 1892 several socialists stood for election to their local Board of Guardians to try to make these forbidding places more humane while simultaneously organising to abolish them. The elected guardian, George Lansbury, author of a pamphlet, *Smash up the Workhouse!*, described his first encounter with Poplar Workhouse:

> . . . [K]eys dangling at the waist of those who spoke to you . . . stripped and bathed in a communal tub, and the final indignity of being dressed in clothes which had been worn by lots of other people . . . ill fitting and coarse . . . floors were polished, but of goodwill and kindliness, there was none.[2]

Workhouses, night shelters, and living rough were the lot of the poorest Eastenders. Crowded sweatshops, dingy workshops, factories paying starvation wages, and the daily scramble for a few hours casual work on the docks were grim realities for those one rung higher. Hard-earned pennies disappeared in rent for cramped, dilapidated lodgings. 'The East End', wrote J.H. Mackay, 'is labour and poverty, chained together by the curse of our time – servitude.'[3]

---

1 Booth defined the poverty line as the level of income for a family of four or five to subsist on: 18 shillings to 21 shillings a week.

2 G. Lansbury, *My Life*, London: Constable & Co. 1928.

3 J.H. Mackay, *The Anarchists*, Boston, MA: Benjamin R. Tucker, 1891, p. 12.

It seemed inconceivable that such distress could exist indefinitely alongside the stockpiling of vast riches a stone's throw away in the City of London without breeding rebellion. But in April 1888, Friedrich Engels lamented that nowhere were people 'less actively resistant, more passively submitting to their fate . . . than in the East End of London.'[4]

Within weeks Engels was proved wrong. A spontaneous two-week strike by 1,400 factory workers ignited a wave of industrial unrest that shook the capital and reverberated nationally. The dispute at Bow's Fairfield Works match factory, owned by the Quakers, Bryant & May, spawned a Union of Women Matchmakers and catalysed other dramatic disputes among low-skilled and unskilled, poorly paid workers. By the early 1890s workers were embracing a 'new unionism', and the East End was the cradle of this exciting development.

The striking matchworkers in summer 1888 were female, working class and many were of Irish heritage, but Louise Raw identifies these three 'disadvantages' as positive drivers of change.[5] During the nineteenth century, 100,000 Irish emigrants, mainly from rural southern and western counties, settled near the Thames, in Southwark and Bermondsey and in London's East End, where work was plentiful though poorly paid and often casualised.

The streets leading towards Bow from Mile End have Welsh names such as Aberavon Road, Rhondda Grove and Morgan Street, rather than Irish names. Sir Charles Morgan combined his

---

4   Letter to Margaret Harkness who published searing accounts of urban deprivation in London under the male pseudonym, John Law. https://www.marxists.org/archive/marx/works/1888/letters/88_04_15.htm (accessed September 2018).

5   L. Raw, *Striking a Light: The Bryant and May Matchwomen and their Place in History*, London: Continuum, 2009.

Tredegar-based iron industry with east London's shipbuilding industry and developed the land around Tredegar Square from the profits. Many enterprises close to the docks were connected with shipbuilding: ropemakers, candlemakers, sailmakers, and timber yards. Other East End districts had their own distinct industries. Bethnal Green and Shoreditch had a large furniture trade; Stepney and Poplar had many bootmakers and shoemakers. But the East End's most enduring industry was clothing. Flemish weavers settled locally in the fourteenth century. French Huguenot refugees, specialising in silk-weaving, were conspicuous in seventeenth- and eighteenth-century Spitalfields and Bethnal Green. The clothing industry expanded greatly in Whitechapel among Irish and East European Jewish immigrants. And as the Jewish presence declined in the 1960s, Bengali immigrants from the Sylhet region arrived and continued this tradition.

Booth's cousin, Beatrice Potter, was both fascinated and repelled by immigrant Jews' sweatshops – a 'new province of production, inhabited by a peculiar people' – where minutely subdivided tasks were performed by unskilled, often unregulated workers. Their system, she claimed, super-exploited Jewish and non-Jewish women performing low-status tasks, and harmed indigenous English tailors who followed 'one man, one garment' methods, with regulated pay and hours. Potter noted that even when women performed the same tasks as men they were paid less money. Her sharp economic analysis, however, was blunted by anti-Jewish prejudice: '[L]ove of profit', she wrote, is 'the impelling motive of the Jewish race.'[6]

Labour within east London's industries was sharply divided

---

6 Article on the Jewish community, in Charles Booth (ed.), *Life and Labour of the People in London*, London: Williams and Norgate, 1889.

by gender. Men carried out hard, physical work, especially on the docks and in furniture workshops. But wherever workers could assemble products through repetitive, unskilled tasks, for exhaustingly long hours, East End employers preferred to hire women, who could be paid less than men.

In Lancashire, many women joined trade unions, especially textile workers, but, until the late 1880s, London's trade unionists were mainly men – builders, carpenters, printers, shoemakers, stonemasons and tailors. The East End's female workers had no vehicle for challenging their conditions and most male workers, fearing their wages would fall if women infiltrated their industries, offered little solidarity.

During the 1880s a sustained economic depression brought high unemployment. Rumblings of discontent turned into rebellion. The Salvation Army founder, William Booth, claimed that many east Londoners fared worse than a cab-horse, which usually had 'shelter for the night, food for its stomach, work allotted to it by which it can eat its corn'. Regular employment, however poorly paid, had kept families afloat. As unemployment pulled this fraying rug from under their feet, a new wave of political radicals encouraged struggling workers to fight back collectively.

Before 1880, London's political radicals campaigned mainly to expand democracy and challenge the Church's authority. But the 1880s produced new organisations, spreading Marx's idea that the working class was the motor of social change. The Stratford Dialectical and Radical Club emerged from the local Secular Society. It held meetings on Mile End Waste – a space previously dominated by street preachers – and transformed itself into the Labour Emancipation League

(LEL). The LEL formed branches in Stratford, Canning Town, Bethnal Green and Hackney, calling for 'political equality with equal social rights for all'. Hyndman's SDF created east London outposts, including one on Burdett Road, Mile End. When William Morris's Socialist League split off, it established premises nearby on Bridge Street. But increasingly, new organisations spreading rebellious ideas in working-class areas focused on outdoor spaces.

East London's liveliest pitches were at Dod Street, Limehouse, Victoria Park in Bethnal Green and Mile End Waste. In Dod Street, to the government's alarm, thousands of workers gathered to hear speakers call for revolutionary change. In 1885, police arrested several socialist activists there, while leaving religious preachers undisturbed. One activist, Annie Besant, formed an organisation to give legal assistance to arrested socialists, and saved SDF member and Jewish tailors' union leader, Lewis Lyons, from a threatened custodial sentence.

Radicals encouraged workers to challenge economic injustice and also targeted Britain's coercive policies in Ireland. The Metropolitan Radical Federation, the Irish National League, the SDF and Socialist League, called a major protest on 13 November 1887 in Trafalgar Square against attacks on Irish civil rights campaigners and the imprisonment of Irish MP William O'Brien. Meanwhile, Sir Charles Warren, an ex-military man appointed to head the Metropolitan Police in 1886, asked the Home Secretary to ban meetings by unemployed workers camping out in Trafalgar Square, London's principal free speech venue, nominally owned by the Crown. Three separate issues – Ireland, unemployment and free speech – each felt strongly in east London, led 30,000 protesters to converge on Trafalgar Square in processions from

Bermondsey, Peckham and Battersea, Paddington, Clerkenwell and east London. They endured savage beatings from mounted police and troops both in the square and in the surrounding streets, where police attempted to prevent them from reaching the square. Hundreds of demonstrators were arrested, including several socialist speakers, in what became known as 'Bloody Sunday'.

Annie Besant was aggrieved because she *wasn't* arrested. Born Annie Wood in London in 1847, she came to socialism via radical secularism, and felt the Irish issue keenly. 'Three quarters of my blood and all my heart are Irish', she wrote.[7] Educated by an evangelical Christian, Annie married Reverend Frank Besant at 20 and had two children, Digby and Mabel. Reverend Besant's abusive treatment of Annie prompted her to question her faith.[8] After they separated, Annie met secularists and political radicals through South Place Ethical Society,[9] and was strongly influenced by the 'poor-man's lawyer', William Prowting Roberts, a former Chartist who said the poor were 'the working bees, the wealth producers with a right to self-rule [and] justice not to charity'. She began writing for Charles Bradlaugh's secularist *National Reformer*, and told Christians: 'I don't deny God, but deny your [interventionist] God who is an impossibility.' Her pet hate, though, was Christian charity, which gave

> . . . a hundredweight of coal and five pounds of beef once
> a year to a family who could earn a hundred such doles

---

7 A. Besant, *Annie Besant: An Autobiography*, London: Theosophical Society, 1893.

8 Besant also attributed her early doubts about Christianity to a 'merciful God' allowing her daughter Mabel to suffer a life-threatening illness in her early years.

9 See Chapter 5.

if Christian justice allowed him a fair wage for the work
he performs. It plunders the workers of the wealth they
make, and then flings back at them a thousandth part of
their own product as charity. It builds hospitals for the
poor whom it has poisoned in filthy courts and alleys.[10]

In her first major speaking engagement, a lecture in August 1874
on women's political status,[11] Besant said she longed for the day
when women and men would be '[c]o-workers in every labour,
co-partners in every righteous project, co-soldiers in every
just cause'. They could bring different and complementary
talents: 'The man . . . his greater strength and more sustained
determination, the woman her quicker judgement and purer
heart, till man shall grow tenderer and woman stronger, man
more pure, and woman more brave and free . . . free to grow, to
strengthen and to rise.'

A week after the first Bloody Sunday demonstration, at which
male police and soldiers hid their tender side, protesters held
a huge rally in Hyde Park and a section of them attempted to
return to Trafalgar Square. Again the authorities responded
fiercely. A 41-year-old legal clerk, Alfred Linnell, unattached
to any political grouping, was knocked down by a police horse,
and beaten by police in Northumberland Avenue, close to the
square. He died a few days later from his injuries. Annie Besant,
under the auspices of the Law and Liberty League,[12] organised
a mass funeral parade from Central London to Tower Hamlets

10 Besant, *Autobiography*, p. 182.

11 At the Cooperative Hall in Castle Street, W1.

12 Formed in 1887 by Annie Besant and William Stead to defend civil liberties and assist
    victims of police brutality.

Cemetery (known locally as Bow Cemetery). The Chief Police Commissioner forbade the procession from starting at the place where Linnell had fallen, which the league had planned. They had to start near Aldwych. The Socialist League's *Commonweal* reported:

> An open hearse with four horses was used; on top . . . a shield painted black with large white letters 'Killed in Trafalgar Square' . . . behind . . . three flags, green, yellow, and red, for the Irish, radicals and socialists . . . the train stretched in an unbroken length for nearly a mile, with a large number of banners, mostly red, and several bands playing slow marches . . . Bow cemetery was reached at half past four, when it was already dark.[13]

At the graveside William Morris said that Linnell's 'hard life and hard death' illustrated the need to transform society. Morris sensed that change was in the air. In January 1888, he wrote:

If rebellion is . . . our future, then we must look back at the past year with hope . . . no one who witnessed the sympathetic demeanour of the huge crowds that accompanied . . . Linnell's funeral procession could . . . deny that the masses of London are on our side. Democratic ideas tending towards socialism have been evolved from the Irish struggle and men's minds have been familiarised thereby with resistance to authority; the precariousness of livelihood under the capitalist has been brought home . . . the class war is becoming obvious to all.[14]

---

13 *Commonweal*, 24 December 1887.

14 *Commonweal*, 7 January 1888.

In June 1888, at a Fabian Society lecture, Besant heard Clementina Black discussing 'Female Labour in London'. From the floor, a former artillery officer named Henry Hyde Champion lit his pipe theatrically, then described conditions at Bryant & May's match factory in Bow, where women worked 12-hour shifts for paltry wages.[15] Their health was undermined by having to eat at their workstations where they used dangerous materials.[16] The following evening, Besant and three colleagues from her left-wing paper, the *Link*, waited by the factory gates to interview women coming off their shift.

Bryant & May acquired this former candle, crinoline and rope factory in 1861. As Quakers and Liberals, they considered themselves enlightened employers.[17] But the workers corroborated Champion's charges, and Besant published a strident exposé in the *Link*. Describing a 16-year-old earning just four shillings a week, Besant said this sum was subject to deductions

> ... if the feet are dirty, or the ground under the bench is left untidy, a fine of 3d ... for putting 'burnts' – matches that have caught fire during the work – on the bench is ... and one unhappy girl was once fined 2s/6d for some unknown crime. If a girl leaves four or five matches on her bench when she goes for a fresh 'frame' she is fined 3d ... some departments a fine of 3d is inflicted for talking

15 Born in Poona, India, Champion often wore an eye glass, a dress suit and silk hat. He resigned his army post while on leave, in protest at Britain's Egyptian campaign with which he profoundly disagreed; 'the next night', he said 'I was preaching socialism in Clerkenwell Green'.

16 Charles Dickens wrote an article in 1852 on health hazards in matchmaking. See Raw, *Striking a Light*, p. 93.

17 Quakers had established some early industries of the East End and established some hospitals and schools.

... One girl was fined 1s. for letting the web twist round a machine ... to save her fingers from being cut, and was sharply told to take care of the machine, 'never mind your fingers'. Another, who ... lost a finger thereby, was left unsupported while she was helpless.[18]

Besant sent a copy to the company directors. Bryant replied by telegram: 'Nothing but a tissue of lies. Will receive legal attention.' Factory foremen tried to bully the workforce into signing a statement confirming that conditions were satisfactory. When the women refused, the management summarily sacked several 'ringleaders'. In response, the women spontaneously walked out. The next day, a male activist urged picketing matchworkers to stay strong and form a union. The police arrested him for obstruction, but were followed to the station by pickets who demonstrated until he was released. He was Lewis Lyons, the Jewish tailors' leader Annie Besant had bailed out in 1885.

During the dispute, she and SDF member Herbert Burrows helped the women form a Union of Women Matchmakers. The women were determined to stay out until the company reinstated those sacked workers; ended the system of fines; and agreed to create a separate area for eating during their long shifts without contaminating their food.

The strikers sought community support. On 8 July they held a rally at Mile End Waste featuring Clementina Black, Cunningham Grahame MP, and radical preacher Stewart Headlam. They marched through the City into the West End returning with donations, and stopping for tea and solidarity at a Workers' Club

18 'Slavery in London', the *Link*, 23 June 1888.

in Berner Street opened by Jewish anarchists. Matchwomen took a petition to Parliament with thousands of signatures, and gained sympathetic press coverage. On 13 July Bryant & May declared that nothing would make them concede. They threatened to recruit new workers from Glasgow and talked of relocating to Scandinavia, but within two weeks, they acquiesced to the strikers' demands. The matchwomen's victory provided a template for action by other low-paid, low-skilled workers.

The factory closed in 1979 but its red-brick buildings remain. Today, Fairfield Works is the gentrified, gated Bow Quarter. Its blocks, called Arlington, Lexington and Manhattan, mask continuing hardship in the East End with a veneer of New York sophistication. Its on-site leisure centre includes a pool, sauna, dance studio and gym. Under the Arlington Arch, inside the gate, a display recounts the factory's history, including the strike, but the public are excluded.

Its outer wall has a plaque commemorating the strike, 'led here by Annie Besant'. Bryant & May always claimed that contented workers were radicalised by outside agitators. Counter-narratives also portray the women as passive and docile, needing leadership by educated socialists. The names of those who actually led the strike – Alice France, Kate Slater, Mary Driscoll, Jane Wakeling and Eliza Martin – struggle for wider recognition.

Louise Raw has convincingly shown that Besant was a *supporter*, rather than leader of the matchwomen's cause. She favoured a boycott over industrial action. Raw discovered that the women, largely from close-knit, politically aware Irish communities, had initiated earlier (unsuccessful) strikes and some of them knew Besant from pro-Irish political platforms. She quotes Booth's survey material, describing the women as 'a terrible

Bryant & May match factory, 1890s.

rough lot' displaying insolent confidence rather than docility.
'[D]ecent people scarcely dared to go down the street when they
were coming out of work.'[19] Excitable behaviour, though, was not
new to Fairfield Road: a plaque on the former Poplar Town Hall
reveals that the Whitsun Fair, which gave the street its name, was
closed in 1823 because of 'rowdyism and vice'.

Annie Besant contributed to east London's progressive campaigns from 1885–90, before her growing interest in
theosophy diverted her. The strike gave heart to local unskilled
workers, and had enduring consequences. London's industrial

---

19 Raw, *Striking a Light*, p. 151.

expansion was powered by gasworkers, including thousands of Eastenders working twelve-hour shifts as at Beckton, near West Ham. An unusual leader emerged among them. Neither Will Thorne nor his wife could sign their marriage register because they were illiterate. They made a 'mark' instead. At six years old, instead of going to school, Thorne worked twelve hours a day, five-and-a-half days a week turning a wheel at Rob's Rope Walk in his native Birmingham and worked in his uncle's barber shop for much of his weekends.

Despite his illiteracy he was a powerful orator and excellent organiser. He was 24 when he first arrived in London in 1881, having lost his job as a gas stoker in Saltley after a failed strike. Leaving his pregnant wife and child behind, he set off for the capital on foot, promising to send for them when he found regular work. He worked at Old Kent Gas Works in south London, but was a victim of the 'last in – first out' rule when the company reduced its workforce the following summer. Returning home, Thorne temporarily found work again at Saltley Gas Works before he came back to the Big Smoke for good, settling in Lawrence Street, Canning Town after being taken on at Beckton Gas Works.

Thorne joined Hyndman's SDF in 1884. His local branch had 14 members and met in a member's house in Lansdowne Road. He added another affiliation in 1885 – the Temperance Union – good for his health and his pocket. Through the SDF he mixed with socialist thinkers and activists such as Eleanor Marx, George Bernard Shaw, John Burns and Tom Mann. He assisted the Federation's struggles to establish outdoor pitches to spread their ideas, especially in east London, and gained experience in addressing mass audiences.

Acutely aware of east London's growing unemployment, he participated in the 'Bloody Sunday' demonstrations, experienced a ferocious police charge and saw colleagues arrested. He returned home injured and more determined to transform the lives of fellow workers and those starving through lack of work. He knew these struggles required patience but, eager to make an immediate difference, he helped to establish a soup kitchen in a temperance bar at 144 Barking Road, East Ham, a venue that would soon play a bigger role in Thorne's union struggles. On Saturday nights Thorne and colleagues visited food shops seeking contributions of bread and ingredients for soup. Zibach, who helped run the Temperance Bar, allowed them to use his kitchen equipment.

Thorne discussed socialist and trade union ideas at work 'in the lobby, in the mess room, wherever the opportunity permitted'. Meanwhile, management introduced new technology, called the 'Iron Man', that increased productivity but made work harder, and compelled randomly selected workers to work eighteen-hour shifts on a Sunday, instead of twelve. Anger and frustration were growing. Thorne called a meeting in Canning Town for 31 March 1889 with a platform of rousing speakers. Thorne himself led a contingent from Barking, 'with a band I paid for out of my own pocket. We had an old van for a platform . . . the atmosphere was electric when I mounted the platform.'

Acknowledging the workers' inhuman treatment by their employers, he greeted the crowd as 'fellow wage slaves'. They responded with a great cheer. He told them:

> . . . we have protested, but . . . we have been sneered at,
> ignored and have secured no redress . . . you will never

get any alteration in . . . your conditions or wages unless you join together and form a strong trade union . . . it is easy to break one stick, but when fifty sticks are together in one bundle it is a much more difficult job.[20]

He promised the workers that if they organised as a union, 'within six months we will claim and win the eight-hour day, a six-day week and the abolition of the present slave-driving methods in vogue not only at the Beckton Gas Works, but all over the country'.

'Will you do this?' He asked his rapt audience. 'There was one loud roar of "We will!"', he recorded. Thorne described this moment as 'the last birth pain of the union'.[21]

Some 800 members enrolled at that meeting. They gathered at 144 Barking Road on Sundays and sent out groups of workers on a 'crusade' to win union members at other gas works and local factories. Within weeks they had 3,000 members and a provisional committee. Union dues were kept at two pence a week, and membership was spread across a range of jobs. Members received a union card with the motto: 'Love, unity, fidelity'.

Some workers favoured campaigning for a pay increase of one shilling per day, but most backed Thorne's strategy, to fight for the eight-hour day, 'Shorten the hours and prolong your lives', he said. He recruited able co-workers, including Eleanor Marx – a multi-talented organiser, translator, drama worker and writer, who drew up the union rules and helped with administration.

When Thorne judged that they had sufficient muscle to

20 W. Thorne, *My Life's Battles*, London: G. Newnes, 1925, p. 68.

21 *Ibid.*, pp. 68–9.

challenge their employers, he petitioned the company directors and informed them that thousands of union members were willing to strike, but preferred to negotiate. The petition landed on their desks just as the employers' fear of competition from electrical power was intensifying. After several weeks Thorne received word that the directors had conceded the eight-hour day. There were still productivity issues to resolve but negotiations concluded with a spectacular victory for the union. Two twelve-hour shifts were replaced by three eight-hour shifts. More workers were taken on, and existing workers whose hours were reduced suffered no loss of pay.

Will Thorne's Gas Workers and General Labourers Union was later renamed the General Municipal and Boiler-Makers Union (GMB). He was proud that this union was 'one of the very few in which men and women are on equal terms', stating 'We want unions of *workers* not of workingmen and workingwomen.' As an Executive Committee member, Eleanor Marx took special responsibility for two all-women branches.

Ben Tillett, another rising figure in east London's labour movement, also began working young. At seven years old he worked long days at Roach's brickyard in Bristol, though he was probably relieved to get away from home, where his alcoholic father and a succession of stepmothers mistreated or neglected him. After two failed attempts to run away, he escaped with a circus troupe, who taught him acrobatics. He took a stray dog with him. The circus troupe gave him a Shetland pony to look after. At night he slept next to the pony, and the dog kept the rats away. One of Tillett's five sisters tracked him down and took him to relatives in Staffordshire, where he had two years of schooling before being apprenticed to a shoemaker. At 13 he joined the Royal Navy, visiting various European ports, Philadelphia and the Caribbean, and learned to read and write with the help of a Scottish friend. Fittingly, in terms of his future activism, he sailed on one ship called *Resistance*. Between voyages he stayed with his sister's mother-in-law in Bethnal Green, east London. He finally settled there at 16 years old, working at Markie's boot factory, and joined the Union of Boot and Shoe Operatives.

Tillett married Jane Tompkins and they shared her mother's flat in Hunslett Street. Determined to expand his intellectual horizons, he became the librarian at his local church, taught himself basic Latin and Greek, and attended lectures at Bow and Bromley Adult Education Institute. He struggled to overcome a stammer by reading Dickens to Jane in the evenings.

He began working on the docks, describing the humiliating 'call-on' system in a powerful speech at Whitechapel in 1887, later published as *A Dock Labourer's Bitter Cry*:

> We are driven into a shed, iron-barred from end to end, outside of which a foreman or contractor walks up and down with the air of a dealer in a cattle market . . . choosing from a crowd of men, who, in their eagerness to obtain employment trample each other under foot, and where like beasts they fight for the chances of a day's work.

A 'day's work' was usually less. Dockworkers often walked great distances to a job, unloaded cargo non-stop for two hours, and were then told to go home. Tillett himself recalled a 40-mile round trip on foot. Beatrice Potter noted the 'hidden irony in the dockers' fate', touching all things but enjoying none as 'the luxuries of our elaborate civilisation pass familiarly through the dock labourer's hands'.

The supply of dock labour constantly outstripped demand, driving wages down. One contemporary account describes how dockers 'faint from over-exhaustion and want of food . . . are ruptured, their spines injured, their bones broken, and their skulls fractured . . . to get ships loaded and unloaded a little quicker and a little cheaper'. This was not a socialist propaganda leaflet but the prestigious medical journal, *The Lancet*.

Tillett was working as a tea cooper at Monument Tea Warehouse in spring 1887 when a dispute broke out among counterparts at Cutler Street Warehouse. They sought Tillett's advice and he helped them to form the Tea Operatives and General Labourers' Association (TOGLA) – a union that would help to challenge the main companies exploiting the dockers.

Tillett was elected as TOGLA's Union Secretary and spent most Sundays speaking and recruiting at the dock gates. His personal diary from 1888 recorded disappointments and successes: frustratingly small meetings in March, when snow still covered the ground after a harsh winter; optimism in April when he met well-organised stevedores and sold copies of *Bitter Cry*. In June he noted large meetings at the dock gates, while 'enthusiastic crowds' attended indoor evening meetings. When industrial disputes broke out among some dockworkers in October and November, he invited Annie Besant and Herbert Burrows to talk to them about the matchworkers' successful struggle. These dock disputes ultimately failed, but Tillett glimpsed the prospect of wider action. His final diary entry in 1888 recorded, 'Cold worse than ever. Went to chapel. Old year out. Like to live next year a more useful life than last.'[22] He would. By early 1889 momentum was building. Hundreds of TOGLA members paid regular union dues and thousands of dockers expressed growing enthusiasm in meetings around the docks. TOGLA established branches in Tilbury, Poplar and Canning Town.

Participants and historians dispute when the Great Dock Strike began. Will Thorne described a meeting at South Dock gates on Monday 12 August 1889 when he and a stevedore, Tom McCarthy, addressed a large, disgruntled crowd before the 8 o'clock call-on. McCarthy listed their grievances and Thorne urged them to form a union and refuse to work. The workers unanimously supported a strike. Simultaneously, dockers unloading the *Lady Armstrong* in the South Dock basin of West India Docks were withholding their labour because a promised bonus had not been paid. Their leader wrote to the dock authorities on Tuesday 13 August with demands that included a minimum four-hour call-on (instead of the usual two or three); wages to be sixpence an hour (eight pence for overtime), and an end to piecework. Ben Tillett had sent similar demands the previous week, but the dock authorities had not responded. On Wednesday 14 August, Tillett met the *Lady Armstrong* workers. On Friday that week the Amalgamated Stevedores Union announced that dock labourers were on strike, and appealed to 'engineers, fitters, boiler-makers, ships' carpenters, coal heavers, ballast men and lightermen', for solidarity action, and for help from the community.

A collective leadership emerged. Tillett, Tom Mann, John Burns and Tom McCarthy mobilised support. Eleanor Marx took on key administrative tasks and Henry Hyde Champion, whose

---

22 The Modern Records Centre at Warwick University holds Tillett's 1888 diary.

Striking dockworkers, 1889.

comments in June 1888 prompted Annie Besant's explosive articles about Bryant & May, acted as press officer. Will Thorne described Tom Mann as 'human quicksilver, here, there and everywhere, commanding, pleading, cajoling, enthusing', while Tillett possessed 'a spark of genius' and 'planned a picket system for the whole 50 miles of London's docks'.[23] As well as demands over hours and pay, the strike committee crucially demanded union recognition throughout the port. Without it, companies could break agreements without being held to account.

---

23 Speakers' Corner orator Bonar Thompson said that Mann's oratory combined 'fire, vehemence, passion, humour, drama and crashing excitement'.

In the last week of August many East End industries were idle. That week the female workforces of Frost's Ropemakers in Commercial Road and Peek, Frean and Co.'s biscuits in Bermondsey walked out. Women also collected donations and organised rent strikes. In Hungerford Street, near Watney Market, a banner defiantly declared: 'As we are on strike landlords need not call.'

Neither TOGLA nor the Amalgamated Stevedores Union held substantial strike funds, so the committee focused on sustaining the strikers' families through meal tickets redeemable at certain shops. The Salvation Army's hall on Whitechapel Road supplied thousands of loaves of bread each day to strikers' families. Local churches opened soup kitchens. Following the matchwomen's example, striking dockers marched through the area and beyond, holding meetings on open spaces.

On 25 August 1889 a spectacular parade, 50,000 strong, headed for the City. Brass bands, banners proclaiming 'Unity and Victory' and horse-drawn boats carrying strikers in fancy dress, lent it a carnival appearance. Street theatre players contrasted dockers' and employers' lives: plates with a director's dinner piled high next to a docker's crust of bread and a tiny herring; puppets represented a docker's scrawny child in rags and a well-fed, well-dressed director's child, and their cats – one thin, the other the director's 'Fat Cat'.[24] They returned with donations totalling hundreds of pounds. Weekend marches ended in huge rallies, some at Tower Hill, others in Hyde Park, where at the end of August, 100,000 people gathered around twenty speakers' platforms.

---

24 The expression 'fat cat' may be based on this. Others claim it was first used by political commentators in 1920s America.

On 27 August the *Evening News* estimated that 130,000 workers were on strike, and it was spreading: '. . . even factory girls are coming out. If it goes on a few days longer, all London will be on holiday . . . the proverbial small spark has kindled a great fire which threatens to envelope the whole metropolis.'

That spark had been lit by the 1,400 women who walked out at Bryant & May's Fairfield Works the previous year and became role models for their brothers, husbands and uncles, many of them dockworkers.

As August drew to a close, the strike entered its most critical period. The extraordinary effort and sacrifice by workers, with solid community backing, had not persuaded the dock employers. Daily collections could not feed all the strikers' families. Hunger was sapping morale. The strike committee considered calling on workers across the capital to come out indefinitely in solidarity. A general London strike might pressurise the employers to settle, but could risk losing a significant section of public and press support and be difficult to sustain. On 29 August the committee took that risk and issued the 'No Work' manifesto, which appealed to 'workers in London of all grades and every calling' to stay at home from Monday, 'unless the directors have before noon on Saturday . . . officially informed the committee that the moderate demands of the dock labourers have been fully and finally conceded'.[25]

Key members of the strike committee expressed misgivings. Within 24 hours the manifesto was withdrawn but with a face-saving appeal to London's workers to contribute generously towards the strike fund. On the other side frustrated ship-owners

---

25 T. McCarthy, *The Great Dock Strike, 1889*, London: Weidenfeld and Nicholson, 1988, p. 125.

pressured the dock companies to compromise, and the dock employers scented victory, believing time favoured them.

Suddenly a game-changing donation of £1,500 arrived – from the Brisbane Wharf Labourers' Union of Australia – with a promise that more would follow. Over a relatively short period, their Antipodean counterparts telegraphed thousands of pounds to the dock strike committee, collected though unions and amateur football clubs. The prospect of the docks remaining idle for several more weeks forced the companies to negotiate. The Archbishop of Westminster, Cardinal Manning, mediated, and the strike was settled by mid-September, with the dockers winning their 'tanner' – sixpence per hour (and eight pence for overtime), and a minimum four-hour call-on in most cases.

Within a short time Tillett's pioneering efforts at dockside unionisation had helped to create a Dock, Wharf, Riverside and General Labourers Union with 18,000 members. By 1890, in the light of the matchworkers', gasworkers' and dockers' successes, commentators acclaimed a 'new unionism' born of rebellion, not only against their employers but also against earlier, inward-looking trade unions representing what Engels termed 'the aristocracy of labour'. East London was the cradle of these struggles.

A more traditional trade unionist, George Shipton considered 'new unionism' too militant. His critical article in *Murray's Magazine* in June 1890, however, gave Tom Mann and Ben Tillett – respectively President and Secretary of the post-strike dockers' union – the opportunity to explain the difference between old and new unionism to its readers. Tillett and Mann said the old unionists '. . . do not recognise, as we do, that it is the work of the trade unions to stamp out poverty from the land . . . We are prepared to work unceasingly for the emancipation of the workers. Our ideal is the Cooperative Commonwealth.'[26]

Although Mann and Tillett cherished the new means of struggle, which transcended the narrow confines of individual workplaces, they valued and honoured the courage of 'old union' activists, whose day was passing. To be a unionist then 'was to be a social martyr . . . with the hue and cry against them of police and Parliament'.

By 1892, Engels had cheered up. He described the new unionists as 'rough, neglected' toilers, 'looked down upon by the working-class aristocracy', but with an immense advantage, as their minds 'were virgin soil, entirely free from the inherited "respectable" bourgeois prejudices which hampered the brains of the better situated old unionists'.[27]

The rebels who triumphed over powerful economic forces and revolutionised struggles for workers' rights, created new possibilities for those following in their footsteps into the twentieth century. The first significant branches of the suffragette movement in London grew in the east, where female match-workers had fought for their workplace rights. Close to Beckton Gas Works, West Ham returned a pioneering socialist MP in 1892, James Keir Hardie. Tom Mann's grassroots organising in workplace struggles prepared him for a pivotal role in the growth of the syndicalist movement that believed true political advances would come only through economic struggles.

Ben Tillett developed his self-confidence and showed courage

---

26 Their reply was later produced as a pamphlet, *The New Trades Unionism*, London: Green & McAllan, 1890.

27 Kenneth Lapides (ed.), *Marx and Engels on the Trade Unions*, New York: Praeger, 1987, p. 163.

in the face of powerful enemies. He urged the next generation of activists to be brave and radical, telling students at Ruskin (trade union) College in 1913: 'I don't want you to be statesmen, don't for God's sake be politicians: they have always been evils. I want you to be idealists.' Unfortunately, he failed to follow his own advice. He become the MP for Salford, Manchester, in 1917, and moved to the right politically, but others continued the grassroots rebellion.

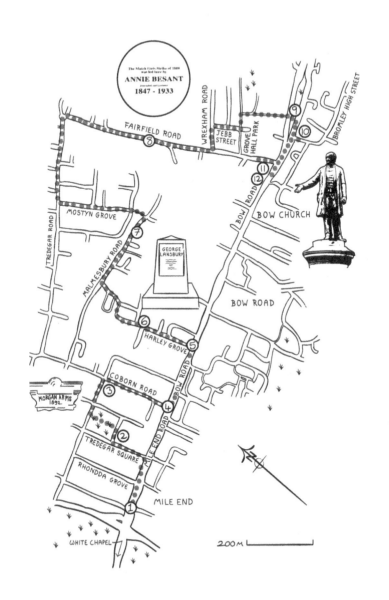

The Match Girls Strike of 1889
was led here by
ANNIE BESANT
Journalist and Lecturer
1847 - 1933

FAIRFIELD ROAD

WREXHAM ROAD

JEBB STREET

GROVE HALL PARK

BROMLEY HIGH STREET

⑨

⑩

⑧

⑪

⑫

MOSTYN GROVE

TREDEGAR ROAD

MALMESBURY ROAD

BOW ROAD

BOW CHURCH

⑦

GEORGE LANSBURY

BOW ROAD

⑥

HARLEY GROVE

⑤

COBORN ROAD

MORGAN ARMS 1892.

③

④

②

MILE END ROAD

TREDEGAR SQUARE

RHONDDA GROVE

① MILE END

WHITE CHAPEL

200M

WALK

Start at Mile End station, E3 4DH.

1. Mile End station
The original designation of Mile End was a stone, one mile east of the White Chapel that stood in St Mary's Garden (now Altab Ali Park). Cross the road and turn right to Tredegar Square, passing Rhondda Grove on the way.

2. Tredegar Square
Walk through the gardens in Tredegar Square, one of several Welsh names marking the land developed by the iron magnate Charles Morgan. He lived within the block of grand white houses on Morgan Street. The pub on the corner with Coborn Road bears his name. Turn right into Coborn Road.

3. Coborn Road
A carved stone mounted on a wall marks the parish boundary of Mile End Old Town. Earlier it delineated two large estates: Morgan's and Coborn's. It later signified the Metropolitan Borough boundary between Stepney to the west and Poplar to the east. Before 1800, Coborn Road was known as Cut Throat Lane. Stop on the corner of Coborn Road and Bow Road.

4. Coborn Road/Bow Road

The building opposite, now converted into Community Land Trust housing, was constructed as the City of London Union (Bow) Workhouse in 1849. It became an infirmary in 1874, before being renamed St Clements Hospital in the 1930s. Turn left into Bow Road.

5. Bow Road/Harley Grove

A plaque embedded in stone stands in front of the estate that replaced the house of *Daily Herald* editor and rebel Labour MP George Lansbury, who lived here with his wife Bessie. He began his political career as a Liberal but his experiences supporting the dock strike in 1889 helped turn him towards socialism. Continue up Harley Grove.

6. Harley Grove

On the right is the side entrance to Phoenix School, built on the former site of Bow Open Air School, which had been constructed out of wood, and designed for children with respiratory problems. The building was destroyed in the Second World War. The Sikh temple at the end of Harley Grove replaced a synagogue that opened in 1927, which, in turn, replaced a Methodist chapel built in 1854. As Jews settled in east London in the late nineteenth century, the Conservative MP for Bow, Captain John Colomb, said: 'I object to England with its overcrowded population, being made a human ashpit for the refuse population of the world.' Cut diagonally through the estate to the right on to Malmesbury Road and turn right.

7. Malmesbury Road

In the distance you will see the red chimney of the former Bryant & May match factory. Go left under Tom Thumb's arch, along Mostyn Grove. Turn right into Tredegar Road, which once housed the Tredegar Silk Mill, then turn right into Fairfield Road.

8. Fairfield Road

Halfway down the road is the gated Bow Quarter estate, converted from the original Bryant & May match factory where the 1888 strike took place. The factory closed in 1979. A plaque celebrates Annie Besant's role in this dispute. Continue along Fairfield Road. Turn left into Wrexham Road, then right into Jebb Street, left into Grove Hall Park then turn right and exit Grove Hall Park through an alleyway alongside the Nunnery Gallery on to Bow Road.

9. Bow Road (island in the middle)

Cross to the road island which incorporates Bow Church. The statue of Liberal politician William Gladstone was donated by Theodore Bryant, a director of the match factory. The factory workers were given half a day off for the unveiling. Annie Besant claimed that matchwomen cut themselves and daubed blood over the plinth when they understood that a shilling had been deducted from their wages to pay for it, although this may be confused with an incident at a fountain donated by Bryant & May further west on Bow Road. In honour of the original story, activists periodically daub red paint on Gladstone's hand. Cross to the south side of Bow Road.

10. Bow Road

The East London Federation of Suffragettes (ELFS), who are discussed in Chapter 9, had their first organising centre at 198 Bow Road on the site of a disused bakery within a parade of shops that has since been cleared for flats. It would have been almost opposite the church. Continue west along Bow Road. The ELFS held street meetings on the corner of Bow Road and Bromley High Street. Cross back at the traffic lights to the corner of Bow Road and Fairfield Road.

11. Fairfield Road

On the side of the former Poplar Town Hall is a small plaque that recalls the closing down of the Whitsun Fair (also known as the Green Goose Fair) in 1823, as a result of raucous behaviour. Turn back towards Bow Road, then turn right.

12. Bow Road/Fairfield Road

The old Poplar Town Hall, built in the late 1930 (now offices), replaced Bromley Vestry Hall. Look up at the mosaic on the canopy entrance of dockers unloading a variety of goods, and reflect on Beatrice Potter's observation that 'the luxuries of our elaborate civilisation pass familiarly through the dock labourer's hands', and remember the strikers of 1888 and 1889 who created the 'new unionism'.

East End tailoring sweatshop, early 1900s.

4

COMING IN FROM THE COLD

Immigrant Agitators and Radicals in Spitalfields

In September 1889, as the docks lay idle, local newspapers claimed that the whole of the East End was 'infected with Strike Fever': '. . . coal men; match girls; parcels postmen; car men . . . employees in jam, biscuit, rope, iron, screw, clothing and railway works have found some grievance, real and imaginary, and have [come] out on strike.'[1]

There was nothing 'imaginary' about the clothing workers' grievances. They were among London's most exploited workers, slaving 14–18 hours per day, six days a week, in 'unhealthy and dirty dens', many on piece rates rather than regular wages. Forming effective unions in this industry was extremely difficult, and owed much to Lewis Lyons's pioneering efforts. Born in 1862 to German-Jewish immigrants, Lyons worked as a tailor from the age of eleven.

As the docks dispute intensified, a 16-strong Strike Committee led by Lyons called clothing workers out against the 'unbearable' hardships 'inflicted . . . by the Sweater'. Five months earlier, gasworkers at Beckton, led by Will Thorne, opted to fight for shorter hours rather than higher pay, and won the eight-hour

---

1   *East London News*, 7 September 1889.

day. The clothing workers followed suit. They downed presses, scissors and needles, and left sewing machines idle, until their employers agreed that their 'hours be reduced to 12', including 'one hour for dinner and half-hour for tea', consumed off-site. They further demanded that no work should be sent home to complete 'after working hours'.

Lyons's Strike Committee met at the White Hart public house on Greenfield Street (renamed Greenfield Road), Whitechapel. The pub stood within a triangle bordered by Whitechapel Road, Commercial Road and Jubilee Street, which housed an immigrant ghetto of Jews who had fled Tsarist Russia. Many of the 7,000–8,000 *shnayders*[2] who walked out were first-time strikers. A trickle of Yiddish-speaking Russian and Polish Jews came to London in the 1860s and 1870s, but cataclysmic events in the Russian Empire in 1881 turned a trickle into a flood.

A revolutionary group, *Narodnaya Volya*,[3] threatened to assassinate Tsar Alexander II, who ruled over an authoritarian state. The revolutionaries believed their action would create a period of chaos in which new forms of popular power might emerge. A bomb exploded and the Tsar was dead. But a new Tsar, Alexander III, quickly restored order from chaos, and increased repression.

One member of the assassination squad was Jewish. Hesya Helfman had found refuge among revolutionaries after escaping a threatened arranged marriage. The new Tsar blamed the Jews for the chaos that followed his predecessor's demise. Mobs launched

---

2 *Shnayders* – the Yiddish term for 'cutters', used generically to describe tailors and makers of clothing.

3 The People's Liberty (Narodnaya Volya) emerged from *Zemlya Volya* (Land and Liberty), an earlier group organising among peasants, students and workers, especially in the Ukrainian and Volga regions.

pogroms on the Jews in their towns and villages, looting and burning shops and homes, wounding and killing people while the authorities looked on. Fear gripped Jewish communities as the new Tsar's 'temporary measures' intensified the restrictions already undermining their lives. Facing random attacks, bound by discriminatory laws, and struggling economically, many Jews began to migrate towards their 'promised land' – America. Britain was a halfway house, but many remained there. Others paid unscrupulous travel agents in Hamburg for tickets to New York, which were actually marked 'London'. Most Jewish immigrants to Britain gravitated to London's East End, finding work as *shnayders* (tailors), *shusters* (boot and shoemakers) and *stolyers* (cabinetmakers) for employers who spoke their Yiddish mother-tongue.

City and West End firms dominated London's clothing industry. They profited handsomely by subcontracting work to East End sweatshops, where a continuous flow of 'greeners' (new immigrants) enabled employers to depress wages. Middlemen also directed government contracts for army uniforms to East End workshops, which typically employed 10–25 workers, few enough to avoid inspection under the 1867 Factory Act.

The thousands who walked out in 1889, closing hundreds of workshops, struck against co-religionists, including *landslayt* (neighbours from their old towns) and even *mishpokhe* (family members). Some tailors struggled with this; others, though, had already lost their innocence in Russia's new factories. Jews who had already imbibed trade union ideas in Russia assisted Lyons in forming unions.

Four weeks into the tailors' strike, employers refused to compromise and strike funds were almost exhausted. Stitchers, cutters and pressers faced the grim prospect of returning to work having won nothing. But, emboldened by the 'Strike Fever', a tailors' delegation headed for the Wade's Arms, in Jeremiah Street, Poplar, to lobby the Docks Strike Committee.

Many dockers were immigrants too, or sons of immigrants – Catholics from the Emerald Isle. As Jews swarmed into Whitechapel, the Irish community shuffled closer to the docks. Stepney became a patchwork of mainly Jewish and Irish enclaves, plus seafarers from India, China and Somalia; Italians and Greeks selling food provisions; and German bakers and sugar refiners. But this was no melting pot. Communities kept to their own familiar streets. Physical confrontations, like today's postcode wars, were commonplace among young Jews and Catholics

Late in life the former dockers' leader Ben Tillett told Jewish trade unionists that he first became an agitator in Riga, in 1877, where he had disembarked with other sailors. At the market square, local police grinned while young wealthy Russians intimidated Jewish stallholders. Tillett saw an old Jew thrown to the ground. 'As the young Russian lifted his foot to kick [him] I lifted it higher and got him down,' he recounted. The British sailors cleared the police from the square, too.

Tillett saw how Jews suffered under Tsarism. Yet, in the late 1880s, he described Jewish immigrants as the 'dregs and scum of the continent' who 'make more foetid, putrid and congested, our already overcrowded slums'. He told one gathering of Jewish workers: 'You are our brothers and we will do our duty by you, but we wish you had not come.' However, after the tailors' delegation outlined their case, the Dock Strike Committee promised £100 – the largest donation the tailors received throughout their dispute.[4] With their strike fund refreshed, they now had the upper hand. Their employers could not afford to suspend production much longer and caved in by the beginning of October. Despite Tillett's antipathy towards immigrants, Irish Catholic dockers' solidarity helped to ensure victory for immigrant Jewish workers.

Cross-community solidarity was further cemented two months later, when a Federation of East London Labour Unions was launched at Mile End's Great Assembly Hall. The *Eastern Post* reported: '2,800 were present . . . and speeches were made in different languages and translated.' Non-Jewish union leaders, such as Tillett and Mann, spoke alongside Jewish militants representing tailors, cap-makers, stickmakers, furriers and carpenters. The Chair, Charles Adams, was tasked by the Alliance Cabinet Makers' Association with organising Jewish immigrant carpenters, chaired. He said, 'if ever labour is to rise successfully . . . it must rise as a whole . . . This new organisation must be composed of people of all creeds and of all nations', and never let employers 'exploit one against the other'.[5]

A Jewish militant, William (Woolf) Wess, drove this initiative. A shoemaker at twelve, he worked as a machinist in Dvinsk before arriving in London, aged 20, in 1881. Wess lived on Clark Street, behind the London Hospital, before moving to Cressy House, Stepney Green.[6] He came to London with radical ideas, which developed through involvement in the Socialist League and the 'anarchist-socialist' journal, *Freedom*.[7]

---

4   Other non-Jewish unions such as the London Society of Compositors contributed funds.

5   *Eastern Post*, 4 January 1890.

6   Several immigrant Jewish anarchists lived in Cressy House and its neighbour, Dunstan House.

7   With some breaks, *Freedom* was printed from October 1886 until April 2014, before going mainly online. Freedom Bookshop is in Angel Alley, E1 (stop number 2 on the walk).

Several years before the tailors' strike, Wess and his comrades laid foundations for activism among immigrant workers by forming unions and establishing an International Workers' Education Club in Berner Street,[8] committed to the 'social and political enlightenment of its members'. It provided a venue for *shnayders*, *shusters* and *stolyers* to eat, drink, play chess or read newspapers after work.

One newspaper they read avidly was *Arbeter Fraynd* (Workers' Friend), a radical Yiddish weekly, later printed on the premises. During major industrial disputes it became a daily strike bulletin. The *Arbeter Fraynd* held a mirror to immigrant workers, reflecting their harsh daily experiences but offering a glimpse, too, of future liberation. It reassured them that workers elsewhere also suffered relentless exploitation but that they could challenge their circumstances and change the world if they acted collectively. This newspaper inspired and motivated rebellious Jewish immigrants.

An energetic German political exile, born in 1873 and raised in a Catholic orphanage, immersed himself in Jewish immigrants' struggles and amplified these messages. As a teen, Rudolf Rocker was apprenticed as a bookbinder, and joined *Die Jungen* – the German Social Democrats' youth section – which proved too radical for the parent party. Rocker and his friends were expelled, propelling them towards anarchism. After several of his friends were arrested, Rocker went into voluntary exile and resurfaced in Paris, where he first encountered Yiddish-speaking revolutionaries. Rocker shared an apartment and working materials with a

---

8   Renamed Henriques Street honouring the Sephardi Jew Basil Henriques, who established the Oxford & St George's (boys)Youth Club in Berner Street. His fiancée Rose Loewe later opened a parallel girls' club.

radical Russian-Jewish bookbinder, Shloyme Rappaport.[9]

In 1895 Rocker reached London, arriving on a foggy morning into 'a world of ghosts . . . people flitted through the murk like shadows. There was a thick clammy yellow mist over everything.'[10] He settled in cosmopolitan Soho, among exiles from the 1848 upheavals onwards. One acquaintance, Otto Schreiber, took Rocker to the city's poorest districts, introducing him to the East End, Deptford and Rotherhithe. Rocker saw

> . . . an abyss of human suffering . . . squalid courts and alleyways, with dreary tumbledown hovels . . . And in these cesspools of poverty, children were born . . . nowhere was the contrast so vast between assertive wealth and indescribable poverty as in the great cities of Britain. Riches and poverty lived almost on top of each other.[11]

He rented a room in Shoreditch from an immigrant Jewish activist and met campaigners who won reduced sweatshop hours in 1889 but still suffered poor conditions and low pay. He knew these conditions even more intimately after he began dating a sweatshop worker, Milly Witkop, the eldest of four sisters born to orthodox Jews in Zlatopol, Ukraine. Milly came to London unaccompanied, aged 17. Her London experiences challenged her religious beliefs. She witnessed 'pious' Jews operating as heartless slum landlords, or forcing employees to complete urgent work orders on the Sabbath. Hebrew prophets were trumped by

---

9   Rappaport became a renowned Yiddish playwright after he returned to Russia. Under the pseudonym An-sky, he wrote *The Dybbuk* in 1914, later adapted for film.

10   R. Rocker, *The London Years*, Nottingham/Oakland: Five Leaves/AK Press, 2005, p. 14.

11   *Ibid.*, pp. 24–5.

secular profits. Religious observance in London felt devoid of the spirituality Milly knew in Zlatopol. At an enthusiastic meeting for striking bakers in September 1894, she encountered the *Arbeter Fraynd*-ers, joined their clan, and rejected God.

The bakers frequently worked shifts longer than 16 hours in poorly ventilated basements. East European immigrants established around 60 Jewish bakeries in the East End, typically employing a few workers based around a family. This made union organisation extremely difficult but workers *did* organise, uniting where possible with Catholic and Lutheran German bakers working nearer the Thames.

When negotiations failed in the 1894 dispute, their fledgling union rented part of 52 Brushfield Street (alongside Spitalfields Market) as a workers' cooperative bakery. The night before the opening, immigrant capmakers, cabinetmakers, tailors, and shoemakers convened a rally at Christchurch Hall, Hanbury Street, urging workers' families to support the co-op.[12] The *Westminster Gazette* reported the opening day:

> ... [O]fficials and organisers among the Hebrew workers
> ... were seen wheeling about barrows of 'union bread',
> each loaf properly labelled and supplied to the grocers,
> restaurant keepers and others who had pledged themselves
> to patronise 'union bread' ... By 10.30 the crowd
> surrounding the premises numbered some thousands ...
> the band struck up the Marseillaise while the doors of the
> shop opened amid vociferous cheers ... the bakers came
> out dressed in white hats, shirts and aprons, carrying a

---

12 Christchurch Hall was used for trade union and political rallies. Annie Besant and Eleanor Marx spoke there in support of matchworkers and gasworkers respectively.

large cake on a pole and headed by banners for the various
trade unions . . . the crowd formed a procession in the
midst of which was a cartload of new bread . . . meeting
everywhere with much sympathy.[13]

Bad debts ultimately defeated the cooperative, but consumers'
commitment to 'union bread' took hold, workers fleetingly
experienced control over hours and pay, and they glimpsed a
different world. Wherever workers negotiated acceptable work
conditions and the right to organise, master bakers could use the
union label. The Bakers Union asked the Chief Rabbi to give
this label his *hekhsher* (religious endorsement). His claim that it
was beyond his remit reinforced Milly Witkop's cynicism about
religious leaders.

Relations between immigrant radicals and religious leaders
were often antagonistic. Rabbis berated strikers in Sabbath
sermons and supported employers whose donations helped
maintain the synagogues. In February 1889, a committee representing unemployed Jewish workers asked Chief Rabbi Adler
to deliver a Sabbath sermon on sweating, unemployment and
demands for an eight-hour day. He eventually refused. However,
the *Arbeter Fraynd* had already announced that Adler would
preach this sermon on 16 March. Nearly 3,000 marchers left
Berner Street for his synagogue at Duke Street, Aldgate. Adler
was absent. City police prevented the marchers from rallying
nearby. They returned to Whitechapel, rallied on Mile End Waste
and had further confrontations with the police.

---

13 *Westminster Gazette*, 18 September 1894 (see Larry Wayne's *Union Bread*, published jointly
    by the Jewish Socialists' Group and Socialist History Society, 2009).

Sabbaths were holy, but Yom Kippur[14] holier still. Even many secular Jews fasted and spent the day in synagogue, entreating God to extend their lives for another year. In London and New York though, Jewish anarchists organised Yom Kippur dances. In 1890, an *Arbeter Fraynd* activist, Benjamin Feigenbaum, held a Yom Kippur meeting in Christchurch Hall, entitled 'Is there a God?' He discussed philosophical ideas about deism for an hour and then gave God two minutes to 'kill me on the spot, so that he may prove his existence'. When the time elapsed, Feigenbaum exclaimed, 'There is no God!' and a band struck up the Marseillaise.[15]

Rudolf Rocker first met Milly Witkop when he was living in the West End. She had gone there to sell anarchist papers. He recalled 'a slim young girl . . . with thick black hair and deep large eyes . . . eager and zealous for our cause'.[16] Their love blossomed in uncertain times. They nearly emigrated to America before settling in Liverpool, where Rocker worked on *Dos Fraye Vort* (the Free Word), a Yiddish anarchist newspaper. He began to master this language with its German-sounding words but mystifying Hebrew script.

Rocker and Witkop returned to the East End when he was invited to edit *Arbeter Fraynd* in 1898. Witkop found sweatshop work but also contributed to the newspaper. *Arbeter Fraynd* activists and supporters inspired and led the struggles locally for democracy and freedom within the immigrant community, rights and dignity in the workplace, and for better lives. They organised Friday night lectures and debates in the back room of the Sugar

---

14   The Day of Atonement, during which observant Jews fast from sunset to sunset.

15   See W.J. Fishman's *East End Jewish Radicals*, London: Duckworth, 1975, pp. 157–8.

16   See Rocker, *The London Years*, p. 39.

Loaf pub at 187 Hanbury Street. Rocker marvelled at the commitment shown by 'badly paid and half-starved' workers to these events: 'crowded together on hard benches . . . they followed the speaker with rapt attention, and as the discussion afterwards showed, with understanding.'[17]

These gatherings attracted women as well as men. Rose Robins's parents forbade her from going to the Sugar Loaf where 'free love' was among topics discussed. 'Red Rose' defied them. One night when she returned late from the Sugar Loaf, her parents had locked her out and she slept on the streets.

A larger venue was needed when the international anarchist celebrity Emma Goldman visited England at the end of 1899. She addressed three packed meetings at Christchurch Hall, offering political analysis and inspiration while raising funds for *Arbeter Fraynd*. Her trip started inauspiciously on an anti-(Boer) war platform at the West End's Athenaeum Hall. 'I had caught a severe cold . . . my speaking was painful not only to myself but to the audience.' Hanbury Street, though, was different: 'I was among my people. I knew their lives, hard and barren everywhere but more so in London. I was able to find the right words to reach them. I was my own self in their midst.'[18]

The *Arbeter Fraynd* struggled financially and there were publication gaps, but from 1903 until 1914, it appeared every week. Rocker was philosophical about the paper's economic circumstances.

I had been promised £1 a week for my work . . . The promise was rarely kept . . . amounts owing to me were

---

17 *Ibid.*, pp. 26–7.
18 E. Goldman, *Living My Life*, Vol. 1, London: Pluto Press, 1988 (1931), p. 254.

entered into a book. When the total . . . got too large they put a pen through it and the debt was wiped out . . . it was a splendid way of keeping the books but it didn't do me any good . . . it was only by Milly working and by my odd jobs of bookbinding that we kept going.

The paper was read not only in London, but also in New York and Tsarist Russia. Across vast distances radical Yiddish newspapers enabled Jewish workers to share and support each other's struggles.[19] Dovid Edelshtadt emigrated as a teenager from Russia to New York and worked in sweatshops making buttonholes. He died from tuberculosis aged just 26, but his labour poems outlived him and crossed continents through Yiddish newspapers. His poem, *In Kamf* (In Struggle) became an anthem sung on May Day marches: 'We are shot and hanged, robbed of our lives and rights, for we demand freedom for downtrodden slaves . . . you can kill our bodies but you will never destroy our spirit . . . new fighters will come . . . we will fight on until the whole world is free.'

Some 25,000 immigrant Jews marched from the East End to a protest rally in Hyde Park after a pogrom in Kishinev in 1903 left 49 Jews dead, approximately 500 wounded and 2,000 homeless.[20] Rocker remembers London's streets lined with people who 'gazed in mute surprise upon the strange procession . . . [when] Edelshtadt's *In Kamf* was heard the onlookers became very solemn and took off their hats to the marchers'.[21]

---

19 For example, Mr Trushkowsky of 113 Brick Lane was treasurer of a committee formed by several local immigrant unions which sent money to striking workers in Bialystok in 1898.

20 Kishinev is in present-day Moldova. In 1903 half of its 125,000-strong population were Jews.

21 *Mir Trogn a Gezang* [We Carry a Song], New York: Workmen's Circle, 1977, p. 80.

The main threats Jews faced in the Russian Empire were physical attacks by *pogromchiks*,[22] ignored or even encouraged by the authorities. Although the mainstream British press rarely reported pogroms, Yiddish newspapers did. Greenstein's bookshop in New Road, Whitechapel, stocked a serialised novel in Yiddish 'from the recent pogrom times in Russia', which described them graphically.[23] One group of exiled revolutionaries – the Bundists[24] – distributed an information sheet in the East End called *Pogromen Blat* (Pogroms Sheet) detailing both attacks and self-defence actions. In 1905 they sent £105 collected from 325 local donors to activists in Tsarist Russia who bought guns and knives to defend themselves.

In America and Canada, Jewish immigrants struggled with overcrowding, exploitation, poverty and hunger, just as they did in London. But in the East End an additional threat emerged, which intensified in 1901 when a grassroots anti-immigrant movement – the British Brothers League (BBL) – was created, claiming that 'their' territory was being encroached upon and transformed. BBL footsoldiers were factory workers, some from Irish immigrant families. Its leaders though included the Tory MPs for Stepney and Bethnal Green South West respectively: Major William Evans Gordon and Samuel Forde Ridley, plus retired army captain William Stanley Shaw. '[T]he other day an Oxford graduate joined us, we have enrolled several city merchants, a bank manager is on our central committee', boasted

---

22 Instigators of mob attacks on communities.

23 This novel was printed by Narodiczky, an immigrant Jewish anarchist with a print shop on Mile End Road.

24 The Bund (Yiddish for union) was a Jewish Marxist party formed in Lithuania in October 1897. Three of the nine people who met in secret in 1898 to form the general Russian Social Democratic Workers' Party in 1898 were Bund delegates.

Shaw. '[M]edical men, clergymen, authors and journalists have written expressing sympathy.'[25] Supportive authors included Marie Corelli, author of *A Romance of Two Worlds*, and Arthur Conan Doyle, who donated ten shillings and sixpence to the League.

The BBL held its first public meeting, at Stepney Meeting House, Oxford Street (now Stepney Way), in May 1901. The *East London Observer* reported: 'The weather was bad but there was a crowded working class attendance' who were 'enthusiastic and unanimous'. Further meetings in August, October and November were equally packed. Four thousand marchers converged from Hackney, Bethnal Green, Shoreditch and Stepney for the BBL's largest rally at the People's Palace, on Mile End Road, in January 1902. Hackney BBL's banner proclaimed, 'Britain for the British'. Inside the hall an organ played 'Rule Britannia!' and 'No Place Like Home'. The meeting was protected by '260 stewards ... dock labourers, chemical workers from Bromley and operatives from Shoreditch, Bow, Poplar, Stepney, Bethnal Green and Mile End', who 'unceremoniously ejected ... "foreigners"'.

The League convinced many local workers that the influx of migrants willing to work long hours for low pay undermined their struggle for better conditions. Instead of unionising migrants, the BBL called for restriction. They denied that their movement was 'aimed at any religious sect or of a racial character' but the presence of MPs representing distant unaffected constituencies (such as Orkney and Shetlands) suggests the BBL tapped a deeper, racialised hostility to Jews. Wolverhampton MP Henry

---

25 *Jewish Chronicle*, 31 October 1902.

Norman was applauded for advising other nations to 'disinfect their own sewage'. 'Englishmen', he added, 'would not have this country made the dumping ground of the scum of Europe'. When local agitator Arnold White stated that aliens were not persecuted refugees but came 'because they wanted our money', audience members shouted 'wipe them out'. That year the League presented a petition to Parliament calling for immigration control. Most of its 45,000 signatures were collected in east London.

Individuals struggled to oppose this rhetoric at such rallies, but immigrant Jewish trade unionists, with support from non-Jewish activists, formed an Aliens Defence League with temporary offices at 38 Brick Lane, and organised public meetings countering the BBL's agenda.

Major Evans-Gordon was among those invited to head a Royal Commission on Immigration, gathering evidence on allegations that he and other BBL agitators had themselves disseminated: that immigrants arrived impoverished, destitute and dirty; practised insanitary habits; spread infectious diseases; were a burden on the rates; dispossessed native dwellers; caused native tradesmen to suffer a loss of trade; worked for rates below the 'native workman'; included criminals, prostitutes and anarchists; formed a compact non-assimilating community that didn't intermarry; and interfered with the observance of Christian Sunday.

The Commission's report led to Britain's first modern immigration law, the 1905 Aliens Act, which permitted government inspectors to exclude paupers unless they could prove that they were entering solely to avoid persecution. Liberals MPs opposed this Tory Act, but enforced it when they governed from

1906. Between 1906 and 1910, approximately 2,000 immigrants were refused entry, and more than 1,000 were later deported for 'wandering the streets without visible means of support'. The Tories lost many London seats in 1906, but Evans-Gordon held his, using the slogan, 'England for the English. Major Gordon for Stepney'.

Rudolf Rocker and the anarchists vigorously defended immigrants and countered antisemitic arguments, but also focused on constructive initiatives. In February 1906 anarchists opened a social and educational centre for workers – the Jubilee Street Club and Workers Institute – near Stepney Green, in a former Salvation Army depot. It held meetings and debates on weekdays, concerts and dramas at weekends, and offered classes using Francisco Ferrer's progressive pedagogy.[26] Like the previous tenants, Rocker and associates promised salvation, but through workers' own enlightenment, empowerment and self-belief rather than through prayer.

The East End's best known adult education providers at this time were Christian social reformers, Canon Samuel Barnett and Henrietta Barnett, who, in 1884, established Toynbee Hall, a university settlement between Commercial Street and Gunthorpe Street. Built to resemble a medieval manor, it initially housed 15 Oxbridge graduates. They worked in the City but lived in the settlement, where they ate and prayed together. They devoted their leisure time to 'provide education and a means of recreation and enjoyment for people of poorer districts ... inquire into the condition of the poor, and advance plans to promote their welfare'.

---

26 Ferrer pioneered the non-competitive, non-punitive *Escuela Moderna* education philosophy used in some schools in Spain.

The Barnetts already worked locally, at St Jude's Church. During the 1870s, a Balliol College student, Arnold Toynbee, assisted them during vacations. He maintained this link as an academic. Determined to see slum conditions at first hand, he frequented dingy, disease-ridden buildings, but died from tuberculosis aged 32. The Barnetts kept his name alive through Toynbee Hall.

The settlement was located close to the poorest people. Canon Barnett instructed the graduates to 'learn as much as to teach', to 'feel out rather than find out what are his neighbours' thoughts' until they themselves become 'the mouthpiece for East London indignation'. Fine aims but coated with paternalism, which groomed residents to act on behalf of poor people rather than empowering them to liberate themselves. The Barnetts made enlightened statements about changing social conditions, but tasked graduates 'possessing habits and customs of culture' with 'improving the working class'.

Labour politician and activist George Lansbury admired Canon Barnett's zeal for social reform, but noted that Toynbee Hall workers mixed with the poor only within the building's 'fine parlours' and speculated whether it might be more a stepping stone for the residents than the recipients. They went to East London full of enthusiasm for the masses' welfare, he observed, but soon discovered that the interests of the poor

> ... were best served by leaving East London to stew in its own juice, while they became members of Parliament, cabinet ministers, civil servants [who] discovered that the problems of life and poverty were too complex to solve ... that the rich were as necessary as the poor, that nothing

must ever be done to hurt the good-hearted rich who keep such places as Toynbee Hall going out of their ill-gotten gains.[27]

One of Emma Goldman's Christchurch Hall lectures deconstructed *tsedoke* (charity). The Yiddish flyers advertising this meeting asked: 'What is charity? Who gives it and why?' Goldman saw charities as a necessary function of an economic system that 'robs man of his birth right, stunts his growth, poisons his body, keeps him in ignorance, in poverty, and dependence, and then institutes charities that thrive on the last vestige of man's self-respect'.

Despite this justified cynicism, many Eastenders *did* benefit from Toynbee Hall's adult education classes, especially literacy classes for immigrants, and housing advice and support through a team of 'poor-man's lawyers'.[28] In 1888, during the match-workers' strike, four independent researchers from Toynbee Hall examined Bryant & May's books and confirmed Annie Besant's claims about the system of fines that the strikers described, but the directors denied.

A more radical grassroots initiative to provide adult education, strengthen cultural life, provide practical support, and build collective strength among Yiddish-speaking immigrants for their political battles, arose from weekly meetings held in Morris Mindel's tenement flat at 184 Rothschild Buildings – a stone's throw from Toynbee Hall. Mindel was a Bundist political exile from Lithuania and, like Rocker, a bookbinder. Bundists, anarchists and socialists formed a secular friendly society called

---

27 G. Lansbury, *My Life*, London: Constable & Co., 1928.

28 Forerunners of the National Association of Citizens' Advice Bureaux.

the *Arbeter Ring* (Workers' Circle). It eventually expanded to 19 divisions (branches), mostly in London – the four biggest in East London. Division 1's committee met at Mindel's flat. In 1912 the organisation rented two rooms at 136 Brick Lane as its activities escalated.[29]

Friendly or mutual aid societies proliferated in working-class communities, providing a non-judgemental mechanism for individuals to give and receive support. Most Jewish friendly societies were organised through synagogues among *landslayt*. Often, a rich benefactor provided start-up funds. The Workers' Circle relied solely on members' subscriptions, arguing that philanthropic donations would compromise its members' dignity and its beliefs in 'liberty and economic equality'.

Formed by immigrant trade unionists, it met workers' needs beyond the workplace, by establishing a reading room on Whitechapel Road, which later relocated to a large house in Great Alie Street, Whitechapel, with 16 rooms, including two large halls, which the *Arbeter Ring* purchased for £2,000 in 1922 as a workers' social, cultural and educational centre. Every night, circle members sipped lemon tea while playing chess, draughts or dominoes in its teetotal cafe. On Thursday evenings brothers Alexander and Frank Fine gave free legal advice. On Friday nights, there were political lectures and debates organised by the Circle's 'propaganda committee' featuring Jewish and non-Jewish speakers. On Sunday afternoons, members' children came to a secular Yiddish supplementary school and on Sunday nights there were Yiddish theatre productions, or classical

---

29 The Workers' Circle officially dates its founding to a meeting in 1909 at Nathan Weiner's Boundary Estate home (see Chapter 6). A parallel group called *Arbeter Ring Farayn* (Workers' Circle Union) hosted weekly literary discussions at Woolf Krasner's home in Umberston Street from 1908. They later merged.

concerts presented by the Circle's own orchestra and sometimes top West End musicians. On other evenings members attended a range of classes and courses.

A group of Polish Jewish immigrants who arrived in the 1920s commandeered a top floor room and established the Progressive Youth Circle. They invited academics, trade unionists and political activists to lead discussions mainly in Yiddish on topics such as free love, communism and Zionism, held talks on Yiddish and English writers, and created *Proltet*, an agitprop Yiddish theatre group.

Despite its meagre resources the *Arbeter Ring* provided board and lodging for striking miners in 1914 who spoke at London meetings, and donated to the Gresford community in 1934 after a mining disaster. It contributed towards the legal defence of Sholem Schwartzbard, a Jewish anarchist who assassinated the Ukrainian pogrom-leader Petlyura.[30] *Proltet* held benefit performances for the International Brigades fighting in the Spanish Civil War, and Circle members collected clothing, cigarettes and food for them.

Its members – anarchists, communists, Bundists and left-wing Zionists – held conflicting political views but the Circle's non-sectarian spirit meant it could play a unifying role in London's working-class Jewish life, especially during strikes and in anti-fascist campaigning.[31] Where possible it supplemented strike pay and hosted meetings to mobilise wider support for strikers. The management committees of local workers' cooperatives included Circle members. Rudolf Rocker, who played a key

---

30 After Schwartzbard was acquitted he went on tour to thank his supporters. Thousands gathered in the street outside Circle House where a packed dinner was held in his honour.

31 See Chapter 11.

role in the 1912 tailors' strike that struck a powerful blow against the sweated labour system, acknowledged the support given by the fledgling Workers' Circle.

The events of 1912 tested immigrant workers' commitment to radical campaigning against exploiters within their own community and the strength of solidarity they could offer others. In April a strike over pay and conditions broke out among West End tailors, composed mainly of native English tailors alongside other nationalities. Their leaders feared that during the strike their work would be subcontracted to East End sweatshops and carried out by poorer tailors desperate to feed their families. Rocker and the anarchists recognised that this could severely damage future relations between the West End and East End tailors, strengthening chauvinists in the labour movement who labelled immigrant workers as unreliable.

The anarchists seized the moment by building support for the West End strike among East End tailors. Rocker argued that if they struck too, they could help the West End tailors and simultaneously challenge the sweating system which they endured. A mass meeting in Mile End Assembly Hall, attended by 8,000 East End tailors, overwhelmingly supported him. As the strike began to spread, bakers and cigarette makers gave free supplies to workers; Yiddish theatres raised money through benefit performances. Community support enabled the strike committee to provide strike pay and distribute food to their families.

Within three weeks the West End master tailors were forced to agree a settlement, which also included those East End tailors employed in men's tailoring and uniforms. They were guaranteed shorter hours, no piecework, better sanitary conditions and that only union labour would be employed. But the largest group of workers in East End tailoring workshops made women's garments – and these workers continued to strike. Their employers saw the season's trade disappearing. Eventually they offered to meet every demand except one – the right to form a union in every tailoring workshop in the East End. A midnight meeting was held at the Pavilion (Yiddish) Theatre on Whitechapel Road, after the evening's programmed drama had ended. Another drama was about to unfold. Many tailors waited outside the packed theatre for news. Rocker was not a tailor, but was a highly respected agitator and organiser. He recorded his feelings as he spoke:

> I saw those pale, pinched, hungry faces . . . of people who had come together at midnight to decide what to do about the strike for which they had sacrificed so much . . . I said that if they held out a few more days . . . they would win. If they decided to go back now the Masters would make them feel they had lost . . . You must decide for yourselves. There was an outburst of applause and from all sides came the cry: 'the strike goes on!'[32]

A formal vote to continue striking was unanimous. The next day employers began signing binding agreements so workers would return. For Rocker and the *Arbeter Fraynd*-ers, the strike showed that the most exploited and vulnerable workers could organise themselves to win, give solidarity beyond their own community and locality, and gain esteem among workers who regarded immigrant unions as a weak link.

---

32 Rocker, *The London Years*, p. 130.

That commitment to wider solidarity was further demonstrated in the tailors' support for dockers, also striking to improve conditions. In May, tailors and dockers had held joint strike meetings at Tower Hill. As the tailors resumed work, the dockers' families faced starvation. Milly Witkop and other *Arbeter Fraynd* activists formed a committee to place dockers' children in immigrant Jewish workers' homes so dockers' families had fewer mouths to feed. More than 300 dockers' children spent the last weeks of an ultimately unsuccessful dock strike in cramped Jewish ghetto homes. The committee reluctantly refused some offers to take children where family homes were already too overcrowded. Many dockers entered Jewish homes for the first time when they visited their children. Jewish workers had remembered the solidarity shown by the dockers in 1889.

The outbreak of war in 1914 curtailed a remarkable period of struggle among a courageous group of immigrant rebels and dreamers. During that war, Rudolf Rocker was interned as an 'enemy alien' and deported. In 1916, the *Arbeter Fraynd* and Jubilee Street Club were forced to shut down. In 1917, many leading activists of the immigrant Jewish enclave, including half of the Workers' Circle membership, returned to Russia, some voluntarily, others involuntarily. When forced conscription came in, immigrant Jews were reluctant to serve in an army allied with the Tsarist regime from which it had fled. The government insisted that men of conscription age fight for Britain or face deportation to Russia to fight in its army. Despite the efforts of a 'Foreign Jews Protection Committee' formed especially by Bundists and Workers' Circle activists, with support from Sylvia Pankhurst, many were involuntarily deported. Others pressed for an assisted return in a civilian capacity. The land they never truly left behind was in the throes of revolution. Their dreams of liberation for its downtrodden people were only partially fulfilled, their idealism soon betrayed, but few could return to London.

However, in the decades from the 1880s until the First World War, a group of immigrants in a hostile, anti-alien environment, treated with suspicion by many indigenous workers, oppressed by those who claimed moral authority and held institutional power in their own community, were model rebels. Whatever their internal fears and anxieties as newcomers in a strange society, they gave each other strength by organising collectively, they fought for their rights in the workplace, formed their own clubs, unions and friendly societies, created their own newspapers to give themselves a voice, broke taboos, challenged employers, rabbis and xenophobes, and built links of solidarity beyond their own community, seeking a better world for all.

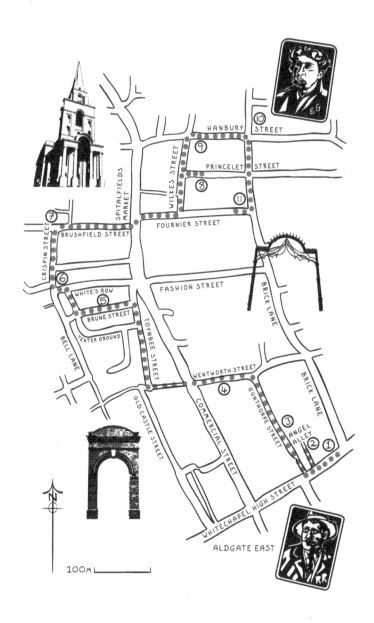

HANBURY STREET

WILKES STREET

⑨

PRINCELET STREET

⑧

⑪

SPITALFIELDS MARKET

⑦

BRUSHFIELD STREET

FOURNIER STREET

CRISPIN STREET

⑥

WHITE'S ROW

⑤

FASHION STREET

BRUNE STREET

BRICK LANE

BELL LANE

TENTER GROUND

TOYNBEE STREET

WENTWORTH STREET

④

OLD CASTLE STREET

COMMERCIAL STREET

GUNTHORPE STREET

BRICK LANE

③

ANGEL ALLEY

② ①

WHITECHAPEL HIGH STREET

ALDGATE EAST

EG

RR

N

100M

WALK

Start at Whitechapel Art Gallery, 77–82 Whitechapel High Street, E1 7QX.

1. Whitechapel High Street

The gallery, which opened in March 1901, now incorporates the old Whitechapel Library building which opened in 1892 and became known as the 'People's University of the East End'. The library was relocated near Whitechapel station in 2005 and renamed 'Idea Store Whitechapel'. The gallery's annual spring exhibition regularly attracted more than 200,000 people in its early years. Walk a short distance in the City direction and turn right into Angel Alley.

2. Angel Alley

Home of Freedom Books, which continues the anarchist tradition established by the *Arbeter Fraynd* newspaper (July 1885) and *Freedom* (October 1886). Along the alley wall, an artistic installation celebrates dozens of individuals associated with libertarian or anarchist thought and action internationally. Rudolf Rocker is on the bottom row and Emma Goldman is in the top right-hand corner. Go back to Whitechapel High Street and turn right.

3. Gunthorpe Street

Just before turning into Gunthorpe Street look at the sign above Albert's shop, crafted by Arthur Szyk. It marks the former offices of the *Jewish Daily Post* – the first (and short-lived) daily English-language Jewish newspaper in England. On the left is Canon Barnett School, named after Toynbee Hall's founder.

4. Wentworth Street

Turn left into Wentworth Street, cross to the archway inscribed 'Four per cent Industrial Dwellings Company', a remnant of the Rothschild Buildings tenement that stood here until 1973. Workers' Circle founding member, Morris Mindel, lived at Flat 184. Sarah Wesker, who led strikes at trouser factories in east London in the late 1920s and early 1930s, lived at Flat 134.[33] Cross Commercial Street, turn right into Toynbee Street then left into Brune Street.

5. Brune Street

On the right hand side is the remarkable façade of the Soup Kitchen for the Jewish Poor, established by Jewish philanthropists in 1902. It closed in 1992. During the early 1930s Depression, it fed more than 4,000 people nightly. Turn right into Tenter Ground, once a field where dyed cloth was dried on frames with hooks called 'tenters' (hence the saying 'on tenterhooks'). Turn left on to Crispin Street.

6. Crispin Street

The sandy-brown building (now housing students) was a night shelter for homeless women (and later men too) run by the Sisters of Mercy from 1861 until 1988. Looking south to Bell Lane, a sky-blue building towers above the shops and flats – student

---

33 Sarah Wesker was the women's organiser of the National Clothing Workers Union and was elected to the Communist Party's central committee in 1930. She was the political role model for Sarah Kahn in her nephew Arnold's famous play, *Chicken Soup with Barley*.

accommodation for a more elite market. The Jews' Free School stood on this site from 1822–1939. Turn right to the junction with Brushfield Street.

7. Brushfield Street

The cafe/restaurant on the corner (number 52) was the site of the cooperative bakery, briefly established in 1894. Turn right, and cross Commercial Street into Fournier Street, named after a philanthropist of Huguenot heritage. Wealthier Huguenot refugee silk-weavers lived and worked in the early eighteenth-century houses in these streets. Turn left into Wilkes Street then right into Princelet Street.

8. Princelet Street

Outside number 6, a pavement roundel indicates the East End's first Yiddish theatre. It closed after seven months when a false fire scare led to a stampede to evacuate the building and 17 people were crushed to death. Secular immigrant radicals established a cooperative *folkskikhe* (people's kitchen) in the abandoned building. A delivery of food to the cooperative on the holy day of Yom Kippur in 1904 led to mass street-fighting between religious and secular Jews. Turn back to Wilkes Street, then go right and turn right into Hanbury Street.

9. Hanbury Street

Christchurch Hall, later called Hanbury Hall, at number 22, was once a venue for political and trade union rallies. Its upper part has been redeveloped as luxury flats. The anarchist Benjamin Feigenbaum held his lecture 'Is there a God?' here. Eleanor Marx and Annie Besant spoke here in support of gasworkers and matchworkers respectively. Emma Goldman lectured here raising funds for the *Arbeter Fraynd*. The Kobi Nazrul centre at number 30 is named after a Bengali revolutionary poet imprisoned several times for anti-Empire activities.

10. Junction of Brick Lane/Hanbury Street

To your left, at 136 Brick Lane (Sheba Restaurant), were the Workers' Circle's first meeting rooms. Along Hanbury Street's extension, across the road, a Jewish anarchist, Barnet Ruderman, had a bookshop at number 71. He was the first publisher of radical Yiddish books in England. The Sugar Loaf pub, which hosted weekly anarchist meetings in its back room stood at number 187. Turn right along Brick Lane then right again into Fournier Street.

11. Fournier Street

The mosque on the corner was formerly Spitalfields Great Synagogue and originally, in 1743 (look up at the sundial), a Huguenot chapel. In the early 1900s, Jewish anarchists taunted religious leaders by eating ham sandwiches opposite this synagogue on Yom Kippur. Rudolf Rocker – a non-Jew – berated his Jewish anarchist comrades for this practice. He felt it antagonised ordinary worshippers instead of solely targeting the religious establishment.

Great Strike of London Tailors

A GREAT

DEMONSTRATION

OF

TAILORS

WILL TAKE PLACE IN

HYDE PARK,

On SUNDAY, Sept. 29th, 1889,

Which will be joined by various other Trades and Organisations.

Among the Speakers the following were invited and are expected to attend :—

JAMES MACDONALD, JOHN TURNER,

WILLIAM MORRIS, W. M. THOMPSON,

FRANK KITZ, CHAS. MOWBRAY, TOCHATTI,

JOHN BURNS, TOM MANN,

KEILEY, CLARK, CONNOR, and others.

The Procession from the East End will start at 1.30 p.m., from Buck's Row, and will March by Whitechapel, Commercial Street, Great Eastern Street, Old Street, Clerkenwell, Theobald's Road, Bloomsbury, Oxford Street, enter the Park by Marble Arch at 3 p.m.

By Order of the Strike Committee.

"WHITE HART," Greenfield Street, E.

Leaflet published by the Strike Committee of the 1889 tailors' strike.

Conway Hall in Red Lion Square, Holborn.

5

NO GODS, NO MASTERS

Radical Bloomsbury

Many areas of London are being transformed beyond recognition by the scale and pace of rebuilding, but Bedford Square, at the heart of Bloomsbury, provides a window on the past. Built between 1775 and 1780, it is London's last surviving fully intact Georgian square. The name 'Bedford' is one of three gracing several streets and squares in this district; the others are Russell and Tavistock. They are one family. William Russell, the 5th Earl of Bedford, became a duke in 1694 and was given the title Marquis of Tavistock. The Bedford Estate is still Bloomsbury's largest private landowner.

Bloomsbury was kept exclusive partly by property leasing arrangements which listed more than 60 commercial activities forbidden in the squares owned by the Bedford Estate. These included: baker, chimney-sweeper, publican, coffin-maker, bone-burner, hatter, plasterer, printer, soap-boiler and tripe-seller. Booth's 1889 map of poverty in London West shows a dark blue block just east of Russell Square, indicating 'Very poor . . . chronic want', and similar blocks just south of New Oxford Street. The heart of Bloomsbury, in contrast, is a sea of red and pink, indicating 'well-to-do middle classes'. Traditionally, its squares were the homes of judges, retired military men, leading professionals and their families, and others of considerable means, including many owners of slaves in the Caribbean. A database created through a 2013 research project, detailing compensation payments made to owners of slaves when the government abolished slavery in the British Caribbean in 1833, reveals many beneficiaries in this locale.[1] Among them are the Whig politician James Baillie, of 45 Bedford Square, who had owned 801 slaves in British Guiana and 202 in St Lucia; Reverend Thomas Harrison of 6 Bloomsbury Square, who had owned 140 slaves in Anguilla; and Benjamin Greene of 45 Russell Square, who received compensation for the loss of his 224 slaves in St Kitts.

An unlikely location, then, for political rebels. But the Trinidadian Trotskyist writer C.L.R. James enjoyed staying in its student and young writers' quarter from 1932, living in Heathcote Street and frequenting Russell Square's Student Movement House, where many African radicals who would go on to play key roles in independence and liberation movements, socialised and talked politics. James felt that he had fitted into Bloomsbury 'as naturally as a pencil fits into a sharpener'. Its vibrant cultural and intellectual atmosphere enthused him: 'Anyone who lives in this place for any length of time and remains dull need not worry himself,' he said. 'Nothing he will ever do will help him. He was born that way.'[2]

In 1935, C.L.R. James and Amy Ashwood Garvey launched the International African Friends of Abyssinia, whose office was located at 63 New Oxford Street. That year it held a mass rally in

---

1 See 'Legacies of British Slave-ownership', www.ucl.ac.uk/lbs (accessed 21 January 2019).

2 C.L.R. James, *Letters from London*, Oxford: Signal Books, 2006.

Trafalgar Square, mobilising against Mussolini's plans to invade Abyssinia, addressed by James and Garvey, Jomo Kenyatta, who James had met at Student Movement House, fellow Trinidadian-born socialist George Padmore, and Chris Braithwaite, a Barbadian-born seamen's union organiser living in the East End. These same individuals formed the nucleus of the anti-colonial International African Service Bureau that James launched in London in 1937 which established headquarters in Paddington.

By this decade, though, Bloomsbury was more commonly associated with the well-heeled 'Bloomsbury Set' – intellectuals, writers, artists and philosophers whose flexible living arrangements reflected their radical ideas on aesthetics, feminism, sexuality and pacifism. The American satirist Dorothy Parker said the set 'paints in circles, lives in squares and loves in triangles'. Several members of this elite network shared a common background – public school followed by Trinity College or King's College, Cambridge. The writer Ronald Blythe described them as 'Cambridge in London'.[3]

Acres of literature have been written about the Bloomsbury Set's twentieth-century lives – much of it obsessed with their personal dalliances. Unfortunately, this has obscured the rebellious ideas and activities that flowered in this very comfortable area in earlier decades. Several individuals who were living or working within Bloomsbury, more diverse in background than the Bloomsbury Set, challenged the political and economic orthodoxies that dominated Victorian and Edwardian Britain: the power and authority of the Church, and belief in God; nationalism and unquestioning patriotism; education as a privilege, not

3   Ronald Blythe, in David Daiches (ed.), *The Penguin Companion to Literature,* New York: McGraw-Hill, 1971.

a right; the use of military intervention to settle international conflicts; differing spheres, rights and duties for men and women; and the assumption that capitalism benefits everyone.

Who were these earlier radicals? Some were members of the Bloomsbury Socialist Society, formed in 1888: key organisers of London's first May Day march in which hundreds of thousands of workers participated. The society usually met in the Communist Club at 49 Tottenham Street, close to Goodge Street.[4] Its 1890 manifesto declared: 'We aim at realising socialism . . . a condition of society in which wealth will be enjoyed by those who produce it . . . removing all conditions whatever that render it possible for an idle class to exist.'

The Society's members, including Eleanor Marx[5] and Edward Aveling, whose home was directly opposite the British Museum on Great Russell Street, lived mainly in Bloomsbury, Soho and Fitzrovia. They devoted themselves to producing political propaganda aimed at educating 'the people' in 'social and political matters'. They wanted to put all 'political power into the hands of the people'; their cause – 'the cause of all those who labour'. The Society's manifesto closed with the call: 'Workers of the World, Unite!'

One even earlier proponent of workers' rights based in Bloomsbury was Devon-born Thomas Wakley, MP for Finsbury from 1835 to 1852. He lived at 35 Bedford Square. Wakley came to London in his late teens to train as a doctor at St Thomas's and established a surgery on Regent Street. He became friendly with

---

4   In 1902 the club moved round the corner to 107 Charlotte Street and hosted the initial sessions of the Russian Revolutionary Party's second congress the following year during which the party split into Bolshevik and Menshevik factions.

5   The youngest daughter of Jenny von Westphalen and Karl Marx.

the radical pamphleteer, William Cobbett, in 1821, and founded the medical journal *The Lancet* two years later, which he used as a vehicle to challenge the autocratic power of the Royal College of Surgeons' governing council.

Wakley was elected to Parliament as a Radical. He spoke in the House of Commons in support of Chartism, Irish independence and medical reform, but his maiden speech defended the Tolpuddle Martyrs, a group of farm workers in Dorset led by a Methodist lay preacher, George Loveless, who planned collective action to defend their living standards. They were convicted for taking a secret oath – which contravened the 1797 Mutiny Act – to form a Friendly Society of Agricultural Labourers, and refuse to accept wages below 10s a week. They were exiled for seven years to a penal colony in New South Wales, Australia. A huge protest movement forced the government to remit their sentences two years after their conviction; Wakley was its leading London spokesperson. When the Tolpuddle Martyrs returned to Britain, Wakley was the keynote speaker at a dinner in their honour at White Conduit Tea-House in Islington.[6]

He was an enthusiastic campaigner against the stamp duty imposed on newspapers, which restricted the distribution of radical material. Many activists responded by ignoring the Stamp Act and publishing penny papers until they were forced to stop, often by arrest and imprisonment. Wakley published six issues of an unstamped paper called *A Voice from the Commons* – perhaps the nearest thing to a nineteenth-century blog.

He strongly opposed the 1834 Poor Law, condemned by

---

6   A restaurant occupies the rebuilt tea-house site which has 'White Conduit House' etched across its façade. The nearest turning south of this site was renamed 'Tolpuddle Street' in 1986 to mark the 150th anniversary of the dinner for the martyrs.

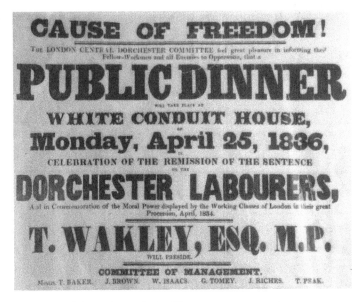

CAUSE OF FREEDOM!

The LONDON CENTRAL DORCHESTER COMMITTEE feel great pleasure in informing their Fellow-Workmen and all Enemies to Oppression, that a

PUBLIC DINNER

WILL TAKE PLACE AT

WHITE CONDUIT HOUSE,

Monday, April 25, 1836,

IN

CELEBRATION OF THE REMISSION OF THE SENTENCE

ON THE

DORCHESTER LABOURERS,

And in Commemoration of the Moral Power displayed by the Working Classes of London in their great Procession, April, 1834.

T. WAKLEY, ESQ. M.P.

WILL PRESIDE.

COMMITTEE OF MANAGEMENT.

Messrs. T. BAKER.　　J. BROWN.　　W. ISAACS　　G. TOMEY.　　J. RICHES.　　T. PEAK.

Invitation to celebration dinner of Tolpuddle Martyrs support campaign.

Chartists for creating the workhouse. Wakley was an outspoken proponent of Chartist ideas and actions which sought to defend the poor, raise working-class consciousness and expand the political franchise, but did not support their demand for annual parliaments which they felt would maximise accountability. He believed that an election every three years was preferable – but the Chartists nevertheless saw him as a strong ally.

Wakley's Finsbury constituency included the Clerkenwell House of Detention. When he visited the prison in a medical capacity in 1839, he was shocked at the treatment of remand prisoners who were 'subjected to the lowest possible diet' for the first 14 days of their confinement and in some cases made to do hard labour. He told the House of Commons that he 'could not conceive on what principle it was recommended that a man should be subjected to punishment before he was tried'. Wakley also strongly criticised the use of solitary confinement, which he termed a 'demoniacal system'. His concerns about punishment extended to army discipline too, and he demanded an end to the practice of flogging.

The army, though, had high status in Victorian England, and it was hard for critics to get a hearing. London's pacifist movement, which challenged militarism and army practices and campaigned for peaceful conflict resolution, is often considered a twentieth-century creature that surfaced during the First World War and matured in its aftermath, when War Resisters International (WRI) and the Peace Pledge Union (PPU) came into existence. WRI was formed at a 1921 conference at Bilthoven, Holland, on the initiative of Kees Boeke, a Dutch Quaker peace activist, and moved its international secretariat to London in 1923.[7] The prominent Independent Labour Party (ILP) campaigner Fenner Brockway was secretary of WRI from 1926 to 1934, and George Lansbury held the post from 1937 to 1940. The PPU was set up in 1935 by Dick Sheppard, canon of St Paul's Cathedral. In a letter, published in the *Manchester Guardian*, Sheppard invited people to send him a pledge on a postcard, saying: 'I renounce war and pledge never again to support another.' Within weeks, some 30,000 people had signed the pledge, and the PPU held its first mass meeting at the Albert Hall in July that year, attended by more than 7,000 supporters.

John Passmore Edwards, who lived at 51 Bedford Square, was a peace activist during the Second Boer War (also known

---

7   Originally called 'Paco' – Esperanto for 'peace'.

as the South African War), which began in 1899. A carpenter's son from Redruth in Cornwall, he moved to London, became a journalist and later a successful publisher. He was a supporter of Chartism and committed to improving opportunities for working-class people, using his wealth to fund 24 free libraries and several free hospitals, mainly in London, as well as art galleries and convalescent homes, some of which still bear his name. More locally, within Bloomsbury, he funded the Passmore Edwards Settlement, in Tavistock Place, which opened up educational opportunities for people who had little access to them. It moved there from temporary accommodation in 1897. Young professional men, especially lawyers, lived in the Settlement building and, in return for board and lodging, they taught academic and practical subjects to adults, and organised music, chess and debating societies. They also ran classes and recreation sessions for children from the surrounding area, after school, while their parents were still at work. Modelled on Toynbee Hall in the East End, the Passmore Edwards Settlement operated a busy 'poor man's lawyer' service. The Settlement's work was led by a Russell Square resident, Mary Ward, who was committed to increasing educational opportunities for women and girls.

Passmore Edwards's record of peace activism went back several decades before the Boer War. He was part of the London Peace Society in the late 1840s, and published its journal, *The Peace Advocate*. He actively pursued his pacifist agenda during the Crimean War, arguing that a war commenced for one purpose 'not infrequently originates or develops other blazing issues, which have to be quenched in blood, if quenched at all'.

In 1855, the Stop the War League (STWL) published Passmore Edwards's lecture, *The War Condemned*. In the STWL, Passmore

Edwards collaborated closely with Chartist Bronterre O'Brien, the republican journalist John Hamilton and anti-slavery activist George Thompson.[8]

His opposition to militarism also included internal army discipline. Like Thomas Wakley he spoke out against the use of flogging and he argued against all forms of corporal punishment in prisons and schools.[9] In a period when wars were fought between professional rather than conscript armies, Passmore Edwards identified the effect on 'the common people' who, he said, 'suffer most by wars . . . can do most to prevent wars, and would be the greatest gainers if wars were prevented'.

One campaigning trade unionist who worked in the West End and later became a Liberal MP for Haggerston in Hackney expressed similar sentiments. William Randal Cremer, usually known by his middle name, was a carpenter and joiner who moved to London in 1852 in his mid-20s. He was a strong campaigner for the nine-hour day (which cost him his job) and a founder member, alongside Karl Marx, of the International Workingmen's Association, which emerged from a conference of socialists, anarchists and radicals who met in St Martin's Hall in Covent Garden in 1864. He was a close friend of Mazzini and Garibaldi and strong supporter of the radical Italian unification movement. In 1870, Cremer, with support from other working-class activists, formed the Workmen's Peace Association in London, later rebranded as the International Arbitration League (IAL). Like Passmore Edwards, he foresaw that ordinary workers and civilians would suffer most from future wars.

---

8   See P. Laity, *The British Peace Movement, 1870–1914*, Oxford: Clarendon Press, 2002, p. 18.

9   Passmore Edwards was a member of the Committee for the Abolition of Flogging in the Army and Navy.

His organisation campaigned for disarmament and for international conflicts to be resolved through arbitration. His decades of work for this cause were recognised at a banquet held in May 1904 at the Holborn Restaurant in Bloomsbury, a popular venue for local radicals and peace activists.[10] The event also celebrated Cremer as the very first winner of the Nobel Peace Prize. He received £8,000 but donated £7,000 of it to the IAL for its campaigning work.

If Cremer was ahead of his time in his concern about civilians during wars, he was behind the times when it came to political equality for women. He was one of the founders of the Anti-Suffrage League in 1906, arguing that women were 'creatures of impulse and emotion and did not decide questions on the ground of reason as men did'. The founding president of the Anti-Suffrage League was Mary Ward, of the Passmore Edwards Settlement, who advocated strongly for women's education but against their political participation.

In the early twentieth century, Bloomsbury's tradition of anti-war activism was upheld by one of the Duke of Bedford's family members – Bertrand Russell. From 1911 to 1916 he lived in Bury Place, close to both Little Russell Street and Great Russell Street. A mathematician and philosopher, his political views veered between liberalism and socialism, but his abiding commitment was pacifism.

Shortly after Britain entered the First World War, he joined a newly established group called the Union of Democratic Control (UDC). This organisation was less sinister than its name suggests: it called for democratic parliamentary control over foreign policy,

---

10 Close to Cremer's office in Lincoln's Inn Fields where he lived, with a turn-up bed and a small gas stove, after the death of his second wife.

believing that Britain had been dragged into war by secret treaties with France and Russia. The UDC announced itself to the public through letters to the press in September 1914 and soon won support from well-known political and cultural figures and built a national membership of 10,000 organised in 100 branches.[11] In London, apart from its West Central and Hoxton branches, its support mainly came from the suburbs. It built up a speakers' panel of 45 lecturers undertaking outreach work, and during the first few months of 1915 its London membership soared from around 600 to over 1,500. The 'patriotic' press characterised this Union as pro-German. The *Daily Express* whipped up public hostility, labelling a UDC event in Farringdon in November 1915 as a 'meeting to promote British surrender'. A group of soldiers obtained forged tickets and stormed the platform.

During that month the No-Conscription Fellowship was founded, and Russell shifted his active involvement from the UDC into the Fellowship. Conscription became government policy in January 1916, coming into force in March of that year. As well as campaigning against conscription the Fellowship gave material and legal support to families of conscientious objectors. Russell was fined in June 1916 for publishing a leaflet supporting conscientious objection and exposing the case of Ernest Everett, an objector who had been sentenced to hard labour for two years. Russell was forced to leave his academic post at Trinity College, Cambridge, because of his anti-war views. He was determined to get himself imprisoned to generate publicity for the objectors' cause but magistrates kept frustrating him. On one occasion

---

11 There was some crossover with suffragette activists. Muriel Matters and Israel Zangwill were prominent members (see Chapter 8). It agreed a resolution in February 1915 that 'democracy must be based on the equal citizenship of men and women'.

when he was fined he refused to pay the fine, but instead of jailing him the court ordered that books be taken from his home to the sum of the fine and auctioned off. He was eventually imprisoned for six months in February 1918 after publicly urging that Britain should take up Germany's offer of peace talks.

Throughout the twentieth century, Tavistock Square Gardens, at Bloomsbury's northern end, accumulated peace memorials in the form of trees, statues, plaques on benches remembering peace activists, and, since 1994, a large stone dedicated to conscientious objectors. Sitting serenely in the middle of the gardens is a statue of Mohandas Karamchand 'Mahatma' Gandhi, pacifist and advocate of non-violent struggle for change.[12]

When Russell was incarcerated, a prison warder, fulfilling administrative duties, asked him his religion. He replied 'agnostic', a term the warder didn't recognise. In situations where he could express his ideas more freely, Russell described religion as a harmful phenomenon that impeded knowledge and fostered fear. Religion still commanded great respect in First World War Britain, but Bloomsbury was known for comprising both individuals and institutions that challenged belief in God and the authority assumed by the Church.

The most significant local institution to challenge religious authority was University College London (UCL). It was founded in 1826 in the face of strong opposition from the Church of England, as a secular alternative to Oxford and Cambridge, which accepted Anglican Christians alone. A battle with the Church raged for ten years before UCL obtained a Royal Charter confirming that it could award degrees. The university was proudly secular and no minister of religion was allowed to

---

12 'Mahatma' means honourable or venerable.

sit on its College Council. This earned it the designation, 'that Godless institution in Gower Street' from Thomas Arnold, Head of Rugby School (and grandfather of Mary Ward). Its very existence provoked a formal educational response, and King's College on the Strand was created as a religious rival to UCL.

Jews comprised one of the categories excluded from Oxford and Cambridge universities at this time, but the investors in the UCL site, who included Isaac Goldsmid, a Jew, were adamant that their college was created for students of all faiths and none. The college's enlightened and progressive philosophy sat uneasily, though, with the origins of its investors' wealth. Council members, such as the merchant banker Alexander Baring and the coal industrialist John William Ward (Earl of Dudley), had acquired considerable wealth through slavery in the Caribbean, and Goldsmid accrued much of his wealth through his work for the British East India Company, which made huge profits exploiting workers in India.

Many secular radicals who stayed within the Bloomsbury area, though, had either studied or taught at UCL. Edward Aveling, the son of a non-conformist minister, later became a central figure in the Bloomsbury Socialist Society. He took an unusual academic trajectory, completing his initial studies at UCL and then taking a teaching post at King's College. He ran into conflicts at King's over his increasingly strident atheistic and socialistic views. These came to a head after Aveling became vice-president of the National Secular Society, and published a book on Charles Darwin's religious views, which claimed that Darwin was an atheist. Aveling was encouraged to seek an academic post elsewhere, and became a lecturer in anatomy and biology at the London Hospital.

On Bloomsbury's eastern edge, Richard Congreve, a Leamington-born Comtean philosopher,[13] who worked closely with Edward Beesly, a history professor at UCL, established a 'positivist temple' in 1870. Beesly had chaired the first meeting of the International Workingmen's Association. Their atheistic project ultimately became known as the Church of Humanity and was located, ironically, in Chapel Street.[14] In this 'church', human achievement was honoured in secular ways through rituals that had no reference to a god. Congreve told his congregants, 'We meet as believers in humanity' who used the 'wise utterances of the past' including those developed through religion, 'but we admit of no revelation and no being outside of man.'[15]

In the same year that his positivist temple was founded, the Education Act supported a national primary education system and insisted that this included religious education. Through the Church of Humanity, Congreve established a 'free school' for local children and adults, which included no religious instruction or worship. One of its unanticipated functions was to teach English to children of radical refugees, who had fled from France after the Paris Commune was crushed in 1871. This atheist church suffered a serious schism in 1878; a number of members left, complaining that Congreve's rituals had become too religious in nature, but they eventually reunited and the church continued to function until 1932.

The Bloomsbury building that most clearly symbolises this questioning of religious ideas and authority by local thinkers

---

13 The French philosopher Auguste Comte was the founder of positivism which rejected religious belief as unscientific and argued for belief only in that which can be proven by science, mathematics and logic.

14 Later renamed Rugby Street.

15 See 'Not the Messiah' by Alain de Botton, *New Statesman*, 19 July 2010.

and writers through the Victorian period and the early twentieth century was established in Red Lion Square, near Holborn, in 1929, by the South Place Ethical Society. Conway Hall was named in honour of the nineteenth-century Unitarian-cum-freethinker and American anti-slavery activist, Moncure Daniel Conway. The South Place Ethical Society started life as a dissident church congregation in the 1790s, rebelling against the doctrine of eternal hell. During the nineteenth century it evolved through Unitarianism to secularism and, ultimately, to atheism/humanism. Conway had played a leading role helping to steer it through these transitions from the 1860s to the 1890s. In the foyer of Conway Hall, a board commemorates successive leaders of the Ethical Society. All those who preceded Moncure Conway had the appellation 'Revd'. Conway had 'Dr' instead, as have all those who came after him, symbolising the move away from any religious trappings. Conway Hall, like its predecessor in South Place, has provided a regular meeting place and platform for radicals.

Another Bloomsbury institution constructed in the 1850s, within an older establishment, did not deliberately set out to provide a rendezvous for radicals, but came to fulfil precisely that role. The British Museum, built in the 1750s, opened an attractive circular reading room in May 1857. This was the brainchild of its principal librarian, Anthony Panizzi, who had arrived in Britain as a political exile via Switzerland, from Modena, where he had been active in a radical Italian nationalist society.[16] Before it was officially launched, the doors of the Reading Room were opened for the public to view, and had 62,000 visitors in eight

---

16 Panizzi was friendly with Giuseppe Mazzini, when Mazzini was exiled in London.

days. Its handbook confirmed its democratic access policy: 'The reading room of the British Museum is open to men and women of any country, or shade of political or other opinions.' Users had to apply for a reading card, be at least 21 years old, have a literary purpose – 'study, reference or research' – and needed to supply a reference confirming their 'respectability'.

Karl Marx used the Reading Room for nearly three decades. Many pamphlets, polemics and manifestos of London's burgeoning socialist movement were researched and written in this beautiful space. Annie Besant began to use the Reading Room in 1874. Clementina Black, whose lecture on female labour in London had prompted Besant to investigate and campaign about the matchworkers in Bow, obtained her reading card in 1877, the same year as Eleanor Marx, who lived nearby from 1884 with Edward Aveling. Charlotte Despard, a vegetarian socialist of part Irish background, who was to play a major and dissident role in the early-twentieth-century suffragette movement, began using the library in 1894. During the same decade, a fellow vegetarian socialist of Irish background, George Bernard Shaw, a prolific writer of socialist polemics, penned many lectures and pamphlets in the Museum's Reading Room, mainly for the Fabian Society.

The novelist Edith Nesbit, a founding member of the Fabian Society, whose work included *The Railway Children*, wrote many of her stories in the Museum's Reading Room, and she frequently met there with Annie Besant and Eleanor Marx. Nesbit described George Bernard Shaw as a 'clever writer and speaker' with an 'irresistible' fund of dry Irish humour. She also said he was 'the grossest flatterer . . . horribly untrustworthy . . . very plain like a long corpse with dead white face – sandy sleek hair, and a loathsome small straggly beard, and yet is one of the most fascinating men I ever met'.[17]

Untrustworthy or not, George Bernard Shaw's pithy one-liners encapsulated many of the challenges to late Victorian and early Edwardian orthodoxies that emerged from Bloomsbury's radicals. 'I'm an atheist and I thank God for it', he said, adding that 'All great truths begin as blasphemies.' He described patriotism as: 'your conviction that this country is superior to all others because you were born in it.' Shaw advised people not to 'waste your time on Social Questions. What is the matter with the poor is Poverty; what is the matter with the rich is Uselessness.' At the turn of a century in which forces of hate would display an unimaginable barbarism, he wrote about the importance of human empathy and solidarity: 'The worst sin toward our fellow creatures is not to hate them, but to be indifferent to them: that's the essence of inhumanity.'[18]

In 1902, the British Museum's Reading Room was frequently visited by a revolutionary exile in his early thirties, who stayed with his wife, also a revolutionary, close to King's Cross. Mr I. Mitchell, secretary of the General Federation of Trade Unions, provided the necessary reference for one Jacob Richter, who obtained a reader's card at the Museum in April 1902. Richter was the pseudonym of Vladimir Illich Ulyanov Lenin, who was taking extra precautions to avoid surveillance by the authorities. He continued to use the Reading Room library on intermittent trips to London over the next few years, his last recorded visit being on 11 November 1911.

---

17 Julia Briggs, *A Woman of Passion: The Life of E. Nesbit*, London: Penguin, 1989.

18 *The Devil's Disciple*, 1901.

The presence of so many women among the radicals using the Reading Room was emblematic of the high profile that radical women thinkers and activists had in the area. In Coram Street, south of Tavistock Square, Emily Faithfull opened a women's publishing company called Victoria Press. She had been part of the Langham Place Group, a circle of middle-class female social reformers, struggling, in particular, for more diverse educational and employment opportunities for girls and women. She had herself been trained in the almost exclusively male profession of typesetting, by a secularist publisher called Austin Holyoake.[19]

Faithfull, who lived on Taviton Street, near Gordon Square, cascaded her skills down to 16 other women who worked at the press alongside male printers. Facing down criticisms that 'the female mind is not mechanical', that women would 'sink under this fatigue and labour', and that women engaging in printing would drive down wages in the industry, her press printed the *English Women's Journal*, the *Law Magazine*, the *Journal for Promoting Social Science* and also poetry collections. It was successful enough to move to bigger premises in Farringdon after a few years.

Researching the hazards of the printing industry, Faithfull discovered that the average life expectancy of printers was 48 years, and that they often died from breathing disorders. She made sure that her premises had excellent light and ventilation, and bought in specially commissioned high-stools so women could sit rather than work on their feet all day. There was a staff kitchen, and the women had regular lunch breaks; there was also a degree of profit-sharing. In 1865 Faithfull launched a penny weekly

---

19   His brother was the Chartist and freethinker, George Holyoake.

journal aimed at working-class women called *Work and Women*, and in the early 1870s undertook lecture tours in America on this theme. The 1860s and 1870s saw the beginnings of campaigning in London for women's political rights, and, from the 1880s, one of the earliest prominent campaigners, Millicent Garrett Fawcett, lived in Gower Street, close to Bedford Square.

The radical writer and lecturer Annie Besant, who lived close to Regents Park, often combined a session in the Reading Room with a visit afterwards to 8 Russell Square, where Emmeline and Richard Pankhurst settled in 1886 after moving to London from Manchester. In the 1850s Richard graduated in law from UCL and in 1867 was called to the bar at Lincoln's Inn, just south of Bloomsbury. During their time in Russell Square, Emmeline Pankhurst created the Women's Franchise League, which campaigned for votes for more women in local government, a precursor to her later militant activism in the Women's Social and Political Union.[20] Their three young daughters, who all became political activists, grew up knowing Annie Besant, William Morris and the Russian anarchist, Peter Kropotkin, as family friends and frequent visitors.

Many Bloomsbury rebels who developed their ideas for the radical transformation of society nevertheless continued to live bourgeois lifestyles. In 1883, Thomas Davidson, a Scottish philosopher and educationalist, brought together a set of ethical socialists who attempted to 'live' the politics to which they aspired. They formed the Fellowship of the New Life. Some of its members established a commune at 29 Doughty Street, where they sought to practise 'harmonious living' based on

---

20 At the time, approximately a third of women had the vote in local government.

'unselfish regard for the general good'. Members of the Fellowship included the gay rights campaigner, Edward Carpenter, the feminist activist Edith Lees, her future husband, the sexologist Havelock Ellis, animal rights activist Henry Salt and the novelist Olive Schreiner. The tension between campaigning to change their own lives while also campaigning for change in the wider society eventually led to a schism. A significant faction broke off in 1884 to form a new group, which called itself the Fabian Society. George Bernard Shaw joined this new group shortly after it was established.

Social justice and women's rights were recurrent combined themes among the agitators, reformers and rebel thinkers of Bloomsbury who were challenging the mainstream orthodoxies of the age. These themes were embodied *par excellence* in Eleanor Marx, thinker and activist, socialist and feminist. She joined the Social Democratic Federation, but departed along with the faction that created the Socialist League, and was then a co-founder of the Bloomsbury Socialist Society. As a radical activist who moved in both the rarefied political circles of Bloomsbury and the mean streets of east London, where she assisted with campaigns led by the poorest and most exploited workers, she was perhaps more acutely aware than many in her immediate environment of the contradictions of class.

In her 1886 pamphlet, *The Woman Question*, co-authored by Edward Aveling, she wrote:

Women are the creatures of an organised tyranny of men, as the workers are the creatures of an organised tyranny of idlers. Both the oppressed classes, women and the immediate producers, must understand that their emancipation will come from themselves. Women will find allies in the better sort of men, as the labourers are finding allies among the philosophers, artists, and poets. But the one has nothing to hope from man as a whole, and the other has nothing to hope from the middle class as a whole.

The personal is political and the political is personal. Sadly for Eleanor, her trust in the man with whom she spent her adult life – who, she thought, shared both her political philosophy and basic values – was betrayed in 1898. After nursing him back to health from a serious illness, she discovered he had cheated on her and had secretly married a young actress called Eva Frye. Eleanor committed suicide on 31 March at just 43 years old. Many of the leading radicals of both the West End and the East End spoke at her funeral, including Will Thorne of the Gasworkers' Union, with whom she had worked so closely in fighting for better lives for east London's workers.

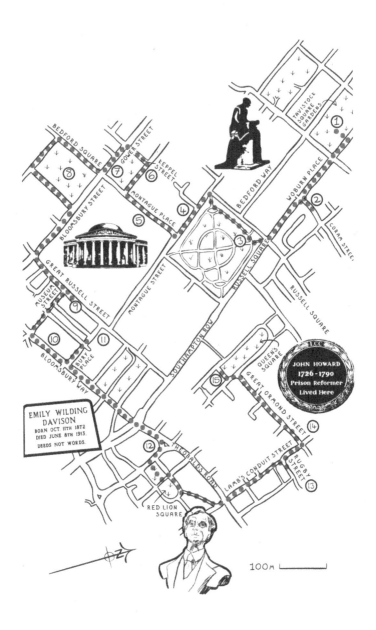

BEDFORD SQUARE

GOWER STREET

KEPPEL STREET

BLOOMSBURY STREET

MONTAGUE PLACE

BEDFORD WAY

WOBURN PLACE

TAVISTOCK SQUARE GARDENS

CORAM STREET

MONTAGUE STREET

RUSSELL SQUARE

RUSSELL SQUARE

GREAT RUSSELL STREET

MUSEUM STREET

SOUTHAMPTON ROW

BURY PLACE

BLOOMSBURY WAY

QUEEN'S SQUARE

GREAT ORMOND STREET

JOHN HOWARD
1726 - 1790
Prison Reformer
Lived Here

EMILY WILDING
DAVISON
BORN OCT 11TH 1872
DIED JUNE 8TH 1913.
DEEDS NOT WORDS.

THEOBALDS ROAD

LAMB'S CONDUIT STREET

RUGBY STREET

RED LION SQUARE

100M

① ② ③ ④ ⑤ ⑥ ⑦ ⑧ ⑨ ⑩ ⑪ ⑫ ⑬ ⑭ ⑮

WALK

Start at Gandhi's statue, Tavistock Square Gardens, WC1.

1. Tavistock Square Gardens

Mahatma Gandhi's statue is the centrepiece of this garden dedicated to the peace movement. Gandhi began to study law at nearby UCL in 1888. He spent most of the next two decades in South Africa. When he returned on a visit in 1906, he was very impressed by the non-violent direct action tactics of the suffragettes. Opposite the northeast corner of the square is the British Medical Association building, formerly Tavistock House. Charles Dickens lived in its spacious and salubrious accommodation when he wrote *Hard Times*. Exit the square and turn right along Woburn Place, then left into Coram Street.

2. Coram Street

Named after a retired sea captain, Thomas Coram, who set up a foundling hospital in 1739. Emily Faithfull established the Victoria Press with the women typesetters she trained at 9 Coram Street. Return to Woburn Place then turn left. Cross over into Russell Square.

3. Russell Square (east)

The square was developed around 1800. Its houses started with number 1 on the southern corner of the Principal Hotel (formerly The Russell) with Guilford Street, and went anti-clockwise around the square to number 64. A Christian socialist,

Frederick Denison Maurice, lived at number 5. He founded the Working Men's College in 1854, which offered evening classes in arts, culture and humanities to workers. The Pankhursts lived at number 8 (northern corner of the hotel) from 1886–93. Mary Ward, leader of the Passmore Edwards Settlement, lived at number 61. Exit the square by the northwest gate and turn left.

4. Russell Square (west)

Number 32 is Stewart House. This was formerly the location of Student Movement House, founded by the Student Christian movement with legacies from three of its members who died in the First World War. A poignant letter to *The Spectator* in September 1938 recalled the house's origins and the role it played as countries edged closer to war again:

> Student Movement House ... was the first, and is still the only Club for University students. It ... admits students of any country, race or creed ... its purpose is to provide a meeting-place for University men and women from all over the world ... For the first fifteen years of its life this international community was exciting, full of possibilities and of hope. But, from 1932 ... there is a different story to tell. The student is no longer a free agent, every turn of the political wheel affects one or other nationality, and we are almost afraid to read the newspapers. Abyssinian students are recalled to fight Italian fellow members of the Club; Spanish students disappear and are not heard of again; refugees come from Germany and Austria, Chinese students are stranded with no money to continue their studies. Youth is by nature hopeful, but even students are

now cynical and almost hopeless; an ever-present fear shows itself in many ways...

Yet ... Chinese and Japanese can and do make friends, within the comparative security of the Student Movement House. Arabs can and do discuss the situation in Palestine with Jewish members. International concerts still produce the music and arts of many, great civilisations.

Turn Right into Montague Place.

5. Montague Place
This is the back of the British Museum, whose Reading Room, opened in 1857, was a place where Bloomsbury's radicals met, researched and wrote lectures, pamphlets and books. Marx wrote the first volume of *Das Kapital* here, and made notes for the second and third volumes, which were published posthumously by Engels. Continue along Montague Place, turn right into Malet Street.

6. Malet Street
On the corner of Senate House is a plaque for Mary Prince, born into slavery in Bermuda in 1788. She lived in a house nearby. She was the first woman to present an anti-slavery petition to Parliament and the first black women in Britain to publish her autobiography. This book played a key part in campaigns of the Anti-Slavery Society. Turn left into Keppel Street then left again into Gower Street.

7. Gower Street
Millicent Garrett Fawcett, a leading figure in the National Union

of Women's Suffrage Societies, lived at number 2 from the mid-1880s, after her husband – the blind Liberal MP, Henry Fawcett – had died. Cross over to Bedford Square.

8. Bedford Square

Walk anti-clockwise round the last intact Georgian square in London. Its houses have since been converted internally into offices. The garden in the middle is only accessible to selected key-holders. The Radical MP Thomas Wakley, lived at number 35. Elizabeth Jesser Reid, a social reformer and anti-slavery activist, founded a women-only higher education institution at number 48. John Passmore Edwards, peace activist, supporter of the Chartists, publisher and philanthropist, lived at number 51. Return to Gower Street. Turn right, then left into Great Russell Street.

9. Great Russell Street

Margaret Harkness, author of six novels exposing working conditions in city slums, lived at number 45; Eleanor Marx and Edward Aveling, stalwarts of the Bloomsbury Socialist Society, lived at number 55. Turn right into Museum Street, then left into Bloomsbury Way.

10. Bloomsbury Way

St George's Church hosted the funeral service of the suffragette, Emily Wilding Davison, who was fatally injured by a horse as she made a protest at the Derby horserace on 14 June 1913. She had lived at 31 Coram Street, northeast of Russell Square. Her coffin was borne on a horse-drawn carriage amidst a march by 6,000 suffragettes. Her body was taken to Morpeth and buried in a family plot. Her gravestone was marked with the suffragette slogan, 'Deeds not Words'. Turn left into Bury Place.

11. Bury Place

A plaque marks the house where pacifist activist and humanist philosopher Bertrand Russell lived just before and during the First World War. Return to Bloomsbury Way. Turn left. Cross into Theobalds Road, then across again to Red Lion Square.

12. Red Lion Square

At the west end of the square, just inside the garden, is a statue of Fenner Brockway, who became a Liberal early in his life but switched to the Independent Labour Party after interviewing James Keir Hardie in 1907. He was an energetic member of the No Conscription Fellowship and War Resisters International and active later in the anti-colonial movement, Liberation. He was also active in the secularist movement. The opposite end of the square has a bust of Bertrand Russell. Exit the gardens along the north side and turn right to the humanist centre, Conway Hall. On the first floor is the Humanist Library. Inside its grand hall above the stage are the words spoken by Polonius in *Hamlet*, recast as a humanist statement: 'To thine own self be true'. Continue along the alleyway, turn left and cross Theobalds Road into Lamb's Conduit Street. Turn right into Rugby Street.

13. Rugby Street

Rugby Street was formerly called Chapel Street, and number 20 was renumbered from 19. The original 19 Chapel Street was the location of Richard Congreve's atheist Church of Humanity.

Return to Lamb's Conduit Street; turn right, then left into Great Ormond Street.

14. Great Ormond Street

At number 23 a plaque commemorates John Howard, a Hackney-born social reformer who campaigned to ameliorate conditions in prison. The Howard League for Penal Reform was created in 1866 in his honour. Continue to Queen's Square.

15. Queen's Square

The Passmore Edwards Settlement, now called the Mary Ward Centre, moved here in 1982 from Tavistock Square. The after-school activities that Mary Ward established there in the early 1900s initiated the playcentre movement. Mary Ward herself described the settlement as 'a place for ideals, a place for enthusiasm'.

Rent strike at Quinn Square, Bethnal Green, 1938 © *TopFoto*

6

LIFE ON THE BOUNDARY

Fighting for Housing in Bethnal Green and Shoreditch

MURDER! Workmen, why allow yourselves, your wives and children to be daily murdered by the foulness of the dens in which you are forced to live?

It is time the slow murder of the poor, who are poisoned by thousands in the foul, unhealthy slums, from which robber landlords exact monstrous rents, was stopped.

You have paid in rent the value over and over again of the rotten dens in which you are forced to dwell. Government has failed to help you. The time has come to help yourselves.

PAY NO RENT to land-thieves and house-farmers who flourish and grow fat on your misery, starvation and degradation.

Leaflet for the No Rent Campaign[1]

These were the words of a leaflet produced by Charles Mowbray, a tailor, printer and self-proclaimed anarchist-communist. Born in Bishop Auckland, Mowbray settled in Boundary Street, Bethnal Green in 1882, on the edge of the 'Old Nichol', one of London's

---

1   Reproduced in Sarah Wise, *The Blackest Streets: The Life and Death of a Victorian Slum*, London: Bodley Head, 2008.

worst slums.[2] There, more than 5,700 people were crammed into 652 houses in 20 narrow streets and alleys, the widest just 28 feet. Some streets were barely seven feet wide. There were 43 empty houses (too dilapidated for use), 12 pubs or 'beer shops', 21 other stores and workshops, and two registered lodging houses. The few open spaces were filled with costermongers' carts, livestock and horses

Journalists and social commentators disparaged this district, declaring: 'Industry is the exception, robbery is the rule.' The population 'live by pilfering. Its streets are the most dangerous for strangers to be found anywhere in London. Children and women are in the thieving line as well as the men ... No respectable person – and the police only on rare occasions – ever ventures there.'

Here, Mowbray shared a one-roomed house with his wife Mary, daughter of an exiled Paris Communard,[3] and four children. From a free-speech pitch near the bandstand in Victoria Park, Mowbray promoted the No Rent Campaign, which encouraged tenants to force landlords to make urgent repairs through rent strikes. Another outstanding orator, Frank Kitz, had moved into the Old Nichol, and joined Mowbray in his agitational work. Kitz recalled:

We occupied a floor there as a cooperative printery . . . The furnishing of our printery was a model of economy and simplicity. Our seating accommodation was made of packing cases. A paving stone was our marking up stone

---

2 Boundary Street marked the boundary between the east London districts of Bethnal Green and Shoreditch.

3 The people's insurrection in Paris against the French government lasted from March to May of 1871.

and ink slab combined. Candles stuck in the composing cases was our lighting installation, and a roller handpress our machinery.[4]

Mowbray and Kitz raised money for printing materials through concerts and lotteries. Additional materials, Kitz recalled, 'were supplied by involuntary contributions from printing firms where some of our members were employed . . . a well known firm of government printers furnished us with some excellent ink, paper and other requisites for printing our revolutionary manifestos and addresses.' Their collective 'sallied out on nocturnal bill-sticking expeditions . . . despite the destruction by the police of some of our handiwork, we managed to placard the East End with incendiary manifestos.'[5]

And beyond. One leaflet making an 'Appeal to the Army, Navy and Police' found its way into several garrison towns. It was worded so strongly, though, that 'the comrade setting it up . . . suddenly threw down his composing stick and declared that he would not go on with it'. Another compositor with fewer scruples completed the job.

The paving stone had one last role to fulfil. When Kitz and Mowbray absconded, owing rent, they left it in the middle of the room for the landlord, with a message saying it was 'akin to his own heart'!

They met through the Labour Emancipation League, of which Kitz was a founder member and regular speaker at open-air meetings in Mile End and Clerkenwell Green. Born in Kentish

---

4   Frank Kitz, *Recollections and Reflections*, London: Freedom Press, 1912.
5   *Ibid.*

Town, he had worked as a professional dyer for the furniture and wallpaper designer and socialist, William Morris.

In the late 1880s, Mowbray, Kitz and Morris were among the editors of *Commonweal*, the newspaper of the Socialist League, which had splintered from the Social Democratic Federation. Mowbray founded the Socialist League with William Morris and Eleanor Marx, hardly the most conventional socialists, but he and Kitz sought to reach out to a constituency of outcasts beyond trade unionists or typical members of workingmen's clubs or radical associations. Mowbray argued, 'We should preach to the thieves, the paupers and the prostitutes.'

He did that, but he also immersed himself in struggles to form trade unions and helped them to lead strikes for immediate gains. Mowbray was one of the minority of non-Jews among the sixteen-strong strike committee that led the tailors' strike of Yiddish-speaking sweatshop workers in 1889. He addressed the mass meeting held in December that year to inaugurate a Federation of East London Labour Unions.[6] But he was more comfortable engaging in direct action than patiently building the infrastructure of workers' organisations. Below the mundane details of starting time, location and other speakers on his No Rent Campaign leaflet, there was a rhyme:

Hurrah! For the kettle, the club, and the poker
Good medicine always, for landlord and broker
Surely 'tis better to find yourself clobber
Before paying rent to a rascally robber

---

6   See Chapter 4, p. 115.

Housing was the most pressing issue for London's poor in the nineteenth century: most of the housing stock belonged to slum landlords. London's population grew from barely a million in 1801 to more than six million by the end of the century, one third of whom had been born outside London. That population growth, alongside rapid industrialisation, included inward flows from the countryside, but also from beyond Britain's borders. London's Irish population grew significantly following the potato famine in Ireland.[7] From the 1880s, large numbers of East European Jews arrived.

There was no legislation at all governing the quality or quantity of housing for the working classes until the 1850s. Acts passed in 1851 and 1853 laid down stipulations about sanitation standards in the growing number of lodging houses, also known as 'doss-houses' or 'kip-houses'. Some 80,000 Londoners slept in a lodging-house bed every night during the 1850s. The social investigator Henry Mayhew described a typical inner London lodging house in which 60 people slept in bunks. They comprised 'pickpockets . . . street beggars, a few infirm old people who subsist occasionally . . . upon charity, 10–15 dock labourers, about the same number of low and precarious callings . . . and a few persons who have been in good circumstances but who have been reduced from a variety of causes.'[8]

In January 1861 bread riots broke out in the East End. Severe weather had prevented any outdoor work. John Hollingshead wrote: 'the distress and suffering that prevail in the metropolis,

---

7   During the nineteenth century the highest number of Irish-born Londoners was recorded in the 1851 census.

8   Henry Mayhew, *London Labour and the London Poor*, Vol. 3, London: Griffin, Bohn, and Company, 1861.

particularly among the dock labourers, bricklayers, masons and labouring classes are truly horrible'. He published *Ragged London* that year, compiled from 10 articles he had written in the *Morning Post*. In the build-up to these riots he noted how, early one week, 'hundreds perambulated the different streets seeking alms of the inhabitants and passers by'. Two days later, thousands congregated in Whitechapel and attacked bakers' shops and eating houses: 'every morsel of food was carried away . . . mounted police of the district were present but it was impossible for them to act against so large a number of people'.[9]

Several of Hollingshead's articles focused on living conditions: 'ill constructed, ill ventilated lurking nests of dwellings'. He described an old mansion 'faded and dilapidated . . . let out to a dozen or 15 families . . . its broad staircase, broken, shattered and muddy is always open to the street, and its long narrow windows are patched with paper . . . its broad closets and store chambers . . . filled with ragged children, who share their beds with coals, coke, wood and a few cooking utensils.' He found 'scores of such houses – containing forty, fifty or even sixty human beings, surrounded by neighbourhoods crowded with gas factories, cooperages and different workshops'.[10]

The metropolis, he concluded, was 'not managed, not cleansed, not relieved from the spectre of starvation which dances before us at our doors. We are . . . surrounded by a dense population, half-buried in black kitchens and sewer-like courts and alleys.'[11] In the age of much-vaunted Victorian prosperity, Hollingshead warned: 'The spreading limbs of a great city may be healthy and

9   John Hollingshead, *Ragged London*, London: Smith, Elder & Co, 1861, p. 3-4

10   *Ibid.*, p. 8.

11   *Ibid.*, pp. 6–7.

vigorous while its heart may gradually become more choked up and decayed.'

Twenty years after Hollingshead's book, when Mowbray and Kitz were agitating, little had changed in the Old Nichol in Bethnal Green. It had just grown more overcrowded, more dilapidated. Royal Commissioners investigating housing and health there in 1884 identified hundreds of insanitary houses. In a quarter of the houses, they reported, the ground floor had sunk to become a cellar, lacking light and ventilation. Bethnal Green's medical officer, George Paddock Bate, filed damning reports in 1889–90. He estimated that 45 per cent of the houses were so damp or dilapidated that that they could not be made fit for human habitation. Fewer than 10 per cent of the houses were in a sound structural condition.

The *British Medical Journal* recorded the population density in the Old Nichol in 1890 as 373 people per acre, compared with an overall Bethnal Green figure of 168 people per acre.[12] It was a breeding ground for diseases. One ten-roomed building in Old Nichol Street housed 90 people. In Old Nichol Street and Turville Street, 'back yards, water closets and sinks can only be reached by passing through dark and dirty underground cellars'. A devastating commentary on health hazards represented a damning moral assessment of typical Old Nichol dwellers:

The class of people living in this unhealthy area are perhaps of the lowest type to be found anywhere in London. The population is largely made up of habitual loafers, unemployed casual labourers, and the criminal

---

12   The Bethnal Green figure was already higher than for London as a whole.

classes, constituting . . . the dregs of the Bethnal Green community.

In Charles Booth's colour-coded poverty maps, many of the Old Nichol's streets are dark blue (very poor . . . chronic want), or black (lowest class, criminal, semi-vicious). Sarah Wise references Booth in her forensic study of this area's history and character, *The Blackest Streets*.[13] But Wise challenges the received wisdom about the Old Nichol – that it was a hive of debauchery, violence and criminality – as exaggerated and inaccurate. Between 1885 and 1895 only one murder was recorded there. The murderer was caught and tried, and local residents gave evidence.

In some Old Nichol courts and alleys there was illegal gaming, dog-fighting and cock-fighting; prostitution was common-place. That was also true of many other poor neighbourhoods in London. The characterisation of Old Nichol's population as 'habitual loafers' was belied by an 1890 survey which listed inhabitants' occupations in alphabetical order. It started with 'Box makers, Button makers, Cabinet makers, Carmen, Carpenters, Chair and couch makers', and ended with 'Shoemakers, Stickmakers and toy makers, Upholsterers, Washerwomen, Weavers, Wheelwrights, Woodcutters and sawyers'. Thirty-two different occupations were listed, in addition to 'various'. The top five, by numbers employed, included skilled cabinetmakers and shoemakers. Many Old Nichol residents, women as well as men, possessed considerable skills, and worked long hours, but their earnings were low and precarious, often on a piece-work basis.

---

13 Wise, *The Blackest Streets*.

The harshest judgements about the area's inhabitants were reinforced in a widely read semi-fictionalised book, *A Child of the Jago*, by a Poplar-born working-class writer, Arthur Morrison. It was published in the mid-1890s as the slum was being cleared, making way for a very different kind of housing development.

Morrison's opening chapter introduces Dicky Perrot, 'a slight child by whose size you might have judged his age at five. But his face was of serious and troubled age. One who knew the children of the Jago might have held him eight.' Any efforts by Dicky to determine his life are thwarted by his environment, 'a howling sea of human wreckage', which draws him into criminality for survival.

In the preface to the book's third edition Morrison remarked:

> It was my fate to encounter a place in Shoreditch, where children were born and reared in circumstances which gave them no reasonable chance of living decent lives . . . fore-damned to a criminal and semi-criminal career. It was my experience to know the ways of this place, and . . . the evils it engendered . . . I hoped to bring the conditions of this place within the apprehension of others.[14]

For intimate details about the character of the Old Nichol's inhabitants Morrison relied greatly on Reverend Osborne Jay (or Father Jay as he preferred to be known). Jay took over as vicar at Holy Trinity Shoreditch, in the Old Nichol, in the mid-1880s. His background could hardly have been more different from that of an Old Nichol dweller. Born in India, the son of missionaries,

---

14 Arthur Morrison, *A Child of the Jago*, third edition, reissue with an introduction by Peter Miles, Oxford: Oxford University Press, 2012.

he returned to England to be educated at Eton, then Cambridge.

Jay worked for three years at a mission in Wapping before the post at Holy Trinity became available. With stables below, it was the only consecrated church in Britain on the first floor. Through his networks of wealthy people, Jay raised thousands of pounds to refurbish the building, so that it eventually comprised a place of worship, a room for mothers' meetings, a working-men's social club in the evenings, and a space for physical training equipped with a trapeze and a boxing ring. Late in the evening it became a lodging house for up to 48 people.

The church offered both spiritual and physical nourishment, providing free children's meals on Sunday mornings. Jay's positive initiatives, however, obscured unholy views about his parishioners' futures that he revealed in an interview as the Old Nichol was being torn down. He described them as a 'submerged and semi-criminal class' with 'physical, moral, and mental peculiarities . . . no nerve nutrition, no energy or staying power . . . their natural gifts are small. Cunning, not wisdom; sharpness, not intelligence, are stamped even on their face.' He believed they were a class of people who, through no fault of their own, 'never had a fair chance of being quickened into life'.[15]

He advocated radical action:

> to stop the supply of persons born to be lazy, immoral, and deficient in intellect. This can only be done by sending the present stock of them to what I will call a penal settlement . . . it would resemble a prison, only . . . far less gloomy . . . possessed of all appliances for physical development

15 Rev. Osborne Jay, 'To Check the Survival of the Unfit', *The London*, 12 March 1896, retrieved from www.mernick.org.uk/thhol/survunfi.html (accessed October 2018).

and well-being . . . To the submerged temperament such
a place would be the best home they had ever known
. . . they would lose some liberty, but gain a better and
perhaps a happier life.[16]

His interviewer, clearly shaken, asked: 'Would there not be a
great outcry against shutting human beings off from all contact
with the outside world?' Jay replied: 'No doubt; but the public
must be educated to the idea.' He conceded that this new method
'sounds drastic and harsh, but . . . a virulent fever cannot be cured
by doses of treacle'.[17]

While Jay rehearsed the eugenicist arguments that would
gain popularity in the coming century, and Morrison's novel
reinforced a view of the area's seemingly hopeless population,
that population itself scattered as the slum was cleared for a new
development. But sadly, few of the previous residents could
access that development.

Before the 1890s only private individuals with money could
undertake substantial housing developments. Sidney Waterlow's
'Improved Industrial Dwellings Company' began work in 1872
on a large tenement block 200 yards north of the Old Nichol. Son
of a small-scale stationer in Mile End, Waterlow was apprenticed
as a printer. He won lucrative contracts with government depart-
ments and built a huge printing firm employing 2,000 workers.
After moving into banking and finance he transferred his energies
into building housing for the working classes. His Leopold
Buildings along Columbia Road were built on land leased from
Baroness Angela Burdett-Coutts. Six storeys high, they provided
affordable housing for 112 families of skilled workers.

---

16 *Ibid.*
17 *Ibid.*

Investors in purely profit-driven housing schemes expected an 8 per cent return on their investment per annum. Waterlow offered just 5 per cent per annum, with the surplus reinvested in new housing stock. His first housing venture, for 80 families in Finsbury, began in 1863. Over three decades he constructed more than 40 estates, housing approximately 30,000 people in several London districts, including Bethnal Green, but they were restricted to the better-off working class. They were not assessed on income alone, though. The historian Anthony Wohl argues that the assessments of candidates for Waterlow's buildings by the company secretary, James Moore, were designed to 'discover the moral character of the prospective tenants'.[18]

Waterlow spoke of 'building for the future' when no family would be compelled to live in just a single room, where neither sanitary nor moral conditions could be satisfied. 'No proper feeling of decency or self-respect can be cultivated in families living in a single room,' he said. He posited a 'trickle-up' theory, whereby poorer quality housing vacated by successful candidates for his tenements would be filled by workers from the next layer down. It remained a theory, for the most part.

Within the nascent local authorities (vestries), people called for the housing crisis of the poor to be addressed, but they had neither mechanism nor resources to effect systemic change. Laws passed in the 1870s gave vestries the right to pull down unsafe insanitary buildings, but did not enable them to take financial responsibility for building new housing based on need.

That was about to change. The vehicle? A London-wide local authority with power to borrow money for substantial housing

---

18   See Anthony Wohl, *The Eternal Slum*, Cambridge: Cambridge University Press, 1977, p. 150.

projects; they would recoup the borrowings in rental income. The local authority would become the landlord. London's council housing revolution was coming closer.

The idea of creating a London-wide elected authority was first mooted in 1837, but the richer boroughs defeated the proposal. In 1855 the government created the Metropolitan Board of Works with a remit to develop infrastructural projects across the capital as its population expanded. But Board of Works members were appointed rather than elected. They were not accountable to the populace and the process of awarding contracts was conducted in secret. Small wonder that critics dubbed it the 'Board of Perks'.

In the 1880s political reformers created the London Municipal Reform League, led by a Liberal MP, J. F. Bottomley Firth, to campaign strongly for London-wide local government. Their efforts bore fruit in 1889. The new London County Council (LCC) held its first elections that year, and a Housing Act passed in 1890 empowered a progressive alliance of LCC liberals, labourites and socialists to embark on council-housing projects.

A few years earlier three prison sites had been suggested for demolition and replacement with working-class housing: Millbank, Coldbath Fields and Pentonville. There was a major slum clearance in the Millbank area, but the Millbank Prison site housed paintings rather than people, as the National Gallery of British Art (now Tate Britain). Pentonville remained a prison. Coldbath Fields Prison was demolished and rebuilt as a postal sorting office. In recent years, much of that site has finally been turned into housing, but London Mayor Boris Johnson controversially stripped the local authority of decision-making over the land and most of the units are being sold at prices well beyond the reach of ordinary local people.

The LCC's first major slum clearance took place on the Old Nichol. It took several years to demolish and replace it with the remarkable, picturesque Boundary Estate, with its blocks radiating outwards from a raised bandstand known as Arnold Circus. The rubble of the old slum lies beneath that bandstand. This estate is often celebrated as London's first council housing. It wasn't. Demolition work began in the early 1890s but the estate was not officially opened until 1900. By then several smaller council-housing projects, for 60–660 people each, had been completed, the first being Beachcroft Buildings off Cable Street, in 1894, which housed nearly 200 residents. Eight other council-house projects were completed in Greenwich, Deptford, St Giles and elsewhere in the East End before 1900.

The process of demolishing the Old Nichol illuminated the social and economic relations within London's housing. The land had been bought up in the seventeenth and eighteenth centuries by lawyers and merchants. While the slum residents never knew their actual landlords – agents came to collect the rents – they suddenly materialised to claim their payments when the LCC offered compensation to owners for the compulsory purchase of their land.

In *The Blackest Streets*, Sarah Wise listed some of these landlords, such as Richard Temple-Nugent-Brydges-Chandos-Grenville, third Duke of Buckingham and Chandos, who 'owned a plantation in Jamaica and 10,482 acres of Britain, including thirty-eight Nichol properties'. His heiress 'Lady Mary Morgan-Grenville, eighth Baroness Kinloss . . . was able to remain masked until 1892 when she had to break cover in order to collect her compulsory purchase compensation for the houses.' Another owner of houses in the Old Nichol was Sir Edward Colebrooke,

1st Baron Colebrooke, a Church of Scotland High Commissioner.

As the slum buildings came down, the population was removed one section at a time. The rat population grew and enjoyed more space and freedom, though their immediate food sources disappeared. Opportunists removed any abandoned materials. Mounted police kept an eye on the area under demolition as rumours spread that criminal gangs had established hideouts in the remaining buildings.

By 1895 the slum was completely cleared and building began on the new estate. A new group was formed within the LCC architects' department: the 'Housing of the Working Classes Branch'. Led by Owen Fleming, they were committed to rational, elegant design, inspired by the Arts and Crafts movement, many of whom were socialists, including William Morris. This group sought to use architectural means to change lives. The Boundary Estate was their model development: individual architects from this branch gave each block its own design flourishes, contrasting with Waterlow's 'improved dwellings', which were solidly built but uniformly designed.

The Boundary Estate features a range of decorative brick- and tile-work, and a variety of roof styles. But the importance of Waterlow's buildings, just north of the new estate, was that it set a standard that the Boundary Estate had at least to match. The vice-chair of the LCC's Housing Committee was David Waterlow (Sidney's son). He ensured that every flat on the Boundary Estate had thicker walls, with better sound-proofing and heat retention, and slightly bigger dimensions, than the Leopold buildings.

Some streets in the Old Nichol had been barely seven feet wide. The streets on the new estate were 50 feet wide, and Calvert Avenue, where shops were built into the ground floor, was 60 feet wide. The first 26 detailed plans of the new estate envisaged a grid system, but plan 27, which was adopted, introduced a bandstand from which the five-storey brick blocks radiated outwards, maximising light and air.

As well as shops there was a central laundry with club rooms above, and 77 artisan workshops for the estate's residents. The existing schools and the church would be refurbished within the plan. But there would be no pubs, and shops on the estate were forbidden to sell liquor.

The Boundary Estate was officially opened on 3 March 1900 by the Prince and Princess of Wales. The Prince was loudly cheered as he affirmed, 'There is no question at the present time of greater social importance than the housing of the working classes.' He assured the crowd that this was 'a subject in which I have long taken a deep interest . . . I heartily congratulate the Council on this outcome of their labours . . . in rooting out a nest of vice and disease and replacing the miserable courts and alleys and insanitary and filthy houses with excellent buildings designed to provide comfortable homes for the working people.'[19]

The *Daily Graphic* marvelled at this 'estate of tall houses and wide streets with a general aspect such that a stranger led there blindfolded might imagine that he was in Kensington', but added: 'Whether it has housed the people it has dispossessed is another matter.'

This was a very pressing matter for the 5,700 plus who mostly moved to other slum accommodation within a one-mile radius. Many displaced families continued to live in one room, and struggled to find the rent every week. Only 15 out of more than

---

19 'Housing of the Working Classes', *Manchester Guardian*, 5 March 1900.

1,000 flats on the new estate were one-room only. Around 90 per cent of the new flats had two or three rooms, commanding rents beyond the earning power of Old Nichol residents; only 11 could afford accommodation there and had their applications accepted. After the LCC's next major slum clearance, in 'The Devil's Acre' of Millbank,[20] the brand new estate offered just two single-roomed flats.

John Honeyman, the esteemed Glasgow-born architect, wrote in the journal of the Royal Institute of British Architects that it was 'a mistake to praise the LCC for erecting artisans' dwellings while they do nothing towards providing suitable dwellings for the poorest class'.[21] He complained that the Boundary Estate's buildings were occupied by a different class. In an atmosphere becoming more febrile towards immigrants, Charles Booth noted, unhelpfully, that this 'different class' consisted largely of Jews. The populist, anti-immigrant British Brothers League, formed in 1901, found strong support in Shoreditch and Bethnal Green.

Immigrant Jews, many with artisanal skills, faced discrimination in seeking employment and private housing to rent. Within a few years they formed approximately 50 per cent of tenants on the Boundary Estate. Zelda Usiskin was born into one such Jewish immigrant family from Russia, who settled on the estate a few years earlier.[22] She had very happy memories of her childhood there before the family moved to Hackney in 1927. Visiting a festival at Arnold Circus in 2010, she stopped at a stall where they were collecting memories from former residents. Zelda recalled

---

20 In 1850 Dickens dubbed this area 'the Devil's Acre' in his magazine *Household Words*.

21 *RIBA Journal*, Vol. 7, April 1900, p. 250.

22 Zelda was the author's mother-in-law.

how the particular layout of the estate had made it such a safe place to play, and also remembered a strong sense of community, with many other family members and friends close by. Her primary school, on Virginia Road, which remains open today, was around 50 per cent Jewish. She recalled good relations on the estate between Jewish and non-Jewish residents, but knew that if she crossed an invisible boundary beyond the estate towards Hoxton she would encounter a different reception. Her brother David attended a secondary school deeper into Bethnal Green, beyond the Jewish enclave, where teachers frequently made anti-Jewish remarks:

> If boys talked in class a master thought nothing of calling them Jewish chatterboxes or referring to us as Jewboys . . . I was taking a French lesson with Mr Wenger, a German Swiss . . . there was one boy Sugarman rather slovenly, not very neat . . . Mr Wenger came up to Sugarman and looked at his work . . . [He said] 'You dirty little Jewish swine' and took the closed book he was holding and thumped him on the head.[23]

The Boundary Estate flourished, but Bethnal Green Council was slow to build more high-quality council estates. An LCC medical officer filed a report in 1911 highlighting conditions in Digby Street and Morpeth Street, a mile east of the Boundary Estate:

> . . . the streets are infested with rats. It is quite common for a father, mother and six children to be living in one

---

23 Personal memoir written for family members in the early 1970s by David Usiskin.

small room. There are underground living rooms in most parts of the area and in one court of tenements there are people sleeping on and under the stairs which are open to the street.[24]

In parliamentary debates shortly after the First World War, which led to a new Housing Act in 1919, ministers promised 'homes fit for heroes' and committed to build half a million homes nationally over the coming three years. Only 213,000 homes were completed. Bethnal Green's Chief Sanitary Inspector commented as the war ended:

Men have gone by the thousands from these nests of misery to fight our battles . . . for civilisation and all that it means. The slums of Bethnal Green provided 12,000 soldiers . . . These men have . . . learned that life holds, or should hold something more than an existence in a gloomy alley four foot wide in a house not large enough to allow one to stand upright in it. They have breathed the pure air of the fields – many of them for the first time in their lives . . . Their whole outlook has been enlarged. What are they going to think when they come back to the sordid dinginess of the modern slum? What will they think of these huts which pass for homes?[25]

Houses that the local authority in Bethnal Green had condemned as unfit for human habitation in 1902 were still inhabited. In a

---

24 Press cuttings held at Tower Hamlets Local History Library archive
25 *Ibid.*

1919 report, Reverend Dick Sheppard[26] identified seven local 'plague spots', which had a death-rate 51 per cent higher than other parts of Bethnal Green. A royal visit that year shone a light on the cramped and poor conditions that many Bethnal Green residents endured. The mayor recalled with embarrassment that 'in one of the houses I had to ask [the Queen] . . . to bend her head . . . the top of her plume touched the ceiling'.

To shore up working-class support during the war, the government prohibited landlords from imposing rent increases. By 1920 that prohibition had been repealed, and landlords were able to increase rents by up to 40 per cent higher than they had been before the war. The Rent Act of 1923 stipulated that when landlords gained control over a house for the first time, they could evict the existing tenants and then charge whatever rent they chose. Voices of protest grew louder as the 1929 depression hit. Unemployment rose rapidly.

A further Rent Act in 1933 stopped further de-control of rents in working-class houses, but landlords were exempted from the Act's restrictions for any house built after the war. The Communist Party (CP) was gaining strength in east London, especially in Stepney, which bordered Bethnal Green. A tenants' defence league, encouraged by party activists, first established itself in Stepney in 1937.[27] Its successes through rent strikes backed by community campaigning boosted tenants' confidence in Bethnal Green too. In 1938 they chalked up a significant victory in Quinn Square, a six-storey block of flats in Russia Lane.

Built in 1882, initially there was a large square in the centre of the Russia Lane buildings where children could play, but that gave

---

26 The same Revd Sheppard who founded the Peace Pledge Union. See Chapter 5.

27 See Chapter 11 for further discussion of the Stepney Tenants Defence League.

way to another block, leaving only a narrow pathway between the buildings allowing air and light to penetrate the flats. The whole estate, including that block, comprised 246 flats, of which only 90 had controlled rents. Sanitation was basic. Each lavatory was shared by two families, each water tap by four families. The flats were in desperate need of repairs: there were broken steps and handrails, lavatory doors with no locks, and washhouses on the roof so dilapidated that no one could use them. The interiors had damp walls, peeling paper and falling ceilings.

The immediate trigger to action was the landlord's attempt to evict a tenant. He claimed that she was behind in her rent. She was on a controlled rent and a quick investigation confirmed that he had been overcharging her. After a further attempted eviction of an unemployed worker, tenants rallied round to resist, and a popular local trade unionist and CP activist, Bob Graves, put out a wider call for solidarity. Despite five policemen assisting the agent and bailiffs, they were unable to carry out the evictions.

At a meeting called at short notice in Oxford Hall, Victoria Park Square, an 18-strong campaign committee was formed, with Bob Graves elected as Secretary. The committee investigated the cases of all families with controlled rents and found that 70 of them were being overcharged. Tenants with de-controlled rents were paying a third more than those whose rents were controlled (and already being overcharged), for similar premises.

The Tenants' Association presented the landlord with a scale of rents according to the size of the flat that would be acceptable to them. In a panicked response, the landlord's agent whizzed round, reducing many rents on the spot. That did not prevent an escalation of collective protest action. The following

Tuesday morning, when the agent came to collect the rent, he met blank refusals on the doorstep, and was followed round by large numbers of women and children booing and harassing him. Campaigners made posters and placards saying: 'Less rent, more repairs', 'Our landlord has made a huge fortune at our expense', 'We refuse to pay high rents', and 'Quinn Square wants a fair deal.'

There were daily tenants' meetings and a picket of the Estate Office from morning till night. Local political figures, such as the Labour MP Dan Chater, and Councillors Turpin, Wilson and King, offered support, as did CP activists, including Ted Bramley, the party's London District organiser.

While enthusiastic support poured in for the tenants on rent strike, the landlord searched for backers. The only group he could muster were thugs from the local branch of Oswald Mosley's British Union of Fascists, whom he instructed to break up the tenants' meetings by force. However, according to Bob Graves, who wrote a pamphlet about the campaign, 'local tenants showed the fascists they were not wanted in Russia Lane'.[28] The landlord was forced to cave in to the tenants' demands soon afterwards. At that time, Mosley himself was busy negotiating the sale of land in Ancoats, Manchester, to Manchester City Corporation, which his ancestor, another Oswald Mosley, had purchased in 1596 for £3,500.

Bob Graves's pamphlet set out what the tenants of Quinn Square had won: a scale of maximum rents which the landlord could not increase; an understanding that necessary repairs would be carried out; official recognition by the landlord of the

---

28 Bob Graves, *Quinn Square Tenants' Rent Strike Victory*, published by the *Daily Worker*, 1938.

Tenants' Association: an agreement that no legal or other action against tenants would occur without consulting the Tenants' Association; and a commitment to address cases of overpayment by controlled tenants.

Back in the 1880s, the anarchist-communist Charles Mowbray urged tenants to organise, recognise their collective strength, and force their landlords to come to heel. Had Mowbray lived longer, he would have relished the victory in Quinn Square.

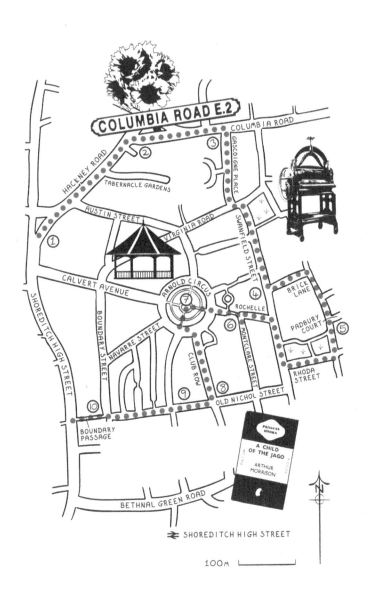

COLUMBIA ROAD E.2

COLUMBIA ROAD

HACKNEY ROAD

GASCOIGNE PLACE

TABERNACLE GARDENS

AUSTIN STREET

VIRGINIA ROAD

SWANFIELD STREET

CALVERT AVENUE

ARNOLD CIRCUS

BRICK LANE

ROCHELLE

PADBURY COURT

SHOREDITCH HIGH STREET

BOUNDARY STREET

NAVARRE STREET

CLUB ROW

MONTCLARE STREET

RHODA STREET

OLD NICHOL STREET

BOUNDARY PASSAGE

PENGUIN BOOKS

A CHILD OF THE JAGO

ARTHUR MORRISON

N

BETHNAL GREEN ROAD

SHOREDITCH HIGH STREET

100M

WALK

Start at St Leonard's Church, Shoreditch High Street, E1 6JN

1. Shoreditch High Street

St Leonard's Church is the latest incarnation of churches that have stood on this spot for more than 900 years. This one was built in 1740. The nursery rhyme words, 'When I grow rich, say the bells of Shoreditch', refers to this church. Behind it lies Boundary Street. This separates Shoreditch from the Bethnal Green parish of St Matthews in Tower Hamlets, which, until the 1890s, comprised the infamous Old Nichol slum. Sensationalist and derogatory newspaper depictions of this district were strongly reinforced by Arthur Morrison's social realist novel *Child of the Jago*, researched in the Old Nichol. Turn right out of the churchyard, and pause at Austin Street. On the right, behind the church gardens, is a sign for Boundary Street, forming one edge of the Old Nichol. The anarchist agitator and founder of the No Rent Campaign, Charles Mowbray, ran a print shop with his comrade Frank Kitz on this street. Bear right into Hackney Road, then right again into Columbia Road.

2. Columbia Road

An impressive block of flats with black metalwork stands on the right. These are the Leopold Buildings built by Sidney Waterlow, who developed the semi-philanthropic 'Improved Industrial Dwellings Company' which built tenements in five areas of London. These tenements were targeted towards 'morally upstanding' families of skilled workers. Waterlow's buildings were criticised by some for 'prison-like architecture'. When the London County Council (LCC) cleared the Old Nichol and built London's first large-scale council housing estate nearby – the Boundary Estate – it knew it had at least to match the room size and quality set by Leopold Buildings. Continue to the corner of Gascoigne Road.

3. Corner Columbia Road/Gascoigne Road

Columbia Road is famous for its flower market. In the distance stands the Birdcage pub. Historically, cut flowers and caged birds were merchandise typically sold by Huguenots. Gascoigne Road, with its French name, is a further indication of the historical Huguenot presence, which included many weavers. Walk along Gascoigne Road, turn left, then immediately right again into Swanfield Street. You soon get your first glimpse of the tall red-brick buildings on the right-hand side that comprise the north-eastern edge of the Boundary Estate. Just behind the flats (Sunbury Buildings) you will see a row of low-rise structures called 'Sunbury workshops'. Built as an integral part of the estate, they indicate that artisan grades of the working classes were the preferred tenants. In 1909, a gathering took place in the home of Nathan Weiner, a cabinet-maker living in Sunbury Buildings. It was the first meeting of the *Arbeter Ring*, a left-wing friendly society formed by Yiddish-speaking Jewish immigrants (discussed in greater detail in Chapter 4). Continue along Swanfield Street.

4. Swanfield Street

A striking-looking old building appears on the left. At street level are the premises of a Mauritian-born foam and mattress seller.

The building was once a weaver's cottage. Turn left then right into the smaller northern section of Brick Lane.

5. Brick Lane/Padbury Court

Stop on the corner of Padbury Court, a narrow street of uniformly built houses. These indicate the dimensions of houses that typically stood within of the Old Nichol slum. In John Henry Mackay's realist novel, *The Anarchists*, written in 1891, he describes one of the central character's first encounters with Brick Lane, approached from the Bethnal Green end:

> Whoever has once slowly sauntered through Brick Lane can say that he has been grazed by the pestilential breath of want; whoever has gone astray in its sidestreets has walked along the edge of the abyss of human suffering ... whoever still believes in the childish dream that the world may be saved by love, poverty relieved by charity, misery abolished by the State ... let him visit the battle-field of Brick Lane, where men do not fall with skulls cracked and hearts shot through, but where hunger cuts them down easily, after want has deprived them of their last force of resistance.

Continue along Brick Lane, turn right into Rhoda Street, right again into Swanfield Street, left into Rochelle Street, then left again into Montclare Street.

6. Rochelle Street/Montclare Street

On the right, a small building with a unique architectural style stands out. It is signposted 'The Old Laundry'. Two blocks had their own washing accommodation but this was the central laundry staffed by an engineer, a stoker, a matron and matron's assistant, paid for by the users' fees. Charges were kept affordable and the laundry was well used. It was equipped with 42 troughs, three box mangles, one roller mangle, 42 drying horses and three centrifugal wringing machines, for use by all on the estate. The laundry was completed in the summer of 1896. Above it there were two club rooms for use by the tenants. Double back to Rochelle Street, then walk up the stairs to the top of the bandstand.

7. Bandstand, Arnold Circus

From the bandstand, built on the rubble of the Old Nichol, you can obtain the best view of the estate's layout: a set of free-standing blocks, each with unique style and influences, which emanate like sun-rays from the bandstand, with much space between them for light and fresh air. The bandstand first appeared in plan number 27 for the estate. On the western side is Calvert Avenue, where shops were built into the estate. No pubs were permitted. North of the bandstand you will see Virginia Road School – one of two schools serving the children living on the estate and the streets around. The original school was built in 1875 and called New Castle Street School. It was enlarged and reorganised in 1887, further improved in 1899 as part of the Boundary Estate scheme, and renamed Virginia Road School. The other was Rochelle Street School, where Montclare Street and Club Row converge on Rochelle Street, opposite the bandstand. It opened in 1879, replacing a 'ragged school' (a charitable school for impoverished and destitute children) on this site. In 1898 it was rebuilt within the Boundary Estate scheme to a design created by the widely respected progressive architect Edward Robson. In 1874, he wrote, 'If popular education be worth its great price, its homes deserve something better than a passing thought. Schoolhouses [should] . . . take rank as public buildings . . . built in a manner befitting their new dignity.' It was through direct contact with schools in the Old Nichol that Lady Jeune, an LCC alderman and co-founder of the School Dinners Association, began her crusade for free milk for schoolchildren. Go down the steps facing south into Club Row.

8. Club Row/Old Nichol Street

The involvement of well-to-do individuals and charitable bodies with the populace of the Boundary Estate is exemplified, too, by St Hilda's Community Centre, which is based on the corner of Club Row and Old Nichol Street. St Hilda's grew out of a settlement established by Cheltenham Ladies' College, with the aim of combating deprivation and social exclusion through education, recreation and social care. It continues to play that role today. Club Row was London's only live animal market, dealing in anything from cats, dogs and chickens through to monkeys and lion cubs. It was the legacy of a bird market established here by French Huguenots. It closed in 1983. Turn right into Old Nichol Street, stop at a playground on the right-hand side.

9. Playground, Old Nichol Street

One of the few buildings that survived the destruction and clearance of the Old Nichol slum was Britain's only consecrated church established on the first floor of a building. It had stables underneath! It could not survive the bombs of the Second World War though, and was never rebuilt. Instead a playground was developed on this site. Holy Trinity Church was turned into a vibrant community hub by Reverend Osborne Jay, who nonetheless harboured sinister eugenicist views about the inhabitants of the Old Nichol, believing that the best thing for them was to be transferred to a penal colony, with men separated from women so they could not bring further 'inferior' generations into the world. Father Jay was a key informant for Arthur Morrison when he was writing *Child of the Jago*. Father Sturt, in Morrison's novel, was modelled on him – and the name 'Jago' is believed to have been derived from 'where Jay goes'. Continue to the junction with Boundary Street; cross over to Boundary Passage.

10. Boundary Passage

At the end of the passage stood Shoreditch High Street, along which those who were already wealthy made their way to the City every day, hoping to add to their fortunes. Unless they ventured down this passage, they could remain oblivious to the plight and daily struggles for existence of the victims of Victorian prosperity, who lived on the edge of the City in the Old Nichol.

'Battersea in Perspective' mural by Brian Barnes, Dagnall Street.

7

STIRRINGS FROM THE SOUTH

The Battersea Four

In 1863 a railway station opened in south London, transforming the local area. A joint venture of two railway lines created a new terminus called Clapham Junction, a name that would soon become an epithet for a noisy, crowded, chaotic scene. Clapham already had an upmarket resonance for Londoners, but the terminus was located in the depressed and impoverished district of Battersea, which at that time had a population of 20,000. By the 1890s a new industrial landscape had appeared, and the local population had grown to more than 160,000, boosted especially by immigrants from Ireland. Battersea's northeastern area, around Nine Elms Lane, became known as the 'Irish Island'.

This rapidly growing workforce was herded into new factories where women made candles, soap, pencils, cigars, hats and caps, army clothing, biscuits, boxes and envelopes, or worked in huge laundries. Men also did factory work, but mainly found jobs on the railways and within its allied industries. With a continuously expanding population, employers could keep wages low. Housing development, based on minimal investment, struggled to keep pace with industrial development. The area soon became as notorious as the East End for its overcrowded, insanitary conditions, and shared similar social problems, especially alcoholism, criminality and prostitution, with the latter centred around Clapham Junction.

Battersea was crying out for people with the vision and ability to change these circumstances. Between the 1880s and the 1930s the area was blessed with four 'tribunes of the people',[1] who attempted in their own ways to do just that. Each of these outstanding figures had the personality and inner strength to make a sustained difference in their own right, and, more importantly, to inspire others with their ideas and optimism that collective effort could bring positive change. One was a power-house of energy from a Scottish background; one, an aristocratic widow from Kent with an Irish father; another, a Liverpool-born photographer of Caribbean background and pan-African political leanings; and the last, a quixotic Indian figure from a Zoroastrian background. Each had their own progressive dreams, and believed they could help to turn dreams into reality.

The powerhouse was John Burns, the youngest of 16 children, born to an English mother and a Scottish father in Vauxhall in 1858. After the father deserted the family, they moved to a basement in Battersea. At ten, Burns was apprenticed as an engineer and, in his late teens, when he was working at Mowlem's construction and engineering company, a French work colleague introduced him to socialist ideas. That colleague was Victor Delahaye, a political exile who had participated in the 1871 uprising that heralded the short-lived Paris Commune. Burns absorbed these ideas and was soon enthusiastically conveying them to others at open-air meetings. He was first arrested in 1878 for defying a

---

[1]   In ancient Rome a 'Tribune of the People' was a champion of the ordinary people's rights, elected by them.

police prohibition against public speaking on Clapham Common.

Burns founded a vibrant local branch of the Social Democratic Federation (SDF) in 1885. The trade union activist Tom Mann, who lived in Battersea in the mid-1880s and joined that SDF branch, said Burns possessed 'a voice that could fill every part of the largest hall or theatre, and, if the wind were favourable, could reach a 20,000 audience in the parks'. Henry Snell, a fellow SDF member and later a Labour MP, claimed that Burns's power as a street orator 'was probably unequalled in that generation'.

Burns organised unions locally at Vauxhall gasworks and at the Nine Elms goods yard and locomotive works. He was one of the key organisers during the Great Dock Strike in 1889. That same year, the SDF and progressive Liberals established the Battersea Labour League. John Burns's credibility grew not only among workers in Battersea but in London as a whole through his determined campaigning against unemployment. On Sundays he led processions of London's unemployed into fashionable churches, including St Paul's Cathedral, forcing their congregations to take notice. On that occasion, when Rev. Gifford delivered a sermon against socialism, Burns stood up and began singing a socialist parody of a hymn, and according to reports 'a disturbance inevitably followed'. In 1886, following a demonstration in central London that escalated into a riot, he and three other socialist leaders were tried for seditious libel. His powerful speech secured acquittal for each of the defendants. He was less fortunate after his arrest at the Bloody Sunday fracas of 1887 and spent six weeks in prison.

Burns knew, though, that change would not come solely through protest but by getting hands on the levers of power. Having built a considerable support base among both socialists and liberals, he contested and won two key elections. He was elected on to the newly formed London County Council in 1889, and defeated the Tory candidate to win the parliamentary seat of Battersea and Clapham in 1892 as a socialist, with significant Liberal Party support. The cooperative relationship he forged between local Labourites, Liberals and Radicals through the Battersea Labour League enabled a broad Progressive Alliance to come into being. Adopting the motto 'Not for me, not for you, but for us', this alliance took control of the local vestry in 1894 and held power until 1909.[2] By then the partnerships within it were sufficiently strained for the Tories to regain control for three years. But during those initial 15 years, with John Burns as its driving force, the alliance enabled Battersea to become the beacon of municipal socialism in London. Gold-coloured bees, symbolising unity and cooperation, adorned the beautiful mosaic floor of its new Town Hall on Lavender Hill, where progressive polices were proposed and adopted.[3]

The alliance reduced the working week to 48 hours for all council employees; created London's first municipal health visiting service – paying special attention to maternity and child welfare; established a sterilised milk depot providing free school milk; and built more libraries, swimming baths and a municipal laundry. But its proudest achievement was one that began to challenge Battersea's biggest problem: poor quality and overcrowded housing. In 1903 Battersea Council opened its first municipal housing estate, the Latchmere Estate. Wired for electricity from the council's own generating station, it comprised

---

2   During which Battersea became a Metropolitan Borough (1900).

3   The former Town Hall building became Battersea Arts Centre in 1979. The Arts Centre was restored after a devastating fire destroyed its Grand Hall in 2015.

173 two-storey dwellings at rents that were affordable for skilled workers. Most properties on the estate had two front doors and housed two families. At the opening ceremony John Burns said: 'The land has communal origin, the streets bear democratic names, the whole plan, history and achievement is redolent of the common victory of the common people.'[4]

On the estate, Freedom Street runs parallel to Reform Street. One street is named after a Boer general (Joubert), another after William Matthews, a stonemason who chaired Battersea's Stop the War Committee during the Second Boer War. All a far cry from the streets a few hundred yards west, such as Candahar Road, Cabul Road and Khyber Road, which celebrate British military adventures of the late 1870s.

Anti-war activism locally was complemented by republicanism. In honour of Edward VII's coronation in 1902, local authorities were instructed to seal a loyal address and organise public rejoicing. When Battersea's ruling Progressive Alliance voted narrowly to refuse to do so, the Liberal-inclined *Daily Chronicle* described it as: 'Battersea versus the British Empire'. The *Pall Mall Gazette* lauded Battersea as 'the only borough council which has the courage to flout the King on his coronation'. The alliance's anti-war stance and proud republicanism had popular support. Councillors adopting these stands continued to be elected, and Burns held the Battersea and Clapham seat in 1900 despite the national Tory surge at the 'Khaki Election'. On Empire Day (24 May), Battersea Council regularly flew its municipal flag rather than the Union flag.

Burns frequently sniped at the style and character of the

---

4   S. Creighton, 'Latchmere Estate: Celebrating its 100th Anniversary' (talk given in 2005), www.seancreighton.com/bwhistory.htm; http://hawkley.ctie.org.uk/History/latchmere_estate.htm accessed September 2014.

wealthy classes. He said: 'The better the dress and position, the bigger the snob and the greater the rogue.' He laid great stress on the virtues of the 'common people', declaring, 'I am not ashamed to say I am the son of a washerwoman.' Nevertheless, an aristocratic widow called Charlotte Despard, who had moved to Battersea's most deprived area, Nine Elms, observed that, on the day in 1892 when John Burns and James Keir Hardie entered Parliament as the country's first elected socialists, Keir Hardie wore plain clothes and a cap, whereas Burns wore an exclusive suit paid for by his supporters. While Keir Hardie consolidated the Independent Labour Party during the ensuing years, Burns edged closer to the Liberals.

Despard was neither shocked nor surprised when Burns accepted a post in the Liberal government that won power in 1906, becoming the first working-class Cabinet member. He argued that it provided an opportunity to make practical policies benefitting working-class people and claimed that many trade unionists supported him. Others regarded it a betrayal of his socialist principles. His radicalism began to fade in government, but some old habits die hard. Having been promoted to President of the Board of Trade, he resigned from the government in 1914 when Britain went to war. He stepped down from political life altogether in 1918, devoting himself to cricket and studying London's history.

Charlotte Despard, of half-Irish background, grew up in Ripple, Kent, as Charlotte French, in spacious countryside accommodation – a dramatic contrast with Burns's circumstances. By the age of ten, though, her naval commander father had died and her mother had been committed to a mental health asylum. Charlotte was packed off to relatives in London and attended by nurses and governesses. As Burns enjoyed upward mobility into the corridors of power, Despard's opposite trajectory found her increasingly immersed in the daily struggles of Battersea's most impoverished residents.

She had married a wealthy businessman, Maximillian Despard, in 1870 and spent many years nursing him. In her spare time she wrote novels, including one about a factory girl in Battersea. After Maximillian's death in 1890, she threw herself into political activity, initially as a campaigner on the Lambeth Board of Guardians, and then on the London School Board. During that decade she joined Hyndman's Marxist SDF and Keir Hardie's ethical socialists of the Independent Labour Party (ILP), campaigned against sweated female labour, and became a Catholic, drawn by spiritual ideas which ultimately led her to Theosophy. Her Catholicism also gave her a strong affinity with the largely Irish population in the congested neighbourhood of Nine Elms – sandwiched between gasometers, a brewery, a coalyard and a railway depot – where she settled.

When Charles Booth interviewed Despard at 2 Currie Street in 1898 for his poverty survey, he found a home converted into a community centre with a club for factory workers, subsidised meals, a dispensary, and a room for mothers' meetings. Booth described her as 'one in 10,000', saying: 'Hardly one I have seen in the whole course of the Inquiry has left so strong an impression . . . If I wanted to read a district with sympathy I should be inclined to borrow her eyes, and if to influence it I should be content with her heart.'[5]

Despite the poverty and degradation around her, Despard believed that the twentieth century would see the 'rise of two great

---

5   C. Booth, *Notebooks*, miscellaneous districts 36/37, Battersea, LSE archive.

movements: Labour and Women'. Teresa Billington-Greig, who recruited Despard to the suffragette movement, described her as 'a visionary and optimist' of 'untiring energy' whose appeal was 'ethical and emotional'. She was 'a dreamer who gave hope and inspiration and courage to those with whom she worked'.[6]

As well as providing everyday practical help to people struggling with their circumstances, she articulated her radical ideas for social change at large outdoor gatherings, speaking regularly at Battersea Park, Wandsworth Common and Clapham Common, and indoors in Battersea Town Hall. Alongside her local work, she was the leading national personality in the Women's Freedom League, a suffragette organisation campaigning not just for the vote but also for equal economic opportunities for all women and against women's oppression in all spheres.[7] Charlotte Despard was extremely effective in supporting the political causes of London's Irish minority, eventually moving to Ireland to campaign there directly.

In 1913, however, newspapers noted Battersea's support for a different minority. An article in the *Chicago Defender*, under the headline 'England More Civilised Than US', reported that a London council had elected its first black mayor. But only just. John Archer, whose father was Barbadian, triumphed by 30 votes to 29 over a West End tailor, W. G. Moore. *The Daily Mail* announced 'Coloured Mayor – Majority of One at Battersea'. In his acceptance speech Archer declared: 'My election tonight marks a new era. You have made history . . . That news will go forth to all the coloured nations of the world and they will look

6   Teresa Billington-Greig papers, Women's Library archive, LSE.

7   See Chapter 8.

at Battersea and say, "It is the greatest thing you have done. You have shown that you have no racial prejudice, but recognise a man for what you think he has done."'

Thetford in Norfolk had elected *Britain's* first black mayor (in 1904), but Archer's appointment to office was novel enough to generate considerable press speculation, much of it uncomplimentary, about his and his parents' ethnic origins. He clarified the issue with delicious sarcasm:

> I am a son of a man born in the West Indies. I was born in a little obscure village in England, that maybe you have never heard of – Liverpool . . . My mother was not born in Rangoon. She was not Burmese. She belonged to one of the grandest races on the face of the earth. My mother was an Irishwoman.[8]

He entered local politics as a Liberal, through Battersea Labour League, and was one of six councillors elected to Latchmere ward in 1906, where he had also opened a photographic studio. But his political interests were wider. He attended the Pan-Africanist Conference in London in 1900, organised by a Trinidadian barrister, Henry Sylvester-Williams, which called on Britain to give 'the rights of responsible government to the Black colonies of Africa and the West Indies'.[9] Archer was elected to the conference's Executive Committee. The conference moved to different national locations over the years and Archer chaired it when it reconvened in London in 1921.

---

8   *Daily Mail*, 10 November 1913.

9   Sylvester-Williams was also elected as a Progressive councillor in 1906 in St Marylebone, where Progressives were the minority.

Following his mayoral election, Archer received congratulations from across the world, but was shocked by the volume of hate mail he received. A month after his election he told a meeting at the Town Hall,

> I have had letters . . . calling my mother some of the foulest names . . . I have been made to feel my position more than any man who has ever occupied this chair . . . because I am a man of colour. My dead mother has been called in question because she married a coloured man.[10]

The Progressive Alliance, which resumed control over the borough in 1912, did not last through the First World War. Labour was emerging as a strong independent force, and the Liberals split off. Archer became a key figure in the local Labour Party, respected particularly for his efforts on behalf of the unemployed and ex-servicemen. He argued that a government that spent millions of pounds a day prosecuting a war 'should be able to find sufficient money to keep out of the workhouse the men who helped to win that war'.

Labour's candidate in the December 1918 parliamentary election was Charlotte Despard, who had taken a strong pacifist stance during the war. Her manifesto put demands of justice and equality for Ireland and India high on the agenda alongside adequate food for children, better education and housing, land nationalisation and a minimum wage. Archer worked hard as Despard's election agent but she couldn't withstand the national backlash against pacifists during this election, and lost the seat

---

10 M. Phillips, *Black Europeans: A British Library Online Gallery Feature, John Archer (1863–1932)*, www.bl.uk/onlinegallery/features/blackeuro/pdf/archer.pdf (accessed 21 January 2019).

to Richard Morris, a Coalition Liberal. Archer proved more fortunate with the candidate he promoted at the next election, a pioneer for his political affiliation as much as his ethnicity.

At a session on colonial freedom during the 1921 Pan-Africanist Congress, Archer welcomed a Parsee Indian, Shapurji Saklatvala, to the platform. Later, Archer became Saklatvala's principal backer for the Battersea North parliamentary seat, aiding his victory in 1922. Saklatvala narrowly lost the seat in 1923 but, with Archer's help, regained it in 1924, holding it until 1929. Saklatvala fought these elections as a Communist Party (CP) member with Labour support. John Archer, a Labour representative, chaired Saklatvala's final election rally in 1924. When he represented Battersea North, Saklatvala was Britain's third Indian MP and its first Communist MP.[11]

Born in Bombay in 1874, Saklatvala came to Britain in 1905 to recuperate from malaria and work in his maternal uncle's firm, the Tata Corporation, in Derbyshire.[12] In his late twenties, Saklatvala had become politically rebellious and outspoken against the damaging effects of British rule. His family prescribed a change of scenery. In Derbyshire he married Sally Marsh, a local working-class woman who had left school at 13. She worked as a waitress at the health centre where Saklatvala was recuperating. Through Sally he began to learn the realities of working-class life in a country enriched by its enormous empire, and saw just how little of that wealth filtered down to the lower classes. He was drawn into left-wing activism after seeing the conditions of ordinary people in Manchester and London.

---

11 Excluding MPs born in India but of white British ethnicity.

12 The corporation established itself in 1868 working initially in steel, energy and textiles.

Saklatvala joined the Social Democratic Federation in 1907 and became a keen follower of Sylvia Pankhurst, whom he first heard speaking at a suffragette demonstration in 1908. The following year he joined the City of London branch of the ILP. He continued to live in two worlds, supremely conscious of immediate issues in his adopted country, but equally aware of the ongoing struggles of Indians under British rule. He connected the two through his campaigning work with the Workers Welfare League for India, set up by two socialists, Charles Ryder and a Battersea-based ILP member, Arthur Field. The Russian Revolution had an enormous impact on him, and after the British Communist Party was established, he was part of a segment of the ILP that split off and joined the Communists in 1921. He had begun to attract the attention of the security services early on and was often followed by a detective. His daughter Sehri recounted in her biography of her father:

> ... it flattered him and gave him importance; he certainly never seemed to resent it. Once, when it was pouring with rain and he went into a restaurant for lunch, he went out and invited the detective to come inside out of the rain; he said he knew he was there and that he was only doing his job, so why get wet?[13]

She also recalled a later occasion when he was due to address a meeting in an unfamiliar part of London and had forgotten the precise venue details: 'He went into the local police station and asked ... where Saklatvala was scheduled to speak that night, and they at once told him!'

---

13 S. Saklatvala, *The Fifth Commandment*, Manchester: Miranda Press, 1991, p. 52.

Saklatvala had increasing contact with John Archer and Battersea's strong trade-union movement. He knew Communist and ILP activists in Battersea, and in 1921 was invited to speak at a rally for striking Welsh miners at the Town Hall. His nomination by Battersea's Trades Council to fight the parliamentary seat was endorsed by the local Communist Party and Labour Party branches. Joint membership was permitted until the Labour Party and CP became locked in internecine warfare in 1924.

He had strong backing from Charlotte Despard, who made a special appeal 'to my fellow Irish countrymen and women in North Battersea' to 'support the Party and support the man, Saklatvala – that will be on your side in the great struggle which is bound to come'.

In his maiden speech to the House of Commons on 23 November 1922, Saklatvala spoke of his constituents who suffered from unemployment. He commented on workers' wages in Bengal too, but his main focus was Ireland, denouncing the Anglo-Irish treaty, which he said was not acceptable to the Irish people as a whole, adding, 'I put forward not my personal views but the view of 90 per cent of those Irishmen who are my electors.'

According to the communist writer J.A. Mahon, Saklatvala's constituents enthusiastically supported his work inside and outside Parliament:

> ... he was known in every [Battersea] working class district as 'Sak'. He placed his legal ability and untiring energy at the disposal of anyone in trouble ... his frequent meetings were crowded with men, women and even children, who absorbed his simple but eloquent explanations.[14]

---

14 Saklatvala file in the Dictionary of Labour Biography archive, Hull History Centre.

Saklatvala's speeches in the House were witty, and his behaviour in Parliament occasionally unconventional. He was slapped down for addressing the Speaker as 'Comrade'. In a debate about the Indian Civil Service, he said it was 'not Indian', had 'no reputation for being civil', and it was 'a domination and usurpation'. Barring these 'great defects, they are all right', he said. His style did not endear him to opponents. One Liberal, Leslie Hore-Belisha, who entered the House in 1923, deplored Saklatvala's 'turbulent' and 'loosely phrased' rhetoric, 'spoken in a slightly raucous voice [with] wild gesticulation'.

As the only Indian MP, he endured racist jibes but answered critics with panache. In a 1924 health debate Saklatvala claimed that the Russian revolutionary government cared more than the British government about workers' health. Austen Chamberlain MP began his reply, 'When Mr Saklatvala knows this country more intimately . . .'. Saklatvala, who had lived in Britain for nearly 20 years, told the *Sunday Worker* that he had 'too good a knowledge of the British ruling class and their politics . . . much more than he considers it good for an Indian to know':

Against one Chamberlain I have the voice of 15,000 British workers in Battersea and during my visits to the provinces . . . I have reason to know that there are as many thousands elsewhere who know I have a far more intimate . . . knowledge of the conditions . . . of the workers of Britain than ever Mr Austen Chamberlain will be able to possess.[15]

---

15 S. Saklatvala, *The Fifth Commandment*, pp. 282–3.

The wrangles at national level between the Labour Party's rival wings affected Battersea's unique situation. Labour's conference in October 1924 forbade party branches from supporting Communist candidates, but Battersea Labour Party rebelled. It voted overwhelmingly to continue supporting Saklatvala. It would not stand a candidate against him, and he retained the seat on a Communist ticket. As a result the local Labour Party was temporarily disaffiliated from the national party.

Battersea and Bermondsey were south London's most militant supporters of the May 1926 General Strike, called by the TUC in support of miners refusing to accept a pay cut and increased hours of work. The miners' slogan was 'not a penny off the pay, not a minute on the day'. Around the country, Councils of Action (COAs) were formed through existing networks of trade unionists. These COAs aimed to maximise local participation in the strike by picketing large workplaces where production was continuing and persuading workers to join the strike; facilitating distribution of food to strikers and their families; and conveying information about the strike's local and national progress in a situation where national newspapers were temporarily closed down.

Within a day of the strike starting, the Lower Hall in Battersea's municipal headquarters was given over to a COA formed by 70 local organisations – mainly trade unions.[16] The local Unemployed Workers' Movement marched through Battersea Square, Battersea Church Road, and along York Road to Nine Elms, stopping to hold meetings outside factories calling workers to join the strike. Every evening, strike updates were given at the

---

16 Battersea COA was chaired by Jack Clancy, who later that year won a seat in a council by-election in Winstanley ward, standing for the disaffiliated local Labour Party against the official Labour candidate.

Prince's Head pub on the corner of York Road and Falcon Road.

But Battersea North's MP could not be present at these updates. He was in jail. Saklatvala had addressed a mass meeting in Hyde Park at the beginning of the strike. Troops were camped nearby. He called on troops to defend the people and not to follow orders to act against them. He was charged with sedition and imprisoned for two months. A huge crowd attended a rally at Battersea Town Hall on 8 May in support of the strike. The main speaker, a South Wales miner, Noah Ablett, was arrested as he left the meeting for supporting Saklatvala's request to the troops.[17]

In the aftermath of the General Strike, the hostility between the Labour Party and Communist Party was ratcheted up further and John Archer ultimately fell out with Saklatvala, fell back in with Labour, and supported a successful Labour candidate against him in the 1929 election.

Between 1932 and 1943, Battersea's four outstanding activists – each of whom had stamped their personalities on the area over the preceding decades, refused to accept the status quo, inspired hope and supported radical change by courageous personal example – departed this earth. John Archer died first, in 1932, a few weeks shy of his seventieth birthday. He was Deputy Leader of the council at the time, representing Nine Elms, where the fight against poverty continued. He was buried in Croydon after a service at Our Lady of Carmel Church, on Battersea Park Road. Mourners said he left a multitude of friends and not a single enemy.

On 20 January 1936, the Bombay-born writer Rudyard Kipling was cremated in a private ceremony at Golders Green

---

17 Ablett was bound over for 12 months and ordered to pay £10 10s costs. In 1911, Tom Mann served six months after making a similar call during the transport workers' strike.

in northwest London, his coffin draped in the Union Flag. The few mourners were surprised to find the grounds littered with red flags and insignia, left behind from a cremation earlier that day. Hundreds had come to pay their last respects to another of Bombay's sons, Shapurji Saklatvala, who had died of a heart attack aged 61. He had suffered his first heart attack in 1929.

Charlotte Despard was buried in Dublin in 1939, having lived to the grand age of 95. In Ireland her political energy was transferred from the Labour Party to Sinn Fein, and, following a trip to Russia in 1930, to the Communist Party. Her religious and spiritual journey took her from Catholicism to theosophy. On her death, the militantly atheist left-winger Harry Pollitt described her as 'the only real saint I've ever met'.

John Burns, who had retired early from active politics in 1918, outlived them all. He was buried by St Mary's Church, Battersea, in 1943. A local primary school is named after him, as is a street leading into the Latchmere municipal housing estate.

In the decades in which these four individuals were so prominent, Battersea gained a reputation for radicalism and internationalism. During the period in which they died, Battersea's people combined these traditions to great effect, especially in their solidarity with the fledgling Spanish Republic's struggle against fascism.

Within days of the Civil War breaking out, the Communist Party organised a public meeting at the Railwaymen's Unity Hall in Falcon Grove, entitled 'Support Spanish Workers Against Fascism'. Speakers included a local communist, Tom Oldershaw, who was cycling for pleasure in Spain when the Civil War broke out. Alongside him was a fellow party member, poet and painter, Clive Branson. Both later joined a band of 'volunteers for liberty' from Battersea who fought in Spain. Six of them, including Oldershaw, never returned. Branson spoke at the next major campaign meeting at Battersea Town Hall in September, which attracted an audience of more than 400.

An ad hoc Aid for Spain Committee helped overcome the tensions between Labour and the CP that persisted from the 1920s. The CP invited the fiery Labour left-winger, Aneurin Bevan, to speak at a meeting about Spain at Battersea Town Hall. Bevan explained that it would be difficult to appear on a CP platform, so the ad hoc committee was formed. More than 1,000 people heard Bevan make a dramatic, prescient speech in which he warned: 'If Madrid fell to fascism, it would be Paris next, and then London.' In December the Trades Council formally established an Aid for Spain Committee that collected food, money and supplies for the Spanish Republic through an Aid for Spain Week and house-to-house collections. The week concluded with a public meeting, with a platform representing more than 20 organisations.

Two venues on Lavender Hill close to the Town Hall became organising and collection centres for the Aid for Spain Committee: the Labour Party headquarters at number 177 and the CP's People's Bookshop at number 115. Inside the People's Bookshop, a group of women knitted garments that were sent as aid to the Republic. The shop's manager, David Guest – a Cambridge mathematics and philosophy graduate, and son of the playwright and suffragette Carmel Goldsmid and a Southwark Labour MP, Leslie Haden-Guest – had a more ambitious project. He wanted to raise £750: the amount needed to send an ambulance to Spain. By the end of January 1937, only £100 had been raised. Guest made arrangements with the central London HQ of the Aid for Spain movement, guaranteeing any shortfall himself. Fellow

Battersea communists, Percy Cohen and Joe Ilean, drove the fully equipped ambulance to Spain. In April 1938 Guest himself joined up with the 15th Brigade, but was killed by a fascist sniper three months later as the brigade attempted to capture a key hill in the Battle of Ebro. Guest's sister, Angela, also volunteered for Spain doing medical work, although she had no medical training at that stage. She survived and became a doctor in 1945.[18]

The local anti-fascist campaigns directed towards Spain from July 1936 gave heart and inspiration to the fight against fascism on their doorsteps. Battersea was one of the few areas in London where the British Union of Fascists had established a working-class base before 1934. Hundreds of campaigners attended Saturday morning open-air meetings. Their local organiser was J.P.D. Paton, a Covent Garden porter, formerly active in the National Unemployed Workers' Movement. Battersea Borough Council repeatedly refused to allow Mosley's movement to meet at Battersea Town Hall.

In April 1938, Mosley himself attempted to hold an open-air rally in the area. Fascist supporters were outnumbered by hundreds of anti-fascists. Instead of speaking from the platform, Mosley had to give his speech from inside a van, through two microphones and six speakers. The rally was abandoned amid a mini-riot by anti-fascists, during which ten of them were arrested. The following month, when the fascists announced a march from Clapham Junction to Clapham Common, fewer than 100 fascists turned up to be met with huge opposition at every step of the route. An area that had provided London with one of its first two socialist MPs in the 1890s, its first black mayor in 1913, its first

---

18 Angela Guest later worked for the World Health Organization, but was killed in a car crash in 1965.

Communist MP in the 1920s, and had sent at least 17 of its most idealistic younger people to Spain to fight for democracy, was in no mood to give ground to those who would destroy these ideals.

JOHN
RICHARD
ARCHER
1863-1932

BIRLEY STREET

DAGNALL STREET

CULVERT ROAD

REFORM STREET

FREEDOM STREET

SHEEPCOTE LANE

EVERSLEIGH ROAD

HOLDEN STREET

GRAYSHOTT ROAD

LAVENDER HILL

BATTERSEA PARK ROAD

ST JAMES'S GROVE

SOUTH STREET

MATTHEWS STREET

BURNS ROAD

LATCHMERE ROAD

LATCHMERE ROAD

FALCON PARK

DOROTHY ROAD

CABUL ROAD

CANDAHAR ROAD

AFGHAN ROAD

FALCON GROVE

ESTE ROAD

FALCON ROAD

GRANT ROAD

CLAPHAM JUNCTION

LAVENDER HILL

100M

226

WALK

Start at Clapham Junction station, Grant Road exit, SW16 2PE.

1. Grant Road

The creation of Clapham Junction station in 1863 brought considerable economic development to Battersea and a huge influx of workers over the next four decades. Turn left into Falcon Road, then right into Este Road.

2. Este Road

Mary Gray, who lived at number 72, was an active member of the Social Democratic Federation and founder, in Battersea, of London's first Socialist Sunday School in November 1892. It began with two pupils, including Mary's own daughter, Florence. By the third Sunday, they had 27 in class. They met in Sydney Hall in York Road, about half a mile from Mary's house. As other Socialist Sunday Schools were created they developed shared songbooks with verses such as: 'We the rebel children sing perish every court and king. We've a world to save and win in the revolution.' This was described as a 'hymn of hate' by the British Empire Union in an early 1920s pamphlet entitled *Danger Ahead*. Go back to Falcon Road, then turn right.

3. Falcon Road

Battersea Labour Club, on the right, is not officially connected to the Labour Party but is indicative of a strong local labour movement tradition. Battersea Labour Party was established in 1908 by a group of Trades Council activists, and this was one of the first areas of London to have a local Trades Council. Continue along Falcon Road. Turn right into Falcon Grove.

4. Falcon Grove

The building at number 5 with long windows used to be the National Union of Railwaymen's Unity Hall. In addition to union meetings, it was used to promote radical political campaigns. During the Spanish Civil War, the first of a series of meetings to 'Support Spanish Workers Against Fascism' took place here. Return to Falcon Road. Turn right and stop on the corner of Afghan Road.

5. Afghan Road

Several residential streets in the next section of the walk were developed by a former carpenter called Alfred Heaver from 1879 and these streets were named to honour British military campaigns between 1878–81. Part of the estate that was subsequently demolished and redeveloped included streets named Kambala, Musjid, Natal and Tugela. Continue along Afghan Road, turn left into Candahar Road then right into Cabul Road, past Sacred Heart Catholic school. Catholic schools in Battersea reflect the large numbers of children of Irish heritage in the area. Pass the former Milton Congregational Hall at 21 Cabul Road, go through Falcon Park, under the railway bridge, left into Latchmere Road then right into Burns Road.

6. Burns Road

This road celebrates John Burns, trade unionist, later Liberal MP for Battersea, and first elected as a socialist in 1892. It leads into the Latchmere Estate – Battersea's first municipal housing project, which opened in August 1903. Turn right into Matthews Street, named after the chair of the local Stop the War Committee during the Second Boer War. Mr Goodman, who lived at number 21, was active in Battersea Labour League and helped to develop the Workers' Educational Association. Turn left into Sheepcote Lane.

7. Sheepcote Lane

Sheepcote Lane was a traditional area for Gypsy families, who camped in the neighbourhood for parts of the year. Continue along Sheepcote Lane. Joubert Street to the left was named after a Boer general; Odger Street recalls a Chartist shoemaker and trade unionist, George Odger, Secretary of the London Trades Council from 1862–72, and one-time president of the International Workingmen's Association (First International). Turn left into Freedom Street. Social Democratic Federation (SDF) activists, Ellen and William Humphreys lived at number 1. Ellen was active in Battersea Women's Socialist Circle and helped Mary Gray to organise the Socialist Sunday School. Turn right into Reform Street.

8. Reform Street

The recreation ground facing Reform Street once housed a controversial brown dog statue, unveiled in September 1906.

Battersea Stop the War Committee, formed in 1900.
Photo courtesy of Wandsworth Heritage Service

Anti-vivisectionists, with strong local support, commissioned the statue following a campaign about vivisections taking place during medical students' training at University College London. The statue's plaque read, 'Men and Women of England, how long shall these things be?' Speakers at the unveiling included George Bernard Shaw and local socialist and anti-vivisectionist Charlotte Despard. 'Anti-dogger' students frequently vandalised the statue and a 24-hour police guard was instituted in 1907. Battersea's Progressive Alliance council supported the anti-vivisectionists, but the Conservative council, elected in 1909, was unsympathetic and in March 1910 it authorised council workers, accompanied by 120 police officers, to remove the statue at night. There were protests calling for its return. It is believed to have been smashed and melted down. In 1985 a new statue was commissioned by the

Anti-Vivisection Society and unveiled in Battersea Park. Walk part-way round the recreation ground and turn right into St James Grove, then right into Battersea Park Road.

9. Battersea Park Road

A plaque above number 214, mounted by the Nubian Jak Community Trust, celebrates John Archer, London's first black mayor, elected in 1913. Archer had a photographic studio/ shop first at number 214, then at number 208. Two roads north of Battersea Park Road, at Overstrand Mansions on Prince of Wales Drive, a blue plaque marks the home of the socialist Irish playwright Sean O'Casey, who lived here briefly from 1927 with his wife, the actress and author, Eileen Carey. Turn right into Culvert Road then left into Dagnall Street.

10. Dagnall Street

Along the side wall of the first building on the right (formerly the Haberdashers' Arms public house) is a remarkable mural called 'Battersea in Perspective', painted by Brian Barnes in 1988. It features nine local heroes. The first four from the left are: black mayor and radical pan-African nationalist John Archer; trade unionist and MP John Burns; Communist MP Shapurji Saklatvala; and wealthy socialist widow, activist and suffragette Charlotte Despard. Turn back then left into Culvert Road. Go through the tunnel then over the railway bridge, left into Eversleigh Road, right into Birley Street, then right into Holden Street.

11. Holden Street

John Burns founded the Battersea Branch of the SDF in 1885 at his home at number 8. The houses in these streets are part of the

Shaftesbury Park Estate, built as a semi-philanthropic venture by the Artisans, Labourers and General Dwelling Company in the 1870s, which provided affordable rented accommodation for skilled workers. The seventh Earl of Shaftesbury – a social reformer – laid the estate's foundation stone. Burns spread the SDF's message on Clapham Common to the south and gained support from many residents in these streets. Turn left into Grayshott Road, then left into Lavender Hill. Cross the road.

12. *Lavender Hill (1)*

In the 1930s, the Communist Party's People's Bookshop was at 115 Lavender Hill, run by Noreen and Clive Branson. Noreen, who sang with the Bach Choir, was Secretary of Battersea Communist Party. Later it was managed by David Guest, who volunteered to fight against fascism in Spain in 1938 and died there. Turn back and walk westwards along Lavender Hill, passing Glycena Road on the right where the Bransons lived.

13. *Lavender Hill (2)*

The building at number 177, which has housed Battersea Labour Party for many decades, was purchased for the party by Charlotte Despard. Continue along Lavender Hill and cross to Battersea Arts Centre.

14. *Lavender Hill (3)*

Battersea Arts Centre occupies the former Battersea Town Hall, built in 1893 to Edward Mountford's design. After Battersea Council was absorbed into Wandsworth in 1965, this building, in which several radical political initiatives were launched, was threatened with conversion into a swimming pool. A vigorous local campaign saved the building. The lobby area floor has a mosaic of bees, representing cooperation and unity. Go through the lobby and up the central stairway. What look like books on a shelf actually form a timeline of Battersea's history, including several radical episodes. The books with red covers have been adapted inside to convey that history through laminated photographs and texts. The Communist Party first held its National Congress here in the Grand Hall in 1922. In 1926, the Lower Hall became the headquarters of the Battersea Council of Action during the General Strike, organising support for strikers and their families. In 1927 Bertrand Russell gave a seminal lecture here entitled, 'Why I am not a Christian', later published as a pamphlet. The Arts Centre sees itself as heir to Battersea's radical traditions. Its Grand Hall re-opened in 2018.

15. Lavender Hill (4)

At number 263, Oswald Mosley's British Union of Fascists established an Unemployed Workers' Centre. Members of this centre, known as the Battersea Boys, were noted for their contribution to Mosley's stewarding force. His movement established a Fascist Union of British Workers to help it recruit among the working class. Its first branch was in Battersea. Today it is used for healthier purposes as an NHS surgery.

Arrest of suffragette, central London.

8

SPEAKING TRUTH TO POWER

Suffragettes and Westminster

In 1883, an imposing venue with two large public halls opened on Caxton Street, Westminster, half a mile from Parliament. This red-brick and pink-sandstone building, which began life as Westminster City Hall, was renamed Caxton Hall and became a celebrated concert venue, a registry office for the marriages of Elizabeth Taylor, Orson Welles, Diana Dors, Ringo Starr and others, and a central location for meetings and conferences touching the further reaches of the political spectrum.

Lenin's notes on the three-day conference on 'Nationalities and Subject Races' held there in June 1910 describe 'speeches by various people living under foreign rule: Egyptians, Indians, Moroccans, Georgians, negro races of Africa, South American Indians and also European nations such as the Irish and Poles'. Any surviving delegates would have been disheartened by the event held there nearly 60 years later, when supporters of several marginal far-right groups – the League of Empire Loyalists, the British National Party, the Greater Britain Movement and the Racial Preservation Society – came together to form the National Front.[1]

---

1   The NF was founded in February 1967. When it split in the early 1980s one faction revived the name 'British National Party'.

The Ministry of Information hosted its wartime press conferences at Caxton Hall, and a plaque celebrates Winston Churchill's presence. On the third anniversary of the outbreak of the war, a Polish-Jewish Marxist, Szmul Zygielbojm, stunned a large Labour Party meeting there, when he revealed the Nazis' first use of gas as a weapon of mass murder, against 40,000 Jews incarcerated in Chelmno, Poland.[2]

On 13 March 1940, Caxton Hall had hosted an equally dramatic meeting organised by the East India Association and the Royal Central Asian Society. The platform speakers included 75-year-old Michael O'Dwyer, who was Governor of Punjab in 1919, when the Jallianwala Bagh massacre took place. British troops fired on a peaceful protest by Hindus, Sikhs, Muslims and Christians, and admitted killing 379 protesters; most Indian sources estimate that more than 1,000 died. O'Dwyer described the troops' behaviour as the 'correct action' in the circumstances.

Udham Singh, an Indian revolutionary, had visited Caxton Hall a week earlier. On the night, as the meeting closed, he stood and fired a revolver towards the platform. O'Dwyer was hit twice in the back. One bullet passed through his heart and right lung, another through both kidneys. O'Dwyer was killed instantly. Lord Zetland, Secretary of State for India, and two other speakers were wounded.

On his arrest, Singh reinvented himself as 'Ram Mohammed Singh Azad' – names representing Indian's diverse religions.[3] In his witness statement he said that O'Dwyer 'wanted to crush the

---

2   In May 1943 Zygielbojm committed suicide at his Paddington flat as a political protest at the Allies' passivity at Nazi genocide. A plaque was mounted on Porchester Road, W 2, in 1996, near to where he lived.

3   The name Azad also means free/independent.

spirit of my people, so I have crushed him', adding at his trial, 'I have seen my people starving in India under the British rule . . . I am not sorry for protesting. It was my duty to do so . . . I am not afraid to die. I am proud to die.'[4] He was hanged and buried at Pentonville Prison. The judge rejected Singh's request to return his remains to India.[5]

Not every meeting at Caxton Hall had such melodrama but assemblies there felt very significant because the venue was so close to Parliament. It became the favoured central London venue for, arguably, London's most successful rebel movement, Emmeline Pankhurst's Women's Social and Political Union (WSPU) or 'suffragettes', which first gathered there on 19 February 1906. Large numbers of East End women stood and sang 'The Red Flag' before formal proceedings opened that day.[6] From 1907, the WSPU held 'Women's Parliament' meetings at Caxton Hall which coincided with the male Parliament nearby reopening after recess. As their alternative sessions closed, the chair would encourage participants to march on Parliament.

With the *Daily Mail*'s unwitting help, the WSPU became popularly known as the 'Suffragettes'. Reporter Charles Hands covered the trial of two members, Christabel Pankhurst (Emmeline's eldest daughter) and Annie Kenney, held after they disrupted a speech by the leading Liberal politician, Sir Edward Grey. Kenney, who had worked in a cotton mill in Saddleworth, Yorkshire, from the age of ten, was fearless. The arresting officer

---

4   See Florian Stadtler's chapter in R. Ahmed and S. Mukherjee (eds), *South Asian Resistances in Britain*, London: Continuum, 2012, pp. 27–9.

5   In 1975 Singh's exhumed remains were returned at the request of the Punjab authorities. His casket was paraded through Punjab's major urban centres, including Amritsar, to Singh's birthplace, for cremation.

6   See Andrew Rosen, *Rise Up Women!* London: Routledge & Kegan Paul, 1974.

claimed they assaulted and spat at him. When Pankhurst and Kenney were convicted they refused to pay the fine and became the first activists for women's votes in Britain to be imprisoned. The news reverberated nationally, and Hands, searching for words to match his outrage at their impudence, mocked them by inventing an adaptation of 'suffragists' designed to demean them. But the movement embraced the name. It offered a simple means of distinguishing themselves from more long-standing suffragist campaigners, who were committed, on principle, to staying strictly legal.[7]

Two early suffragists, Emily Davies and Elizabeth Garrett Anderson,[8] handed a petition to MPs Henry Fawcett and John Stuart Mill several months before the 1867 Reform Act, which doubled the existing franchise to approximately 30 per cent of adult males. Mill proposed an amendment granting equal numbers of women the vote. It fell by 196 votes to 73. When the male franchise doubled again in 1884, women were still excluded at national level. Within a decade, though, the Women's Franchise League, founded in Russell Square in 1889 by Emmeline Pankhurst, whose family had temporarily moved to London (in 1886), succeeded in increasing the limited franchise for women in local government. Pankhurst returned to Manchester, but the ball was rolling.

When she resettled in London, in 1907, local suffragette branches had already sprung up across the capital, especially among women workers in east London. The movement concentrated its mass outdoor activities in Westminster – in Parliament

---

7   Suffragist societies in Britain which formed in London, Manchester and Edinburgh in the 1860s coalesced into the National Union of Women's Suffrage Societies (NUWSS).

8   Stepney-born Anderson became the first female doctor in London. Her sister Millicent married Henry Fawcett in 1867.

Square, Trafalgar Square, Whitehall, Downing Street and Hyde Park. In June 1908 seven separate processions bedecked with green, white and purple flags converged on the park. The *Daily News* said that 'suffragettes have cultivated the art of popular magnetism for all it is worth. Those who dominate the movement have a sense of the dramatic.' *The Times*, not normally given to hyperbole, stated that the organisers 'had counted on an attendance of 250,000 . . . Probably it was doubled; and it would be difficult to contradict anyone who asserted confidently it was trebled.' Eighty speakers on 20 platforms promoted suffragette messages. The *Daily Mail*, which already had form for disparaging women activists, dug itself even deeper when its Special Correspondent opined:

> . . . men take politics so seriously. Women blend with their determination to get votes a delightful resolve to enjoy themselves as much as possible in the getting of them. The idea that the women who want the suffrage are plain, severe, be-spectacled middle aged frumps, was . . . exploded long ago. But . . . a great many people . . . never realised until yesterday how young and dainty and elegant and charming most leaders of the movement are.[9]

Men were present too. The pacifist-socialist Laurence Housman had formed a Men's League for Women's Suffrage together with three radical writers, Israel Zangwill, Henry Nevinson and Henry Brailsford. Zangwill brought his sardonic wit to their campaigning, saying: 'A man likes his wife to be just clever enough

---

9   *Daily Mail*, 22 June 1908.

to appreciate his cleverness and just stupid enough to admire it.'
At the 1910 general election, sympathetic men scrawled 'Votes for
Women' over their ballot papers.

The WSPU held large indoor meetings at the London Opera
House and London Pavilion[10] as well as Caxton Hall, and ostenta-
tious rallies which filled the Albert Hall seven times between 1908
and 1913. These rallies gave confidence to their members and won
new supporters, but the movement was also determined to speak
truth to power, directly. On 9 March 1906, Annie Kenney led 30
suffragettes to 10 Downing Street intent on meeting the Prime
Minister, Henry Campbell-Bannerman: unthinkable today, when
electronic gates guarded by heavily armed police bar entrance
to the whole street. Activists then simply approached the door
of Number 10 with petitions and letters, where a policeman
greeted them. When Kenney was told that the Prime Minister
was unavailable, she clambered on to his parked car, using it as an
impromptu platform to address her sisters.

The suffragettes used traditional protest methods – mass
rallies, petitions, lobbying, propaganda through leaflets and their
own newspapers – but also pioneered new tactics, some to shock,
cause outrage and draw publicity, others provoking the authorities, to force a government response. In 1909, sculptor Marjorie
Dunlop attended a rare gathering when Parliamentarians invited
deputations from suffragettes. She slipped unnoticed into St
Stephen's Hall and left a message with an indelible rubber stamp:
'Women's Deputation. June 29. Bill of Rights. It is the right of
the subjects to petition the King, and all commitments and prose-
cutions for such petitionings are illegal.' Charged with wilful

---

10   This theatre, opened in 1885 on the corner of Piccadilly Circus and Coventry Street, was
     converted to a cinema in the 1930s. It is now part of the Trocadero Centre.

damage, she was sentenced to one month's imprisonment. The previous year, Dunlop had shared a cell with a child killer after being arrested on a protest. This time, she demanded recognition as a 'political prisoner'. When the authorities refused, she began a hunger strike. The government panicked and released her after 91 hours, not wanting a dead suffragette on their hands. Suffragette leaders hadn't authorised Dunlop's action, but quickly grasped its potency.

Many courageous suffragettes came forward, willing to commit actions for which they could be imprisoned. They were prepared to undertake hunger strikes, knowing they might endure tortuous attempts at force-feeding. In 1913, the government passed the 'Cat and Mouse Act'.[11] This sanctioned the release of prisoners when they were weakened by their hunger strike and their re-arrest as their health returned. Upon early release, suffragettes would frequently visit a hairdresser to change their appearance, then stay with friends to frustrate police searching for them.

In 1908, London suffragettes began smashing windows, at first targeting government property, then, from November 1911, attacking private property too – including West End shops, hotels and newspaper offices.[12] This was controversial within the movement. The Women's Freedom League (WFL), led by Battersea socialist Charlotte Despard, which had split from the WSPU in 1907, threw stones at government property alone.

In March 1912, the *Daily Graphic*, founded by the social reformer William Thomas, reported that: 'Bands of women paraded Regent Street, Piccadilly, the Strand, Oxford Street

---

11   The name popularly given to the Prisoners (Temporary Discharge for Ill Health) Act 1913.

12   Window-smashing incidents occurred before this date but it became official policy that year.

and Bond Street, smashing windows with stones and hammers', adding that 221 women and three men were arrested. The *Graphic*'s reporter seemed particularly affronted that Burberry, Liberty and Marshall & Snelgrove were attacked.

These new tactics, however, mostly relied on individual acts of militancy, usually undertaken by middle-class members, substituting for mass collective action involving large numbers of working-class women. Earlier mass demonstrations, to express and strengthen pro-suffragette public opinion, ultimately looked to the Labour Party to emerge as a credible force to implement change. Christabel Pankhurst introduced direct action tactics to shift the movement in a more militant direction, defining 'militancy' as a 'great upheaval, a great revolution, a great blasting away of ugly things'. She rebranded the movement as a radical middle-class pressure group that Liberals and Tories had to take notice of right here, right now. Teresa Billington-Greig, who left the WSPU with Charlotte Despard in 1907 to form the WFL, criticised random militancy and the class politics behind it.

In 1903, Emmeline Pankhurst had sent Preston-born Teresa Billington[13] to London with Annie Kenney to expand the fledgling movement there. Later she sent her to Glasgow to build branches in Scotland. Apprenticed as a milliner, Billington also attended night school and became a teacher. She remained conscious, though, of her roots. The WSPU, she claimed, 'gradually edged the working-class element out of its ranks', becoming 'socially exclusive, punctiliously correct, gracefully fashionable'.

Christabel Pankhurst recognised that violent acts of civil

---

13 When she married Glasgow socialist Frederick Greig, their pre-nuptial agreement insisted both adopt the name Billington-Greig.

disobedience might divide the public, but, she argued, 'public opinion' was: 'shamefully tolerant of hideous wrongs and indignities inflicted upon women ... The sufferings of the militant women they have not felt keenly enough, and the cost of repairing government windows has fallen on them too lightly. That is why private property has now been attacked.'

Few suffragettes would dispute her moral justification: '... there are cases where law may be broken to vindicate a higher law and where violence may be done to prevent a greater violence ... suffragist violence is committed ... to put an end to the violence done to sweated women, to white slaves, to outraged children.'

However, her defence of these tactics sanctioned women acting on behalf of others, rather than encouraging all women to liberate themselves: 'No militant could go to prison merely for her own sake … It is for the sake of other people more helpless and more unhappy than themselves that the militant women are prepared to pay a heavy price.'[14]

Arson was another dramatic form of militant action that caused establishment panic. Lillian Lenton, a dancer and seasoned window-smasher, began a series of arson attacks in London with her colleague Olive Wharry in early 1913. In a 1960 interview Lenton said:

> Whenever I was out of prison my object was to burn two buildings a week … to create an absolutely impossible condition of affairs in the country, to prove that it was impossible to govern without the consent of the governed … no one could ignore arson.[15]

In November 1910, when Prime Minister Asquith ruled there was no time within the parliamentary session for the Conciliation Bill – which would have enfranchised some women – to reach its conclusion, 300 angry suffragettes marched on Westminster. The clash with the authorities, recorded as 'Black Friday', was marked by police brutality and mass arrests. Israel Zangwill believed that this day altered suffragette psychology, after which they resolved, 'to inconvenience oneself as little and society as seriously as possible'.

That day was etched in the memory of Rosa May Billing-hurst, secretary of the Greenwich suffragettes. Billinghurst was

---

14 C. Pankhurst, 'Broken Windows (1912)', in J. Marcus, *Suffrage and the Pankhursts*, London: Routledge & Kegan Paul, 2005, p. 123.

15 See Jessie Street's 1960s interviews with Lenton and other former suffragettes in the Women's Library archive at LSE.

paralysed from the age of five months. Her legs were strapped
in irons and she moved around on a manually propelled invalid
tricycle. Her earlier interest in suffragette activism emanated
from her work helping to rescue young girls from prostitution.
On 'Black Friday', she said, the police

> ... threw me out of the machine on to the ground in a
> very brutal manner ... when on the machine again they
> tried to push me along with my arms twisted behind me
> in a very painful position ... [Then] they took me down
> a side road and left me in the middle of a hooligan crowd,
> first taking all the valves out of the wheels and pocketing
> them so that I could not move the machine.[16]

A hundred years later – almost to the day – students protested on
the same Westminster streets about increasing tuition fees. Many
were shocked by video footage of Jody McIntyre, pulled roughly
from his wheelchair by police. Few knew of the precedent a
century earlier.

Police brutality failed to intimidate Billinghurst. She was
arrested just four days after Black Friday, steering her invalid
tricycle into a police cordon. In March 1912 she served a
one-month prison sentence for participating in the window-
smashing spree. While her sisters rampaged with hammers, she
kept a supply of stones under the blanket covering her paralysed
legs.

She served her final term of imprisonment in January 1913 for
setting fire to a pillar box. Facing eight months inside she began

---

16 See Rosa May Billinghurst papers in the Women's Library archive, LSE.

a hunger strike. The prison authorities attempted to force-feed her violently, damaging her teeth and leaving a deep gash in her cheek. The Home Secretary ordered Billinghurst's release after ten days. She immediately stepped up her campaigning to stop force-feeding of suffragette prisoners.

Between 1912 and 1914 the suffragettes escalated their tactic of burning pillar boxes until their demands were addressed. In its ability to disrupt the economy through burning correspondence between businesses this was like a modern-day mini-cyber attack. Among the first activists imprisoned for this offence was Emily Wilding Davison, who ultimately gave her life for the movement on Epsom Racecourse in June 1913. On 14 December 1911, she was arrested in Parliament Street. Inspector Powell told the court:

> She was wearing a long coat, which hid her arms ... When she got close to the letter-box ... she appeared to be striking matches ... She was holding a small packet in the left hand, one of the top corners of which was slightly alight. She held it in that position for a minute ... I seized the packet ... and ... extinguished the flame. I took her into custody ... she sat in a room; as I was leaving ... [she] said, 'Do you know I set fire to two in the City this morning, [one] ... in the middle of Leadenhall Street ... the other was facing the Mansion House.'[17]

She told Inspector Powell that she had also set fire to a post office in Fleet Street on the previous Friday. Before she was sentenced, Davison told the Recorder that she had acted without malice:

---

17 Old Bailey Proceedings Online (www.oldbaileyonline.org, version 8.0, 22 January 2019), January 1912, trial of DAVISON, Emily Wilding (36, tutor) (t19120109-20).

It was a purely political act ... to draw the attention of the public to the iniquitous state of affairs ... Technically ... I must be judged to be guilty, but morally ... you before whom I stand ... are guilty; you, the private citizens of this country and the Government that you choose to represent you, who keep women out of their just rights as citizens ... so long as you exclude women from these rights, upon you lies the blame for any act that they may have to commit in order to procure those rights.[18]

Public suffragette activity was heavily focused on the Westminster precinct – marches on Parliament, static protests in Parliament Square, women chaining themselves to railings, and delegations lobbying the Prime Minister. Officers from Canon Row Police station, guarding government buildings, had very frequent contact with the suffragettes.[19] One officer, Harold Brust, recalled a lone suffragette bringing a petition to 10 Downing Street:

She was recognised as a suffragette wanted by the police under the Cat and Mouse Act. She was ... seized by Sergeant Gough ... In a flash the unfortunate sergeant was surrounded by a score of women who sprang into Downing Street from all sorts of odd corners and doorways ... [we] were hopelessly outnumbered, and then the women began to strip the clothes off poor Gough! ... it was an astounding sight to see him, the

---

18 *Ibid.*

19 On 17 January 1908, suffragettes Edith New and Olivia Smith chained themselves to railings outside 10 Downing Street. They were charged with disorderly conduct and imprisoned for three weeks.

centre of a plunging, struggling, shrieking mob ... being
divested of hat, coat and vest. In shirt sleeves, his face
one crimson blush, the sergeant howled protest as they
began to unfasten his trouser braces. It was too much.
Gough released his prisoner and disaster was averted by
two brace buttons.[20]

The suffragette movement achieved most of its goals by 1918.
The new Representation of the People Act abolished most
property qualifications for men over 21 and enfranchised women
over 30 who met minimal property qualifications or those who
were graduates of British universities. This created a national
electorate of 21 million potential voters in the December 1918
general election, of whom 8.4 million were women. Given the
numbers of men killed during the war, women would have
constituted the majority of the electorate if the government had
granted equal suffrage then. Full voting equality was inevitable,
but took another ten years. Millicent Fawcett, veteran of London's
'law abiding' suffragist societies of the late 1860s, lived to see
that day. She died in 1929. But Emmeline Pankhurst, who had
transformed the movement into one unafraid to step outside the
law, that developed new and powerful forms of rebellion, died
on 14 June 1928, less than three weeks before the Conservative
Government finally passed the Act giving all adult females the
vote on the same basis as men.

Victoria Gardens abuts the Houses of Parliament. In the section
nearest to Parliament, a 1930 statue, with two blocks added in the

---

20 H. Brust, *I Guarded Kings: Memoirs of a Political Police Officer*, New York: Hillman-Curl,
1936.

1950s, commemorates Emmeline Pankhurst and the suffragette movement. Even with the later additions it is fascinating for who and what it omits.[21] Eldest daughter Christabel is honoured on one side. On the other is an etching of the 'Holloway brooch' – a portcullis-shaped medal, with a chain, overlaid with a triangle of green, white and purple bars – presented to suffragettes on release from prison. Emmeline's middle daughter, Sylvia, a dedicated suffragette from the WSPU's foundation and a leading figure in its radical east London section designed the medal. But she is not named on the statue.

The overwhelmingly working-class East End suffragettes were increasingly at odds with West End suffragettes over principles and tactics. They allied their activity to daily economic struggles for better lives, and sought 'universal suffrage' rather than 'votes on the same basis as men', which West End WSPU leaders were willing to accept, as this would still exclude many working-class voters.[22] Several prominent women trade unionists including Mary MacArthur and Margaret Bondfield stayed aloof from the WSPU which they saw as a movement led by middle-class women with little in common with working-class men, and little apparent interest in them. They were worried that a limited franchise given to middle- and upper-class women would strengthen conservative forces in society and act as a bulwark against granting votes more widely to the working class.

In March 1914 the political tensions between East End and West End suffragettes reached a point of no return. Emmeline and

---

21 The statue was made by Arthur George Walker and the base by Herbert Baker.

22 Before 1918, approximately 60 per cent of men had the vote on a property-related qualification.

Christabel Pankhurst issued an instruction to Sylvia Pankhurst and another leading east London suffragette, Norah Smyth, to sever their branch's connections with the WSPU, after which the east London suffragettes became an independent movement.[23]

Sylvia's younger sister Adela, imprisoned several times for suffragette activism, is also unacknowledged on the statue, although her latter political involvements may have embarrassed a movement advocating equal rights. After Adela fell out with her mother in 1914, Emmeline bought her a one-way ticket to Australia. In Melbourne, she worked closely with the suffragist and feminist Vida Goldstein's anti-war Women's Political Association. Adela and her husband Tom Walsh were founder members of the Australian Communist Party, but she later had a major political *volte face* that drew her to pro-fascist ideologues. She ultimately joined Australia First, which advanced Nazi biological race theories, and was interned during the Second World War for pro-Japan activity.

Emmeline Pankhurst performed a U-turn too. When she began campaigning for women's political rights, she was active in the Independent Labour Party (ILP) and the Fabian Society,[24] and a close associate of Keir Hardie. In 1926 she was adopted as the parliamentary candidate for the East End seat of Whitechapel and St Georges – by the Conservatives. She died before the election, which Harry Gosling comfortably won for Labour.

The East/West divisions of 1914 exposed continuing class conflict among London's suffragettes. However, the movement's first major fracture took place in London as early as 1907 and,

---

23 See Chapter 9, pp. 274-275.

24 Many of the early WSPU leaders and a high proportion of the first suffragettes sent to prison were ILP members.

ironically, given the movement's democratic goals, it concerned lack of democracy inside the movement. Teresa Billington-Greig had drafted a constitution as requested by Emmeline Pankhurst. At the meeting of 350 suffragette delegates where this was to be discussed, Emmeline Pankhust 'announced that there was not to be a constitution or any voting membership, but that she ... had assumed dictatorship and would direct-govern ... through her selected colleagues or subordinates'.[25]

She tore up the draft document, theatrically trampled it underfoot, announcing that 'the WSPU was not a society but a volunteer army enrolled by her and her officers for one purpose only and that no interference from the ranks could be contemplated'. Billington-Greig describes 'stunned surprise and confusion ... the meeting broke up in disorder'. Delegates asked how they could 'claim the right to vote as citizens of the country and agree to be voteless in the management of our own society'. Seventy activists walked out, later forming the Women's Freedom League (WFL). The League had its own charismatic figure – the vegetarian socialist Charlotte Despard – but she and other officers were elected annually. Their conference made binding policy decisions by majority vote. The League could not match the WSPU's scale of operation but was a key player in major mobilisations while largely working in parallel with the WSPU but maintaining its own approach. The WFL, also, is unacknowledged at the Pankhurst statue.

The novelist and playwright Christabel Marshall[26] described Despard's mesmerising presence at a suffragette demonstration in Hyde Park:

---

25 Teresa Billington-Greig papers, Women's Library archive, LSE.

26 Also known as Christopher Marie St John.

The arms were raised, Cassandra like; the whole thin, fragile body seemed to vibrate with a prophecy ... the white hair, the familiar black lace veil ... On the edge of the great mass of listeners ... I could catch no word, but I seemed to know the thoughts as they passed.[27]

Despard was nearing 60 when the WSPU was formed. She had joined Hyndman's SDF and Keir Hardie's ILP, and saw women's struggle for political rights as intimately linked with wider struggles for equality. In a 1910 letter to a friend, Mrs Solomon, she wrote: 'It is my dream, when the first step is won, to make our league international – for women's freedom everywhere and the lifting up of the oppressed through her ... our cause is not only votes for women but the binding together of all womankind with human rights.'

A pamphlet she published that year, *Women in the New Era*, articulated demands beyond the WSPU's single-issue campaign, ' ... for equal rights, equal opportunities; equal reward for our work; equal justice'. The WFL supported women's workplace struggles, such as the 1908 strike of London teashop waitresses. When negotiations with their employers broke down irretrievably, Despard helped them start a cooperative cafe in Leicester Square.

She urged women to become more self-aware and to prepare for wider equality battles:

We women have been cajoled or forced into a false conception of ourselves. We work first for enlightenment

---

27 Appreciation by Christopher St John in C. Despard, *Women in the New Era*, London: Suffrage Shop, 1910.

... using our own capacities, seeing with our own eyes and not with the eyes of men to understand ... what are our duties and our rights.[28]

Tactically the WFL supported civil disobedience such as window-breaking targeted at state institutions, but it insisted that every form of protest should demonstrate a clear reason for that action. Billington-Greig argued that the WFL's campaigning was 'more marked by sacrifice of self than by aggression against others'. Although many members were pacifists on international conflicts and challenged wartime conscription, they were combative when they faced heavy-handed policing.[29] Charlotte Despard's first prison sentence resulted from her leading large numbers of women from a Women's Parliament meeting directly into police lines protecting the House of Commons. The *Daily Mail* said: 'The women fought like tigers and they received and inflicted many bruises.' After Despard's arrest and conviction, she refused to pay the 40 shillings fine, and spent 21 days in Holloway Prison. One of the early WFL branches was formed in the Holloway area and several members visited the district temporarily! Within the WFL's first three years, 300 of its members had served prison sentences.

Annie Cobden-Sanderson, a socialist activist in Hammersmith and a prominent WFL member, was arrested at the same protest as Despard and sentenced to two months. She told the court, 'I am a law-breaker because I want to be a law-maker.'

---

28 C. Despard, *Women in the New Era*, 1910.

29 The WSPU suspended most of its campaigning work during the war to display patriotic credentials. The WFL opposed compulsory war service for women as long as they were 'denied their share in the government of the country'.

Cobden-Sanderson later helped to establish the Tax Resistance League, inspired by her neighbour, Dora Montefiore, an activist in several socialist and suffrage groups and a tenacious campaigner about unemployment, who lived at 34 Upper Mall, by the Thames. She sat on the SDF executive and was a founder of its Women's Socialist Circles.

Montefiore was a tax-rebel before the WSPU and WFL were born. During the Second Boer War of 1899–1902, she refused to pay income tax because it 'went towards financing a war in the making of which I had had no voice'. In 1906, after informing fellow WSPU activists to prepare support, she defied the tax authorities and barred her doors against the bailiff 'who had appeared outside the gate of my house [and] the "siege" of my house began'. Inside were Dora and her housekeeper, who also strongly supported the suffrage campaign. 'The tradespeople of the neighbourhood were absolutely loyal to us besieged women, delivering their milk and bread, etc., over the rather high garden wall ... The weekly wash arrived in the same way and the postman day by day delivered very encouraging batches of correspondence.'[30]

The six-week siege won sympathetic press coverage. There were day and evening meetings. East End suffragettes trekked across town to Hammersmith after work, to show support.

At the evening demonstrations rows of lamps were hung along the top of the wall and against the house, the members of the W.S.P.U. speaking from the steps of the house, while I spoke from one of the upstairs windows.

---

30 D. Montefiore, *From a Victorian to a Modern*, London: Archer, 1927.

> On the little terrace of the front garden hung during
> the whole time of the siege a red banner with the letters
> painted in white: 'Women should vote for the laws they
> obey and the taxes they pay.'[31]

When the siege ended and bailiffs seized goods sufficient to cover the tax debt, 22 police were sent to protect the auctioneer of the seized goods.

Montefiore attributed the courage and inspiration she needed to take this action to her frequent contact with 'self-sacrificing and self-effacing' Russian political exiles, some of whom had stayed at her house, especially Seraphina, a Russian Jewish woman who had been imprisoned for organising textile workers.

In Russia, the revolutionists sought to overthrow an autocratic monarchy dripping in wealth. One suffragist tax-rebel who might have caused consternation among more socialist comrades was Princess Duleep Singh, resident of Hampton Court Palace and a regular speaker at suffragette branches in Kingston and Richmond. She was prosecuted several times and had a diamond ring, pearl necklace and gold bangle impounded.

The WFL popularised campaigns of non-violent defiance – such as refusal to pay taxes, purchase dog licences, or complete census forms – through its own newspaper, *The Vote*, published from its Robert Street offices, near Aldwych. While the WSPU was abandoning mass action in London in favour of individualised militancy, the WFL continued its inclusive campaigns requiring collective action. These included nocturnal activities. During the night of 12–13 October 1908, WFL members plastered proclamations of women's political rights on hundreds of public buildings

---

31 *Ibid.*

in London, the provinces and Scotland. London targets included ministers' homes, the House of Commons, Scotland Yard and Holloway Prison, as well as countless pillar boxes.[32]

But the WFL also had members keen to perform individual stunts. Australian journalist and actress Muriel Matters had a penchant for aerial activities. She arrived in London in 1905 and became friendly with George Bernard Shaw and the Russian anarchist, Peter Kropotkin. On 28 October 1908, Matters and a WFL colleague, Helen Fox, chained themselves to the grille at the front of the Ladies' Gallery for observing the House of Commons, and began to broadcast suffragette ideas to the MPs below. A third activist lowered a WFL proclamation to the parliamentary floor on a string, and a male collaborator in the Strangers' Gallery dropped a flood of handbills. Unable to break the chains, the police removed the whole grille with the women attached. The grille was never replaced. On another occasion Matters flew over London, showering handbills with suffragette messages from a dirigible emblazoned with the slogans 'Votes for Women' and WFL.

During the war, the WSPU suspended most of its activities, but WFL members and the expelled East London Federation of Suffragettes led campaigns for equal pay, as women filling jobs previously reserved for men were often paid at half or even a third of the wage rate. When the franchise for women rose from zero to 8.4 million overnight in 1918, Emmeline and Christabel Pankhurst believed their work was done. The WSPU dissolved itself but the WFL continued to campaign for full equality and on its wider agenda.

---

32 The WFL also did daytime visits to ministers' homes, making speeches on their doorsteps until they were removed by police.

In her most intensive period of activism, Teresa Billington-Greig argued that:

> The vote cannot secure of itself any single woman's emancipation. It is a tool; and the kind of work that can be done with it depends first upon the nature of the tool, and second, upon the capacity of the person who uses it. Large areas in which emancipation is needed lie entirely outside [its] scope ... a slave woman with a vote will still be essentially a slave.[33]

When the WFL shut down in autumn 1961, Billington-Greig praised the organisation for insisting that votes for women was 'only the first stage of political emancipation' and 'rejecting dictatorship as a false means to a good end'. She added: 'I feel its death as a tragedy. It was born of the spirit of democracy and rebellion.' In London that included a rebellion within the suffragette movement.

On 28 December 1918, Constance Markiewicz, a Sinn Fein activist married to a radical Polish count, was the first woman elected to Parliament. But she sat in Holloway Prison rather than Westminster that day, locked up for campaigning against the conscription of Irish men into the British army. In any case, Sinn Fein boycotted the British Parliament. A Conservative, Nancy Astor, won a by-election in Plymouth in November 1919 to become Britain's first actual female MP. Dr Ethel Bentham won Islington East for Labour in 1929 to become London's first female MP.[34]

---

33 Teresa Billington-Greig papers, Women's Library archive, LSE.

34 Susan Lawrence won East Ham North for Labour in 1923, but at that time it was an Essex rather than London seat.

The period from the 1890s until the end of the 1920s, during which the House of Commons was forced to become more democratic and diverse, also saw the first non-white MPs elected – each one of them in London. The Liberal MP for Finsbury Central elected in 1892, Dadabhai Naoroji, and the Communist/Labour MP elected for Battersea North in 1922, Shapurji Saklatvala, were both Indian Parsees and political radicals who supported women's suffrage. A third Parsee, Mancherjee Bhownagree, Conservative MP for Bethnal Green North East in 1895, was, in contrast, pro-establishment – a staunch supporter of the British Empire.[35] Their breakthrough was short-lived. No other Asians were elected in Britain until Keith Vaz in 1987.

In India, Naoroji had campaigned for girls' education and taught at a girls' school. In 1889, he strongly supported Jane Cobden, one of the first two women elected to the new London County Council. Her official agent was George Lansbury, at that time a Liberal, soon to become a leading east London socialist. Saklatvala's election leaflets were enthusiastically endorsed by women's suffrage campaigner, Charlotte Despard. In summer 1908, he went on his first large demonstration– the suffragette extravaganza in Hyde Park – and was enthralled by Sylvia Pankhurst, who later became a leading figure among east London's suffragettes.

For rebels such as Sylvia Pankhurst and George Lansbury, equality for women was intertwined with the fight for working-class advancement. And east London in the 1910s and 1920s, as the next chapter shows, was the perfect arena for them to play their part in these struggles.

---

35 Bhownagree's campaign was also marked by its disagreeable anti-alien propaganda.

Suffragette being arrested outside Buckingham Palace.

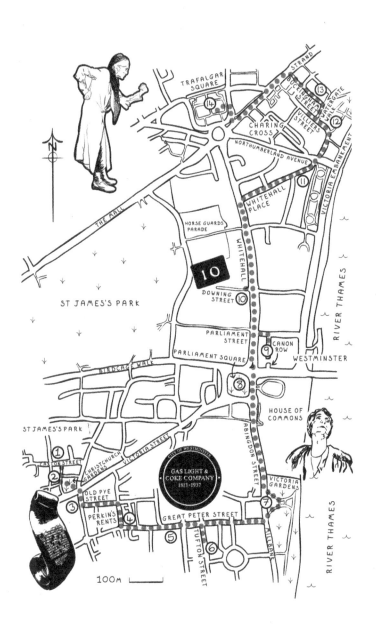

WALK

Start at Caxton Hall, 10 Caxton Street, SW1H 0AQ.

1. Caxton Street
Caxton Hall hosted the Women's Parliament meetings organised by the WSPU. Its Great Hall and York Hall, now demolished, were used for political and cultural events. Its high-society registry office closed in 1979. Cross over into Christchurch Gardens.

2. Christchurch Gardens
Edwin Russell sculpted the 'S'-shaped monument, for the Suffragette Fellowship in 1970. Women's Freedom League member Edith How-Martyn created the Fellowship in 1926 to perpetuate the memory of suffrage campaigns. Former suffragette arsonist Lillian Lenton unveiled the monument. Walk through the gardens, cross Victoria Street into Old Pye Street.

3. Old Pye Street
This area was one of London's worst slums in Victorian times, designated 'the Devil's Acre' by Dickens in *Household Words* and depicted in Gustave Dore's bleak etchings of London's poverty. Slum clearance began in the 1860s and 1870s. Several semi-philanthropic Victorian housing developments remain. Turn right into Perkins Rents.

4. Corner of Perkins Rents and Great Peter Street

The public house, called the Speaker since 1999, was rebuilt in 1794 on the site of an earlier pub – the Castle. The Speaker has three panels on the outside with entertaining facts about parliamentary norms, particularly the role of the Speaker! Turn left into Great Peter Street.

5. Great Peter Street

The plaque for the Gas Light & Coke Company, next to the Seacole Building (one of three buildings comprising the Home Office), marks Britain's first gasworks, founded here by a German, Freidrich Winzer, in 1813. He came in 1799 and changed his name to Winsor. He is also memorialised through Winsor Terrace, which leads to the former site of Beckton gasworks, where Will Thorne organised for the eight-hour day. Turn right into Tufton Street.

6. Tufton Street

A plaque commemorates Eleanor Rathbone MP, both a campaigner for women's suffrage and a beneficiary of the campaign, who lived here. The first woman elected to Liverpool City Council, she later represented one of the former 'Combined Universities' parliamentary seats. Active within the constitutional National Union of Women's Suffrage Societies, she argued that more militant campaigners 'came within an inch of wrecking the suffrage movement, perhaps for a generation'. In April 1937 she joined a fact-finding delegation to Spain during the Civil War, and co-founded a Dependants' Aid Committee to support the families of International Brigade volunteers. Return to Great

Peter Street, turn right, and cross Millbank/Abingdon Street into Victoria Gardens. Follow the path towards Parliament.

7. *Victoria Gardens*

Near the exit back on to Abingdon Street is a statue of Emmeline Pankhurst sculpted by Arthur George Walker, with two side-blocks added in the 1950s. The ceremony unveiling the original statue, further south in the gardens, in March 1930, included the Metropolitan Police Band performing March of the Women. Continue towards the House of Commons. Cross over to Parliament Square.

8. *Parliament Square*

This was the site of the 'Black Friday' suffragette demonstration in November 1910. At another demonstration on the square a year later, 184 protesters were arrested. On the west side of the square is a striking statue of Millicent Fawcett. Around the plinth are 59 miniature profiles of suffragists and suffragettes, several of whom feature in this book. On 'Census Night' in April 1911, Emily Wilding Davison hid in the broom cupboard in the Chapel of St Mary Undercroft in the House of Commons, as suffragettes disrupted the census. In 1991 two MPs, Jeremy Corbyn and Tony Benn, mounted an unofficial plaque on that cupboard, honouring her. Hundreds of activists from the WFL and WSPU spent Census Night at Aldwych Ice Rink, arguing that 'women not considered persons should not be counted as persons'. Cross to the east side of Parliament Street. Walk towards Whitehall. Turn right into Canon Row.

9. Canon Row

This police station opened in 1902 (and closed in 1992). Many suffragettes spent the night singing and shouting in the cells here. Return to Parliament Street. Cross to the west side of Parliament Street and stop outside Downing Street's unwelcoming gates.

10. Downing Street

Suffragette delegations brought petitions directly to the door of Number 10. Barriers were erected at the St James Park end in November 1920. Until 1982 campaigners could walk along Downing Street to hand letters or petitions to the police guarding Number 10. Steel gates were erected in 1989. Walk along Whitehall and turn right into Whitehall Place.

11. Whitehall Place

Charlotte Despard's pamphlet *Economic Aspects of Women's Suffrage* originated as a talk given to the National Liberal Club in Whitehall Place in 1908. Women were not admitted as full members of the club until 1976. Cross Northumberland Avenue into Villiers Street.

12. Villiers Street

At 43 Villiers Street, where Rudyard Kipling lived from 1889 to 1891, Ronald Kidd opened a radical bookshop in the 1920s. On 1 November 1932 Kidd observed protesting Hunger Marchers, who were completing a three-week march, being incited into a physical confrontation with police by the use of police provocateurs as they passed Trafalgar Square into Whitehall. He resolved to create a body to monitor and expose such activities, and defend protest rights. He co-founded the National Council for Civil Liberties. Turn back towards Embankment and step down into Watergate Walk. Halfway along, walk up some stairs into Buckingham Street.

13. Buckingham Street

The Women's Freedom League's first premises (1907–8) were at 18 Buckingham Street, before they moved to Robert Street. Continue along Buckingham Street and turn left into the Strand.

14. Trafalgar Square:

The first suffragette demonstration held in Trafalgar Square was on 19 May 1906. Charlotte Despard, leader of the Women's Freedom League during the period when women were seeking the vote, spoke many times at Trafalgar Square for women's rights, socialist causes and Home Rule for Ireland. Her last speech in the square was at an anti-fascist rally in the mid-1930s.

Demonstration in support of Poplar Council, 1920s.

9

NOT AFRAID OF THE
PRISON WALLS

Rebel Women and Men of Poplar

'How shall we benefit if instead of electing our master – as we do today – we elect his wife to govern us?' asked Rose Witkop, an immigrant Jew in London's East End, who followed her older sister Milly, into the anarchist movement. Her barb, aimed at the suffragettes, may have been fair comment about middle-class West End campaigners, whose 'Votes for Women' call was qualified by the words: 'on the same basis as men'. The 1884 Reform Act increased the franchise but left a property qualification in place that restricted the vote to approximately 60 per cent of adult males. If the government had acceded to the demands of Emmeline Pankhurst's Women's Social and Political Union (WSPU), it would have equalised the franchise gender-wise, while still leaving 40 per cent of the population, living more precarious lives, with no political voice.

In Witkop's Whitechapel milieu of sweatshops and small factories, populated by an immigrant underclass, her cynicism was understandable. But it seems to be an unjust slur on working-class women activists a little further east such as Minnie Baldock and Adelaide Knight who established London's first suffragette group east of Whitechapel in Canning Town, and were organising for every woman's rights, and every man's too. By 1912, six separate suffragette groups worked together under the umbrella of an East London branch of the WSPU. They transformed a disused bakery at 198 Bow Road, Poplar, into an organising centre emblazoned in gold letters with the slogan: 'Votes for Women'. They later moved their centre to Bethnal Green's Roman Road.

While local suffragettes were gaining a higher profile through meetings, processions and protest marches, a controversial decision made by a local politician in 1912 helped thrust debate about women's right to vote into the centre of Poplar's political arena. The parliamentary seat of Bow and Bromley had traditionally swung between the Tories and the Liberals/Whigs. But in 1910 George Lansbury won this seat for Labour.

Lansbury was born in Suffolk in 1859. When he was seven, his parents moved to Albert Road, Bethnal Green. Young George loved Victoria Park, a 'mysterious' place for children, where the park-keepers 'wore top hats, frock coats, red waistcoats and carried sticks'. Later, the family moved into a mainly Irish part of Whitechapel. His political aspirations surfaced early: 'When I was a very small boy I wrote my name in a church prayer book as "George Lansbury MP". I think I even added the name of an East End constituency.'[1] He was at school until fourteen, with a year's break aged eleven to work in an office. From fourteen he was a factory worker, a manual labourer and a wholesale grocer. He became involved with community projects through the Bedford Institute and helped to provide breakfast for 1,000 local homeless people on Sunday mornings.

Married with three children but struggling economically in his mid-20s, he was lured by adverts to seek economic gain in

---

1   G. Lansbury, *Looking Backwards and Forwards*, London: Blackie, 1935.

Australia. His time there was politically formative. 'I knew the bitterness of unemployment, and endured the hardship of being treated just a little worse than a serf.' When he and his family returned, he took a job in his father-in-law's sawmill (which he later inherited), and began attending political meetings. Lansbury became familiar with local anarchists, socialists, radical liberals and freethinkers, and was strongly influenced by the Rector of St Matthew's, Bethnal Green, Christian socialist Stewart Headlam. But Lansbury believed that the Liberals offered the best vehicle for practical change.

He was election agent for Jane Cobden, seeking election to the London County Council's first administration in 1889. She was one of only two women elected. That same year he visited Ireland and returned frustrated at the local Liberal parliamentary candidate's dismissive approach to Irish political concerns. When the dock strike broke out, in August 1889, Lansbury campaigned alongside local socialists. Through the local eight-hour-day committee he helped to organise London's first May Day march in 1890. In 1892 Lansbury left the Liberals and helped found the Bromley and Bow branch of the Social Democratic Federation (SDF), which he designated 'the cockpit of socialism in East London'.

> Our branch was about 40 strong. We were . . . convinced our mission was to revolutionise the world . . . Our branch meetings were like revivalist meetings. We opened with a song and closed with one and often read together some extracts from economic and historical writings . . . Every Saturday we ran dances, telling our critics we were going

to dance into socialism . . . We were firm supporters of . . . equality of the sexes and equal pay for equal work.[2]

In 1903 Lansbury switched to the Independent Labour Party (ILP). He, his wife Bessie, and several of their children were already active women's suffrage campaigners by the time the movement hit the headlines in 1905. The suffragettes' story is replete with individuals making personal sacrifices for the movement, and George Lansbury played his part. Having made a priceless breakthrough for Labour by wresting Bow and Bromley from a succession of Liberals and Tories,[3] he resigned the seat and forced a by-election on women's suffrage. He hoped that the men who put him in Westminster agreed with votes for women. In January 1911, he spoke alongside Charlotte Despard at a crowded and very supportive Labour meeting at Bow Baths, advocating votes for all adult women and men.

When he won Bow and Bromley, an enthusiastic voter wrote to Lansbury, 'you have earned it and ought to keep it now as long as you like (provided you aren't court martialled or shot as a traitor)'.[4] But contesting an unforced by-election on this issue was risky. Labour's Westminster leaders believed the governing parties were very far from accepting votes for women, but could be pressurised into increasing the male franchise. Lansbury took a minority position that the party should only agree to proposals for extending the franchise that enfranchised at least some women.

He contested the by-election without Labour's endorsement. In Lansbury's last speech before the ballot, he argued that it was

---

2   G. Lansbury, *My Life*, London: Constable & Co., 1928.

3   He won the seat in 1910 by a majority of 683 over a Liberal Unionist candidate who opposed Home Rule for Ireland.

4   From Lansbury correspondence 1910–11, LSE archive.

only 'when the women and men are able to stand [together] in the common fight' that they could 'hope to accomplish economic and social emancipation'. Bessie wrote to the local press: 'both of us believe that men and women, united as friends and comrades, can and will save this country from the horrors of destitution, prostitution, and misery'. West End suffragettes parachuted in to support him, though some local suffragettes thought his action premature. Lansbury's Tory and Liberal opponents united behind one candidate. His elder brother James had warned him that Parliament 'is no place for a man of conscience'. George Lansbury lost by 861 votes to a Tory named Blair.

Despite this setback, he stepped up his campaigning work both for socialism and women's suffrage. Supported by trade unionists, he established a left-wing national newspaper, the *Daily Herald*.[5] In 1913 Lansbury was imprisoned for incitement to civil disobedience after making an Albert Hall speech supporting militant suffragette actions. Sentenced to six months, he borrowed the suffragettes' hunger strike tactic and was released within days: 'I took neither food nor drink,' he recalled. '. . . I refused to change my clothes, would not take a bath, and [refused] to be civil to anyone except to the doctor.'[6]

The Lansburys' coupling of women's political emancipation with the struggle against poverty and destitution chimed with the local suffragettes' approach. A far cry from the moneyed 'ladies' who met as the Kensington Society in the 1860s, or those living in London's more fashionable squares in the early 1900s, east London suffragette activists were typically factory workers

---

5   See Chapter 1.

6   Lansbury, *Looking Backwards and Forwards*.

like Flora Buchan, maids and cleaners like Melvina Walker and Daisy Parsons, laundry workers like Nellie Cressall, barmaids like Charlotte Drake, and housewives, many married to dockers.[7] They built a strong, mutually supportive relationship with dockworkers.

Working-class suffragettes argued that winning political rights for women would only be worthwhile if they could use these rights to challenge the economic circumstances that blighted the lives of both women and men of their class. As militant campaigners, committed to collective action, they were worthy heirs to the determined women or 'rough set of girls'[8] who rebelled at Bryant & May's match factory in Bow in 1888. George Lansbury described women in Poplar as 'splendid listeners', who 'never fail to argue and heckle anyone who comes to teach them the way they should go. They are . . . not at all angelic, and are quite capable of taking care of themselves.'[9]

If the matchwomen benefitted from middle-class supporters such as Annie Besant and Henry Hyde Champion, so the east London suffragettes' activism was boosted by the ingenuity of a rebellious middle-class socialist hailing from the Pankhurst family. Estelle Sylvia Pankhurst, who joined the ILP at age 16, had a troubled relationship with her mother and preferred to use her middle name, chosen by her father.

Sylvia was an artist, who had studied in Manchester, Venice and London. As a student she learned important feminist lessons: male art students were groomed for careers as artists; female art students were guided towards teaching.

---

7   Daisy Parsons was later Mayor of West Ham and Nellie Cressall was Mayor of Poplar.

8   As Charles Booth described them.

9   Lansbury, *Looking Backwards and Forwards*.

She lent her professional talents to her political involvements, decorating halls hosting suffragette events and designing posters and banners; in 1906 she designed a banner for West Ham suffragettes emblazoned with the words 'Courage, Constancy, Success'. When she settled in the East End in 1912, she was already known locally. Sylvia proved less flighty than Annie Besant, whose East End involvements were confined to a few years in the 1880s. In 1912 Sylvia promised: 'I am part of the East End now and if still alive, I shall not leave it.'[10] She left in 1924 for Woodford and died in Addis Ababa in 1960, but for twelve years was at the heart of every major suffragette and socialist campaign in east London, demonstrating her commitment and self-sacrifice. She was repeatedly imprisoned during 1913–14, undertaking ten separate hunger and thirst strikes in that period.

Before she settled in east London, Sylvia travelled widely, working as an artist and writer and supporting activism. In 1907 she recorded women workers' conditions in northern England and Scotland through paintings and articles, an experience that deepened both her socialist and feminist convictions. She spent much of 1911 lecturing on the British suffragette movement in the USA and Scandinavia, but she was in Britain in August when women in Bermondsey's jam and biscuit factories fought for economic justice through spontaneous strikes. She went there to hear first-hand about the conditions they were rebelling against.[11] East London's suffragettes consistently supported women's struggles for equal opportunities and fair pay in the workplace.

Suffragettes east and west showed equal determination in the face of hostility, threats and violence, but clear differences

---

10 *TP's Weekly*, 4 July 1914.

11 See Chapter 10.

emerged between them. East London suffragettes, influenced by Sylvia's own attitudes, favoured mass *collective* action by women to emancipate themselves, rather than the individual action on behalf of others favoured by their West End sisters.

East London suffragettes held mass Women's May Day processions that started at East India Dock Gates and ended in Victoria Park. These processions displayed the suffragettes' familiar colours – green, white and purple – but many marchers also wore red 'caps of liberty', affirming their left-wing political radicalism. Victoria Park's free speech site, which attracted the politically curious – and the police – was the backdrop for an imaginative propaganda stunt by local suffragettes in the summer of 1913 – a time of frequent conflict with the police. Dozens of suffragettes carrying folded umbrellas hired boats on the west lake by Crown Gate. Out on the lake and beyond the reach of police, they opened umbrellas overlaid with suffragette slogans in large letters.

The conflicts between East End and West End suffragettes came to a head after Sylvia Pankhurst spoke at a public meeting on 1 November 1913, organised by George Lansbury's Daily Herald League in support of the Dublin workers fighting for trade union rights. Defying her sister Christabel's injunction, Sylvia spoke alongside Sinn Fein supporters and the radical socialist James Connolly, founder of the Irish Citizens' Army.[12] Emmeline and Christabel Pankhurst were simultaneously courting Ulster Unionists, who had promised that an Ulster state would grant votes to women. A few weeks later, Emmeline and Christabel summoned Sylvia along with fellow activist Norah Smyth to

---

12 Other prominent socialist suffragettes such as Charlotte Despard and Dora Montefiore also addressed the meeting.

Paris, where they had fled to avoid police harassment. They ordered Sylvia and Norah to sever connections between the East London suffragettes and the WSPU.

The enforced separation actually liberated both parties. Mainstream suffragette leaders stopped looking over their shoulders at what working-class sisters were doing in their name, and the east London suffragettes relished the autonomy to campaign without fear of censure from the centre. In March 1914, east London WSPU became the independent East London Federation of Suffragettes (ELFS), and launched its own newspaper – *Woman's Dreadnought*.

'Dreadnought' not only symbolised a powerful battle force, but also signified that women fighting for freedom 'must fear nothing'.[13] A family firm, Arber & Co., based near the suffragettes' Roman Road organising centre, printed the paper.[14] On market days east London suffragettes set up a second-hand goods stall near there to raise money for political work and sell the paper. At the stall and through house-to-house sales, they found out about the issues most affecting women's lives locally.

The *Dreadnought* stayed afloat through sales and self-sacrifice. The ELFS organised 'self-denial' weeks, when supporters would go without sugar in tea and butter on bread, would walk to work instead of taking the bus, and stop smoking. They donated the money saved to the paper. Alongside exposés of exploitation in the sweated trades, practical advice on dealing with bailiffs and organising rent strikes, the *Dreadnought* mobilised readers to attend indoor meetings at the Mission Hall in Tredegar Road and Crowder Hall in Bow, and outdoor meetings in Victoria Park,

---

13 Sylvia Pankhurst had proposed *Workers' Mate* as a title but members preferred the *Women's Dreadnought* suggestion made by Mary Paterson, secretary of the Poplar branch.

14 Arber's, established in 1897, finally closed its doors in May 2014.

Priscilla Road, Morris Road and Chrisp Street. It advertised 'elocution' classes to widen the pool of confident public speakers. From May 1914 these classes took place on Monday evenings in the newly acquired Women's Hall at 400 Old Ford Road, above which Sylvia Pankhurst and Norah Smyth shared living space with suffragette supporters and shoemakers Jessie and Jim Payne. The Women's Hall was formerly a Baptist church with two halls, one accommodating up to 350 people, the other 50. It was turned into a radical social centre, housing a library and hosting concerts, plays, a clothing exchange and strike meetings. Trestle tables were supplied free by George Lansbury's timber firm.

While a choir practised at the Women's Hall on Tuesday evenings, the 'People's Army' trained in self-defence techniques, including ju-jitsu, at Bow Baths and sometimes at the Women's Hall. This stewarding organisation, inspired by Connolly's Citizens' Army in Dublin, and composed of women and men (especially dockers), was set up by the ELFS to prevent police from attacking and closing down suffragette meetings. When police raided an ELFS meeting at Bow Baths in October 1913, two women had arms broken and two were knocked unconscious, including Zelie Emerson, later treated in hospital for a fractured skull. Mounted police, whose horses were stabled behind Bow Road police station, launched a fierce assault two months later on a protest attended by hundreds of local suffragettes supported by a contingent of gasworkers, including a brass band, outside the Tomlin's Grove home of Conservative Councillor John le Manquais, who campaigned to bar suffragettes from council property. During the assault, the band's instruments were thrown over a garden wall, and a local publican passing by suffered a broken rib.

The east London suffragettes experienced the police as an oppressive force that sought to deny their right to organise, yet on 28 March 1914 the *Dreadnought* published an anonymous 'Policeman's letter' assuring the ELFS that they 'have the sympathy and support of the majority of the intellectual section of the police'.

The 'intellectual section' was clearly elsewhere on 28 May 1914 when the ELFS held their Women's May Day procession from East India Docks to Victoria Park. Sylvia Pankhurst, threatened with re-arrest under the Cat and Mouse Act,[15] marched with 20 People's Army bodyguards surrounding her. As they reached Victoria Park, the police tried to arrest Sylvia. Women's hats were torn off, their hair pulled, their faces punched, and arms twisted, but they clung on. The police realised that her bodyguards were all chained together. An inspector demanded the keys but none were given. Police hammered at the chains with truncheons until they broke. They took Sylvia Pankhurst away and inflicted further blows on her defiant bodyguards. One guard who pulled a policeman to the ground was seized by another who threatened to ' . . . break your bloody arm and twist your bleeding neck'. Despite the police actions, the procession entered the park, and speakers from different groups, including the Men's League for Women's Suffrage, the Rebel Social and Political Union, and the Actresses Franchise League, addressed the marchers from nine platforms.[16]

In early June 1914 the ELFS requested a meeting with the Prime Minister, Herbert Asquith, explaining that previous delegations were composed of well-to-do middle- and upper-class women, but the bread-winners, child-bearers and home-makers of East End families wanted to state their views too.

---

15 See Chapter 8.

16 Report in *Women's Dreadnought*, 30 May 1914.

On two previous occasions Asquith had refused to meet the ELFS. This time, Sylvia Pankhurst forced his hand by threatening a hunger strike on the steps of the House of Commons. She said: 'I shall not give way, although it may end in my death.' Asquith finally relented.

Like the Women's Freedom League,[17] the ELFS resented the West End suffragette leaders' autocratic practices, so they democratically elected their delegation at branch meetings. Previous suffragette delegations to Asquith had argued for women's votes on the same (restricted) basis as men; the ELFS delegation, composed of six working-class women, sought votes for all adult women and men. They arrived in two cars accompanied by former MP George Lansbury and John Scurr of the Dockers' Union, a former SDF member who was president of Poplar Trades Council. Lansbury and Scurr introduced the delegation, which included Scurr's wife, Julia. Asquith received them warmly and spent over an hour with them.

Each delegate revealed poignant details of their everyday lives. Mrs Ford, a widowed mother of two, spoke about her husband, who became an invalid soon after their marriage. She had taken up trouser-making and pressing, but left because of sexual harassment by a foreman. Mrs Scurr said the difficulties facing widows were very common:

> Our husbands die ... at a much earlier age than do the men of other classes ... by accident and overwork ... we know by bitter experience the terrible struggle with absolute want that our widowed sisters have to face from no fault of their own.

---

17 See Chapter 8.

Daisy Parsons, a cigarette packer, described her piece-work. Young women, paid two pence a thousand, earned less than a shilling some days. Men were allowed time for lunch, women had to eat surreptitiously in the lavatory. She said that if men had to work under these conditions, 'through their trade union or through the vote they would secure an alteration'.

Mrs Savoy was introduced as 'Mrs Hughes' because her husband didn't want publicity.[18] She handed Asquith a brush valued at ten shillings and sixpence and explained that she received two pence for each one she made. She had done this work for 43 years. 'As I have to work so hard,' she said, 'I feel it is very wrong that I cannot have a voice in the making of the laws.'

Mrs Bird described working in a jam factory from the age of eleven and then in a clothing workshop before becoming a mother of six. Her husband, a transport worker, earned 25 shillings a week. 'I have one of the best men,' she said. 'He is a teetotaller but yet I have a great struggle to bring up a family on the wages he earns.'

Collectively they demonstrated that women could not hope to challenge these appalling circumstances without a political voice. Daisy Parsons also referred to brutal police actions against suffragettes, endorsed by superiors who were 'not fit to help rule the country, while we have no say in the matter'. Mrs Scurr said it was 'gravely unjust' that the government passed legislation affecting women's daily lives without consulting them.

Jessie Payne spoke last. She ended by saying: 'We come from the East End and we have the voice of the people, they want us to ask you to give the vote for every woman over 21.'

---

18 It was her mother's maiden name.

Asquith conceded that this delegation was more representative than previous ones. He said he understood, from their 'moderate and well-reasoned' presentations, that women could not get 'substantial and intelligent reform' either in legislation or administration affecting their economic conditions, unless they 'themselves had a voice in choosing their representatives'.

The meeting had clarified his thoughts about the merits of partial changes. 'If the change [women's suffrage] has got to come', he said, 'we must face it boldly and make it thoroughly democratic in its basis.'

This crucial breakthrough, achieved by a rebellious, marginalised section of the wider suffrage movement, was frustratingly put on ice a few weeks later when war broke out in Europe. The war deepened conflict within the suffragette movement and opened up schisms within east London's labour movement. Just after Austria-Hungary declared war on Serbia, Lansbury's Daily Herald League called a 'united labour and socialist demonstration' in Trafalgar Square for Sunday 2 August stating, 'The war must be stopped'. Lansbury warned the government that the labour movement would 'not allow England to be dragged into this fearful crime', where workers of different nationalities slaughter each other. Speakers' platforms were set up all around the square. At one, dockers' leader Ben Tillett told the crowd, 'We don't want to sing Rule Britannia nor God Save the King ... [but] God Save the People', as they would do 'the fighting and the starving'.

The *Manchester Guardian* reported that, 'the crowd overflowed into Whitehall and some distance up the Strand. It was the largest Trafalgar Square demonstration for many years.' The *Herald* said a contingent of 5,000 had marched to the Square from the East

End 'headed by the striking red banner of the National Transport Workers Federation'.

Two days later, women's organisations held a huge peace rally in Kingsway Hall, calling on the British government to stay out of the conflict and on Europe's workers not to kill each other. But that week the situation changed dramatically. Germany declared war on Russia and France, and invaded Belgium. Britain and Serbia declared war on Germany, and Austria-Hungary declared war on Russia. As soon as Britain entered the war, working-class communities were swept up by the wave of patriotic fervour. Several labour and trade union leaders, including Ben Tillett and Will Thorne, now adopted a pro-war position. Mainstream suffragettes ceased campaigning and the government released all suffragette prisoners. The WSPU focused on supporting the war effort and ensuring that women could participate as equals in serving Britain. It later renamed its newspaper *Britannia*.

But rebellious Poplar swam against the tide. Lansbury, the *Daily Herald* and the ILP fought against the war. ELFS leaders instinctively shared these sentiments but stated them less stridently. Many of their supporters' husbands had signed up to fight. They made it clear, however, that they would continue to campaign for equality and women's rights and livelihoods as food prices rocketed and unemployment grew.

On 29 August the *East London Observer* claimed that the best British socialists 'have joined wholeheartedly with the Government in our hour of trial', except the 'Socialists of Bow and Bromley and Poplar, and the Suffragette garrison at Old-Ford' whom it lumped in with 'social maniacs and desperadoes … trying to make capital out of the most awful war'.

In early September, an ELFS delegation to the Board of Trade called for government intervention over food prices. However, knowing that government wheels turned slowly (except for the war effort itself), they developed their own initiatives to support and empower struggling local women. On 5 September the *Dreadnought* announced it had opened a 'cost price restaurant' offering two-course meals for two pence, or soup at a penny a pint. Two sisters, Ennis Richmond and Morgan Brown, both health-food enthusiasts, were soon serving 200 dinners a day. At the end of September, another 'tuppenny restaurant' opened in Railway Street, Poplar, serving suet dumplings, gravy and bread. In January a soup centre opened in St Leonard Street, Bromley. The ELFS began to provide work through establishing cooperative factories and workshops, making boots, clothing and children's toys. The most long-standing one – a toy factory – opened on Norman Road.[19] It supplied toys to Selfridges, Gamages and also Liberty – whose windows had been smashed by suffragettes in 1912! Women were paid five pence an hour, the amount ELFS campaigned for as a minimum wage. Women could work flexitime and leave their children in a crèche between 8 a.m. and 7 p.m. for three pence a day including meals.

The ELFS transformed a disused pub, the Gunmakers Arms on Old Ford Road, into a crèche and maternity health facility, and renamed it the Mother's Arms.[20] Its principal nurse, Maud Hebbes, later worked at Marie Stopes's pioneering birth control clinic. Women's Freedom League activist Muriel Matters,[21] who was trained by Maria Montessori, set up a small school there.

---

19   Later renamed Norman Grove.

20   Israel Zangwill, suffragette supporter and pacifist, who lived at 288 Old Ford Road, said in 1916: '… the hope of the world lies in changing the Gunmakers' Arms into the Mother's Arms.' Sarah Jackson, 'The East London Suffragettes in the First World War', www.eastlondonsuffragettes.com/blog/the-east-london-suffragettes-in-the-first-world-war (accessed October 2018).

21   See Chapter 8.

Meanwhile, the ELFS continued to campaign for equal pay as women were drafted into absent male workers' roles at half or even a third of the normal rate. They lobbied the Board of Trade in April 1915. The following month, ELFS activists also lobbied Home Secretary Reginald McKenna about price controls. As Sylvia Pankhurst was leaving the meeting, McKenna said, 'I must shake hands with you – you are the pluckiest girl I ever knew.' In July, the ELFS organised a large protest march from East India Dock Gates to the House of Commons, demanding equal pay for men and women, that wages should rise with prices, and that women should get the vote.

The ELFS became more openly anti-war, but without diminishing support for East End women affected by the war. After compulsory conscription was introduced, Sylvia Pankhurst was arrested and fined for speaking against the war and the *Dreadnought*'s office was raided several times. In February 1915, Sylvia Pankhurst collaborated with the Lansburys to form the League of Rights for Soldiers' and Sailors' Wives and Relatives, which fought for higher allowances and pensions. One ELFS activist who threw herself wholeheartedly into the League's work was Minnie Glassman, one of seven children born to an immigrant Jewish bootmaker, Isaac, and his wife Hannah (Annie), who grew up on Chicksand Street, off Brick Lane. She had joined the ELFS while working as a primary school teacher. Minnie married the Lansburys' son Edgar, a Labour councillor, then left teaching to work full-time for the ELFS as assistant secretary to Sylvia Pankhurst. Minnie and Edgar settled in Wellington Road, Bow. Minnie stayed politically close to Sylvia as the *Women's Dreadnought* became the more explicitly socialist *Workers' Dreadnought*.

Much further east, in 1917, revolution gripped Russia. Sylvia

Pankhurst's political focus shifted from local to global, and the ELFS morphed into the more revolutionary and mixed gender Workers' Socialist Federation. There was huge support for the Russian Revolution in the East End, not least among its 150,000 Jews who had fled from Tsarist persecution, but east London's workers were more inclined towards radical reform than revolution in their own backyard.

In 1920 Minnie and Edgar Lansbury joined the newly formed Communist Party,[22] but stayed politically grounded in east London, where they contributed to a seismic shift, if not a revolution, which began in 1919. Shortly after the war ended, every adult male still waiting to vote was enfranchised except prisoners, along with 8.4 million women. (Women between the ages of 21–30 remained disenfranchised.) Labour gained dramatically from that wider franchise in the 1919 local elections, especially in east London, where the party won impressive majorities for the first time. In Poplar, Labour won 39 of the 42 council seats. They appointed four aldermen to facilitate the administration. One was John Scurr, who had escorted the ELFS delegation to Asquith. Another was Minnie Lansbury.

Janine Booth, author of a study of Poplar Council from 1919–25, described how the new council 'for the first time ... looked like its electorate. It included railworkers, dockers, labourers, postmen, a road engineer, a toolmaker, a leadworker and a farrier.'[23] At its inaugural meeting, the Labour council elected George Lansbury as its mayor. He accepted the nomination but refused the pageantry of robes and chain that would

---

22 As did Melvina Walker, and two east London sisters and suffragette activists, Nellie and Rose Cohen.

23 J. Booth, *Guilty and Proud of It*, London: Merlin, 2009. More accurately, though, it resembled its predominantly working class *male* electorate.

set him apart from other councillors. Mayor George Lansbury described the new council as 'class-conscious socialists working together', to change people's lives. They drafted schemes for slum clearance to build municipal housing, invested heavily in health programmes, especially maternity and child welfare, reducing infant mortality significantly, expanded the library service, provided many services free to unemployed workers, brought in a minimum wage for council employees, and equalised the wages of men and women employed by the council. Male council employees saw pay increases of 25 per cent on average; the wages of female council employees rose by up to 75 per cent.

The new council worked closely with local trade unionists, and organised public meetings to share its plans with the community. It set what it considered a fair rate to pay for these new and increased services, but they were obliged also to levy a 'precept' paid to the London County Council (LCC) for cross-London services, such as drains, sewage, parks and police. When Poplar Council examined the formula for calculating this precept, it discovered that the burden fell disproportionately on the poorest boroughs. They were newcomers to office, but had a local rebel tradition to draw on. In March 1921, George Lansbury proposed that the council stop collecting the rates for cross-London bodies. They set a rate of four shillings and four pence instead of six shillings and ten pence, putting themselves on a collision course with the LCC and central government, who threatened to prosecute.

Poplar's councillors were summoned to court on 29 July and told that, if they did not levy the precept they would be sent to prison. Minnie Lansbury said: 'Poplar will pay its share of London's rates when Westminster, Kensington, and the City do the same.'

The councillors marched to court with thousands of supporters. Lansbury assured them: 'if we have to choose between contempt of the poor and contempt of court, it will be contempt of court.' The question, he said, was not whether their refusal was legal or illegal but whether it was 'right or wrong'.

John Scurr said the government was 'on the horns of a dilemma. If they send us to prison they will not get their money; and if they don't send us to prison they will bring the law into contempt. Poplar does not care on which horn they choose to impale themselves.'[24] The councillors' legal team included the Fabian Henry Slesser and W.H. Thompson, who had been jailed three times for conscientious objection during the First World War.

They lost. The judge told the councillors to prepare to stay in prison until their contempt was purged. The arrests took place at the beginning of September. Twenty-five male councillors were placed in Brixton Prison; five women councillors, including Minnie Lansbury and other former ELFS activists, including Nellie Cressall, were sent to Holloway Prison, where Julia Scurr was also imprisoned while her husband was locked up in Brixton. Just a few councillors remained to run the administration in their absence. The night before the first arrests, the council discussed how to function with such depleted numbers. Outside the Town Hall, 6,000 supporters gathered. As the meeting ended councillors sang 'The Red Flag', 'bringing particular passion', Lansbury recalls, to the lines 'Come dungeon dark or gallows grim, this song shall be our parting hymn'.

In prison they fought for their rights. Lansbury recalls:

---

24 Booth, *Guilty and Proud of It*, p. 50.

We all refused to … [wear] prison uniforms … [and] to do any work and … drink the tea or eat the food. In a few days the food was changed … we all went on strike against being locked in our cells all day, and as a result we had them opened after breakfast until after supper. Then we went into the police commissioner's room and entertained ourselves with lectures and discussions … we were entertained after 8 o'clock by public meetings and singing outside our windows.[25]

They won daily visits instead of two per week. Family members, MPs, magistrates, churchmen, councillors and council employees, including dustmen, roadsweepers, surveyors and engineers visited. They won the right to hold council meetings in prison, the first one (of 32) held on 11 September. From 27 September, women councillors in Holloway were bussed to Brixton for these meetings.

Lansbury was pleasantly surprised by a comment made by a warder soon after the councillors arrived: 'He said "Don't worry, you'll win. Every cause has to be fought for, and always prison opens up the way to reform".' The government threatened other boroughs that if they followed Poplar's example they would be imprisoned too. The threat backfired. Stepney Council and Bethnal Green Council both voted to withhold the precept too. With the rebellion spreading, the government and LCC backed down. Poplar's rebels were released on 13 October. That same week a conference was convened to equalise cross-London rates.

---

25 Lansbury, *Looking Backwards and Forwards*.

Poplar's rates were partially relieved and one shilling in the pound was added to the rates of Westminster and the City of London.

For the Lansburys though, this victory was soon overshadowed with great sadness. Minnie Lansbury had become ill in prison, and struggled with her health after being released. Over Christmas, a heavy bout of 'flu became pneumonia. She died, aged 32, on 1 January 1922. Thousands took to the streets to pay respects as her coffin was borne on the shoulders of four Poplar councillors, amid a procession led by hundreds of unemployed workers. At Bow Bridge the coffin was transferred to a hearse for a service at Ilford crematorium. Her ashes were later interred in East Ham Jewish Cemetery.

Mourners described her as a 'lover of justice' who dedicated 'a life of toil and labour in the relief of distress and the uplifting of her fellow men [sic]'. William Morris's poem 'All for the Cause' was read:

Mourn not therefore, nor lament it,
That the world outlives their life;
Voice and vision yet they give us,
Making strong our hands for strife.

The struggles for social justice that Minnie Lansbury gave her life for continued to flourish and, as the next chapter shows, they blossomed on both sides of the Thames.

Female Poplar councillors on their way to Holloway Prison.

Male Poplar councillors in Brixton Prison.

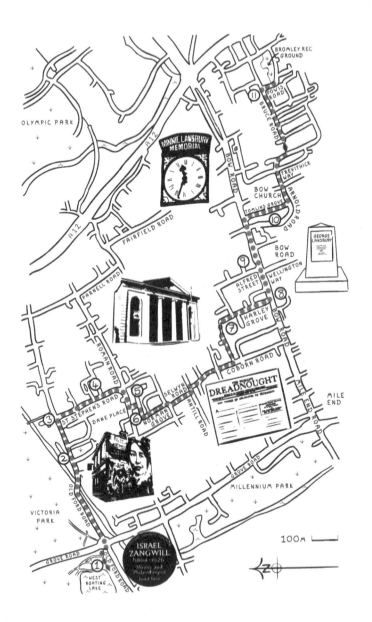

OLYMPIC PARK

A12

A12

FAIRFIELD ROAD

MINNIE LANSBURY MEMORIAL

BOW ROAD

BROMLEY REC GROUND

POWIS ROAD

BRUCE ROAD

TREVITHICK WAY

BOW CHURCH

TOMLINS GROVE

ARNOLD ROAD

11

10

GEORGE LANSBURY

BOW ROAD

9

ALFRED STREET

WELLINGTON WAY

8

BOW ROAD

HARLEY GROVE

7

PARNELL ROAD

ROMAN ROAD

COBORN ROAD

MILE END

DELWYN ROAD

4

5

ST STEPHEN'S ROAD

DANE PLACE

NORMAN GROVE

ANTILL ROAD

6

3

DREADNOUGHT

2

GROVE ROAD

MILLENNIUM PARK

MILE END ROAD

OLD FORD ROAD

VICTORIA PARK

100M

ISRAEL ZANGWILL
1864–1926
Writer and Philanthropist
lived here

GROVE ROAD

OLD FORD ROAD

1

WEST BOATING LAKE

N

WALK

Start at Crown Gate, Victoria Park, E3 5SN.

1. Crown Gate

Enter the park and you will see the lake where the suffragettes carried out their umbrella stunt in 1913. This was a well-established 'speakers' corner' area. Across Old Ford Road, at number 288, lived the writer Israel Zangwill, co-founder of the Men's League for Women's Suffrage. Walk east along Old Ford Road.

2. Old Ford Road (1)

On the side of the Lord Morpeth pub is a stunning mural of Sylvia Pankhurst and local suffragette activity. A plaque on the wall indicates the former site of the ELFS Women's Hall. Sylvia Pankhurst and Norah Smyth lived above it with Jessie and Jim Payne. Continue along Old Ford Road.

3. Old Ford Road (2)

On the corner with St Stephen's Road a plaque indicates the former site of a disused pub, the Gunmakers Arms, converted by the ELFS into the Mother's Arms mother and baby clinic and Montessori school. The director of the Mother's Arms was Bessie Lansbury.

4. St Stephen's Road

Opposite St Paul's Church a housing estate has replaced the earlier buildings that included, at number 103, the timber merchants/sawmill that belonged to Bessie Lansbury's father. Several members of the Lansbury family were connected with this business. Wood from this mill furnished the Mother's Arms and the Women's Hall, and was made into a speakers' platform that the ELFS used outside their Bow Road premises. Continue to the junction then turn right into Roman Road

5. Roman Road

The ELFS office was at number 321 (before street renumbering) near the corner with Appian Road. On the right-hand side looking west was Arber's, the company that printed the *Women's Dreadnought*. The paper was sold from a stall on Roman Road. Bow Baths stood towards the eastern end of Roman Road before Libra Road. A police raid on a suffragettes meeting here in October 1913 caused serious injuries. The ELFS 'People's Army' trained there. Turn left into Dane Place then right into Norman Grove.

6. Norman Grove

At number 45, a plaque recalls the toy factory established by the ELFS, which provided work to local women during the First World War. It was managed by Regina Hercbergova, a Polish woman of Jewish heritage. It closed in 1934. Cross into Selwyn Road, turn left into Antill Road then right into Coborn Road. Turn left into Malmesbury Road, past the school, then turn right into Harley Grove.

7. Harley Grove

The Sikh Temple here replaced a synagogue opened in 1927, which in turn replaced a Methodist Chapel. Continue to the end of Harley Grove.

8. Bow Road (1)

George Lansbury House is a small estate built on the site of his former home at 39 Bow Road. The Lansburys lived there for 23 years. A plaque mounted on a stone facing Bow Road recalls a 'great servant of the people'. Turn left along Bow Road.

9. Bow Road (2)

At Electric House, by the corner with Alfred Street, the Minnie Lansbury memorial clock mounted in the 1930s juts out. It fell into disrepair but was restored in 2008. At ground level right on the corner are two plaques, one mounted when the clock was first installed, and recalling Minnie's 'life devoted to the poor of the borough', the other celebrating the clock's restoration, describing her as an 'East End suffragette' and 'champion of local people'. Minnie lived nearby on Wellington Road, now renamed Wellington Way. Walk past Bow police station, the windows of which suffered attacks by suffragette stones. Turn right into Tomlin's Grove.

10. Tomlin's Grove

In December 1913, a suffragette protest outside Councillor le Manquais's home at number 13 was violently attacked by police. Turn left into Arnold Road, follow round into Trevithick Way, walk up a few stairs and cross into Bruce Road. Turn right into Powis Road.

11. Powis Road

Kingsley Hall was a community centre originally established in a disused chapel nearby by socialist, pacifist Christians Muriel and Doris Lester in 1915, providing educational and recreational facilities. The new Kingsley Hall opened here in 1928. Muriel Lester spoke on suffragette platforms in Victoria Park, and from 1922 to 1926 was an alderman serving Poplar's radical Labour council. The original centre served as a soup kitchen during the 1926 General Strike. That year Muriel Lester travelled to India to meet Gandhi. He stayed at the new Kingsley Hall during the round-table conference on India's future in 1931.

Women strikers outside Pink's jam factory, 1911.
TUC Library Collections, London Metropolitan University

10

PEOPLE'S POWER
IN BERMONDSEY

Cross the Thames from the City over London Bridge and you arrive at Borough High Street – a Roman road boasting smart office blocks and increasingly up-market cafes. On Tooley Street, heading east, tourists queue for the London Dungeon. To the west, pungent smells emanate from a food market with international flavours and exorbitant prices. Beyond the market lies Southwark's cultural quarter: Tate Modern, the rebuilt Globe Theatre and swish restaurants. The sole cultural institution in these streets that testifies to harder times endured by nineteenth-century locals is the Clink Museum, which tells the grim story of London's prisons.

London jails were filled with debtors, pickpockets, petty criminals and, intermittently, with political activists too. Clerkenwell had the highest concentration of prisons but Southwark came a close second. Its accommodation for convicts included the notoriously harsh Marshalsea Prison, which closed in 1842.[1]

When John Dickens, a naval clerk mired in financial difficulties, was caged up there in 1824, his family took lodgings nearby and his twelve-year-old son became the breadwinner. Slaving away in a boot-blacking factory by the Thames inspired young Charles

---

1   This replaced the medieval White Lion Prison.

Dickens's later searing descriptions of London's poverty, notably in *Little Dorrit* (1855), a vivid novel centred on Marshalsea. In *Oliver Twist* (1837), Dickens described Jacob's Island, near St Saviour's Dock, Bermondsey, east of London Bridge:

> ... rooms so small, so filthy, so confined, that the air would seem to be too tainted even for the dirt and squalor which they shelter . . . every repulsive lineament of poverty, every loathsome indication of filth, rot, and garbage: all these ornament the banks of Jacob's Island.

When London was hit by a further cholera outbreak in 1849,[2] Henry Mayhew noted that more than half the capital's deaths over a three-month period occurred south of the Thames, especially in Lambeth, Southwark and Bermondsey:[3]

> ... anyone who has ventured to visit [Bermondsey] will not wonder at the ravages of the pestilence in this malarious quarter, for it is bounded on the north and east by filth and fever and on the south and west by want, squalor, rags and pestilence. Here stands . . . the very capital of cholera . . . Jacob's Island . . . insulated by the common sewer.[4]

Several decades after Dickens and Mayhew had written about Jacob's Island, little had improved. Booth's 1903 poverty survey

---

2   See discussion of 1831 cholera outbreak in Chapter 2.

3   Since 1965 Bermondsey has been incorporated into the London Borough of Southwark. In the 1840s, 'Southwark' referred to the northwestern segment of that borough.

4   *Morning Chronicle*, 23 September 1849, quoted in D. Russell and M. Tichelar, *Class Struggles in South London 1850–1950*, London: Southwark-Lambeth History Workshop, 1981.

of Southwark and its environs described people in 'chronic want' or at best 'very poor'. Many were Irish immigrants from Cork engaged in casualised wharfside work. In St Saviour's, 68 per cent of the population lived on or below the poverty line, infant mortality was 28 per cent, and the average life expectancy, albeit skewed by the infant death rate, was 36.8 years. When Dickens was writing *Oliver Twist*, Bermondsey's population numbered roughly 65,000. Despite the high death rate, it doubled over 50 years, peaking at 136,660 in 1891, when it was regarded as one of the most insanitary, overcrowded and impoverished places in Britain.

George Orwell followed Dickens to Bermondsey 100 years later, staying in a decrepit Tooley Street dosshouse while he researched *Down and Out in Paris and London*. If Orwell had stayed in the heart of Bermondsey, he would have told a different story. Much of the area had been transformed during the 1920s and 1930s by the remarkable pioneering efforts of a socialist council rooted in the idealism of a handful of rebellious activists. Their rebellion was not against a particular political opponent or authority figure, but against the dire conditions and widespread hopelessness around them. They believed that the lives of people in the area *could* be transformed. They won the confidence of local residents and were themselves strengthened by the drive of Bermondsey's people, who grasped that hope and fought for their dignity, emancipation and rights.

On 5 May 1908, 16 people gathered in Yalding Road, Bermondsey, the home of bookbinder Tom Briggs, to discuss the creation of a new radical movement in the area. The only political choice for those lucky enough to vote was Liberal or Conservative, and the Conservatives usually won. Briggs's friends wanted to establish a socialist third force – a branch of the Independent Labour Party (ILP).

Local activists, such as Frederick Lessner, an immigrant German tailor and friend of Karl Marx, had made stuttering attempts to form a Bermondsey ILP in the 1890s. It held outdoor meetings in Southwark Park, and at Dockhead by Lee's Temperance Bar. Harry Quelch, who lived at 21 Southwark Park Road, edited the Social Democratic Federation (SDF) newspaper *Justice*. He met socialist and trade union colleagues at the General Garibaldi pub, close to his house, or at the Bricklayers Arms in Old Kent Road. During the 1887 agitation around unemployment, Bermondsey SDF held a very large meeting there, with William Morris chairing and John Burns speaking, but these initiatives remained fleeting and marginal.[5]

Two people opted out of the incipient group formed in Yalding road, so Bermondsey's first ILP branch was formed with just 14 members. These included a remarkable, idealistic couple, Ada and Alfred Salter, who met at the Bermondsey Settlement, a hub for anti-poverty work in the local community established by John Scott Lidgett, a left-leaning Methodist.

Ada Salter came to the Settlement as Ada Brown, a committed Christian from rural Northamptonshire, whose convictions drew her to social activism among the urban poor. Alfred Salter grew up in Bermondsey's more prosperous neighbouring district, Greenwich. His aspirational lower-middle-class parents were Plymouth Brethren by conviction, but by the time Alfred settled in Bermondsey he had shed these religious beliefs, which he felt

---

5   See *South London Chronicle*, 19 March 1887. Quelch became the business manager of the radical publishers Twentieth Century Press, founded by William Morris, and was a close associate of Lenin during his time in London.

were excessively focused on a glorious afterlife. He wanted social justice for Bermondsey's people here and now.

Salter won a scholarship to study medicine at Guy's Hospital in Southwark. Every day, as he travelled between Greenwich and Guy's, he saw Bermondsey's deprivation and desolation. His professors thought they were grooming a very promising student for a Harley Street career, but Salter had already chosen the mean streets of Bermondsey. He found a crop of other idealistic young doctors, and they formed a cooperative medical practice where they shared approaches to community health and pooled their income. They offered medical consultations at minimal cost, sometimes free, to a desperately poor population frequently exposed to life-threatening illnesses, and soon acquired several thousand patients.

Alfred married Ada in 1900 and they had a daughter in 1902, also called Ada but known mostly by her middle name, Joyce. As a student Alfred had joined the Marxist SDF and then the Fabians, both of which shaped his philosophical outlook. Through these connections he engaged in occasional illicit activities at night by the Thames, helping to smuggle fugitive immigrant radicals into the country, but in general he considered the SDF too concerned with theory over practice.

Across London, the Labour Party was in its infancy. The SDF and Fabians were too small and aloof, so Alfred, reluctantly, and Ada, more enthusiastically, looked first to the Liberals as a possible vehicle for practical social activism. The local Liberals asked Alfred to be their parliamentary candidate for the 1906 election but he rejected the offer. Meanwhile, he was busy converting Ada from liberalism to socialism, and she was converting him back to Christianity – its Quaker variety.

The fledgling ILP branch broadened its support base, not just among men but also among women. Ada Salter played a significant part in this through a fast-growing offshoot of the ILP, the Women's Labour League (WLL), promoting the particular interests of working women. It called for votes for all women rather than the partial enfranchisement demanded by the mainstream suffragettes, and worked to promote women candidates for local council elections. In November 1909 the ILP and the WLL celebrated a major success. Ada Salter became London's second female borough councillor[6] – though she was the sole socialist among Bermondsey's 54 councillors. The night she was elected, Ada, Alfred and fellow activist Eveline Lowe,[7] fantasised about what a socialist local council could do. They would pull down slums and build a tree-lined garden city, with bathrooms in every house and nursery schools for all under-fives. Every hungry schoolchild would be fed; a community health centre would offer free diagnosis by specialists and send TB sufferers to Switzerland for treatment. Ada imagined the red flag flying over the Town Hall. Eveline Lowe added, 'and over the new County Hall'.[8] Alfred dreamt of it flying over Big Ben.

Three months later, their dreams turned into nightmares. Their daughter, Joyce, had suffered two very severe bouts of scarlet fever. Some of the Salters' close friends thought they should have sent Joyce out of the borough to a boarding school or a Quaker school, rather than risk her sharing a local school

---

6   Reina Lawrence was the first, winning a by-election to sit on Hampstead Borough Council in December 1907.

7   Eveline Low had been a founding member of the Women's Labour League, with Ada Salter. Her husband, George Carter Lowe, was part of the doctors' cooperative with Alfred Salter.

8   County Hall was starting to be built, opening in 1922, with further blocks added in the 1930s. After Thatcher's government abolished the Greater London Council in 1986, the building was sold to private investors.

environment where killer diseases were rife. But Alfred and Ada, on principle, refused to allow Joyce privileges inaccessible to other Bermondsey children. Very unusually, she contracted a third bout of scarlet fever, just after her eighth birthday. This time she didn't recover. But instead of destroying the Salters' idealism, this tragedy enhanced their determination to give every Bermondsey child a future.

That night, in November 1909, when they dreamt of transforming Bermondsey, but held just one council seat, Alfred predicted that they would need twelve years to win the borough for socialism. In 1922 the Labour Party, in which the ILP was pivotal locally, won 38 out of the 54 seats on Bermondsey Council. Ada Salter became Mayor, and Alfred Salter won the parliamentary seat for Labour too. In the interim, a campaigning movement with a shared progressive vision was growing, but it needed a physical base.

Soon after the ILP branch was established in 1908, its members collectively rented a shop at 79 Grange Road, converted its main space into a small meeting hall and bought an old printing press, operated by Charlie Gamble, a compositor. Gamble shared his skills with other members, and they printed propaganda leaflets for open-air meetings and Thursday evening debates in the hall. They soon outgrew this space.

On Fort Road, an adult education facility had fallen into disrepair. The ILP rented it for twelve months with an option to buy. The veteran socialist James Keir Hardie officially opened the Fort Road Labour Institute on 8 July 1911. The building's original foundation stone, on one side of the entrance, bore the name of Lord Rosebery, a Liberal. Its new foundation stone, on the opposite side, read: 'Socialism the hope of the world.'

The local branch had barely started to discuss how best to utilise this centre to promote socialism locally, when it was commandeered by a spontaneous movement that suddenly erupted among thousands of Bermondsey's unorganised and impoverished female workers.

Bermondsey's workplaces, like those of the East End, were heavily demarcated by gender. Men were primarily engaged in dock work, transport, engineering and printing. Some worked within a declining leather industry, still recalled in local signs for Tanner Street, Morocco Street, Leathermarket Gardens and the Leather Exchange pub.

Bermondsey Street, which cuts through the former leatherwork area, was home to Christy's, the biggest hat factory in Europe, which employed large numbers of men and women. But women workers were mainly concentrated in a different industry whose products could not be worn. Raw food materials arrived in abundance at the docks, and a food processing and packaging industry grew in the nineteenth century. It began with tea packing, sugar refining, grain and spice milling, and later produced and packaged biscuits, cakes, confectionery, ice-cream, margarine, jam, sauces, pickles, meat and fish pastes, jellies and custards.

Hartley's jam factory and Sarson's vinegar factory were both on Tower Bridge Road. Spillers dog biscuits were made at Jacob Street, while biscuits for human consumption were manufactured at Jacob's factory on Wolseley Street and at Peek Frean's site on Drummond Road, which employed 2,300 workers in 1911. Crosse & Blackwell's jam and pickles plant was in Crimscott Street and Pearce Duff's custard factory was on Spa Road.

At a time when most unskilled male workers generally earned at least 15–20 shillings a week, Bermondsey's female workers usually took home seven to nine shillings, and factory girls under 16, just three shillings a week. Some Bermondsey children, as young as six, did factory shifts after school.

In the summer of 1911, striking tramway workers met at the new Labour Institute. They were earning 25 shillings a week working a ten-hour day, six days a week, and were fighting for 30 shillings a week and an eight-hour day. When the women saw their brothers, husbands and uncles called out on strike by their unions and gaining improved conditions through collective action and solidarity between workplaces, they couldn't help but reflect on their own exploitation. Meanwhile Ada Salter and the Women's Labour League were stepping up their political activities among working women.

On 11 August, the local papers reported 'turbulent scenes in Tower Bridge Road and Old Kent Road' the previous evening, 'which resulted unfortunately in a baton charge by the police'. As the transport strike spread, lorries and vans were waved down and even attacked by militants determined to halt deliveries and persuade drivers to return their vehicles to their workplaces. Mounted and foot police tried to keep the road clear for delivery vehicles but a large body of strikers continued to block it. The police made many arrests.

The papers also reported an unexpected act of solidarity. Female employees of Benjamin Edgington's tent-makers at Duke Street, London Bridge, came out in solidarity with the men. They paraded through Tooley Street 'singing the socialist Marsellaise "Fall in and follow me!"'. Some of Pearce Duff's female workers did just that.[9]

---

9   *South London Press*, 11 August 1911.

These events dominated discussions locally over the following weekend. On the Monday morning, as the solid strikes among Bermondsey's male-dominated occupations continued, hundreds of women at a confectionery factory walked out, demanding a change to their conditions. They had no union but acted spontaneously and collectively. They marched to nearby factories calling their sisters out. Within a day, 14,000 women workers at 21 Bermondsey factories were on strike. One young worker at a chocolate factory told a reporter from the *Southwark and Bermondsey Recorder*: 'We are striking for more pay, mister, and we won't go in till we get it.' The amounts that the strikers demanded varied depending on their existing pay. Not all the women came out – some felt strong bonds of loyalty to their employers, despite enduring long hours for low wages over several years; others feared being victimised by their bosses when the strike ended. But the majority of women struck, and even where production continued, it was severely disrupted. The local papers reported that: 'The women appeared to be in the highest of spirits when they came out on Monday. Armies of them paraded the streets of Bermondsey while the men who had also struck held meetings on the corners of the principal thoroughfares.'[10]

The newspapers' editorial columns, however, condemned the wildcat strikes, which, they claimed, imposed 'flagrant injustices' on decent local firms. Peek Frean's spokesperson, Mr Green, told the *South London Press* that the company 'had no reason whatever to suppose that there was any dissatisfaction whatever among our hands either with the rate of wages or the conditions of employment. While not confessing to be model philanthropists . . . we have always been on excellent terms with our workpeople.'[11]

---

10 *South London Press*, 18 August 1911.

11 *South London Press*, 25 August 1911.

Initially, half the Peek Frean workforce came out, but striking car-men picketed the entrance so no goods could leave the factory. Peek Frean rewarded the loyalty of those who continued to work by giving them double wages during the action. Another Peek Frean representative described the women's tactic of moving as a troop from one factory to another to call other women out as a 'reign of terror'.[12]

Employers were surprised and very alarmed. Around 40 per cent of jam and biscuits consumed throughout Britain were processed and packaged in Bermondsey's factories. Mary Macarthur, a union organiser and ILP member born in Glasgow in 1880, who had moved to London to take a post with the Women's Trade Union League,[13] and later founded a general women's union – the National Federation of Women Workers (NFWW) – was excited rather than alarmed. She had worked as a book-keeper in her father's drapery business which later moved to Ayr. Her father was a significant figure in local Conservative circles. Mary became active in the Primrose League, a body created to popularise Conservative views especially among women. She had aspirations beyond book-keeping. She wanted to become a journalist. Her epiphany came when she went to report on a meeting on the Shop Assistants' Union held locally. She was so shocked at the conditions the workers suffered that she became active in this union, and was elected as branch Chair a few months after joining. Within the trade union world she became more widely known when she led a successful 10-week strike among

---

12 During the Dock Strike of 1889, women there and at other local workplaces – Spratts, Southwell jam factory, Lloyd's tin-plate manufacturers – came out in solidarity with the southern side dockers, and joined striking dockers on protest marches.

13 The WTUL sought to represent women workers in mixed workplaces where men had been allowed to join a union but women workers could not.

chainmakers in Cradley Heath in the Midlands.

She sped down to Bermondsey from the NFWW office in Clerkenwell to meet and support the strikers. From the sheer numbers that came out on the first day, and the enthusiasm and self-organisation they had already shown, Macarthur believed they could make significant gains. The difficulty would be sustaining the strike long enough to succeed.

Back in April she had been powerless to affect the outcome of a seemingly promising movement by women workers at the Idris soft drinks bottling plant in Camden. Initially, 50 women walked out over the sacking of Annie Lowin, a 25-year-old widowed mother of two, who had worked for the company for 13 years. The number on strike quickly rose above 90. The company insisted that they were right to sack her because of 'persistent lateness' and 'incivility to a timekeeper'. On the day she was sacked, she had arrived three minutes late. Macarthur and Lowin's co-workers believed she was being victimised because she had started to take up union issues about poor sanitary arrangements in the factory: women sometimes worked up to their ankles in water; they also had to boil water for tea in the same pails used for washing the floor.

Her colleagues wrote songs for the picket line. One, written to the tune of 'Every Nice Girl Loves a Sailor', said:

> Have you been to work at Idris?
> No we won't go in today
> For we're standing by a comrade
> And we'll never run away
> She stood bravely by the union
> And she spoke up for us true

And if she gets the sack, we never will go back
Whatever they do, whatever they do.

The strikers stood firm and won support from well-unionised
male workers at two nearby factories, who levied their members
to help sustain the women while they were striking. The employer,
though, recruited local unemployed men to fill the jobs left idle by
the pickets. Bermondsey, however, had closer-knit communities
which resisted attempts to recruit scab labour. In Bermondsey
many men were simultaneously striking against their employers.
Women and men supported each other's struggles.

Macarthur, assisted by local ILP volunteers, turned the newly
opened Labour Institute on Fort Road into a strike headquarters. She appealed through the *Daily News* for material support,
requesting not money but food. Local shopkeepers and well-
wishers donated bread, milk and barrels of herrings, and gave
money too. Macarthur's ILP team distributed the food from Fort
Road and Ada Salter set up additional food distribution points.

Despite local newspapers' editorial bias against the strikers,
individual reporters empathised with the women's action and
recognised the hardships they faced while striking:

> . . . every day since Tuesday an immense crowd . . . weary
> and with the pinch of hunger on their faces marched to
> the hall of the Independent Labour Party in Fort Road
> where they were presented with loaves of bread. Clinging
> on to the skirts of the women were the children, piteously
> crying for food, and the bread as soon as it was received
> was split into small portions [for] the hungry children.[14]

---

14 *South London Press*, 18 August 1911.

Outside Pink's jam factory on Staple Street, women held placards stating: 'We are not white slaves. We are Pink's slaves' and 'More trouble at Pink's'.

Throughout the morning of Monday 14 August 1911, striking Bermondsey women marched and chanted 'Are we downhearted?' answering in unison 'No!' They reached Southwark Park for a rally in the afternoon. Dockers' leader Ben Tillett, Poplar MP George Lansbury and Mary Macarthur, of the NFWW, greeted the strikers. Tillett, one of the organisers of the simultaneous strikes among dock and transport workers, promised that the men would not return to work until the women's demands were met.

In concert with the industrial action, women in Leroy Street and Wolseley Street, near Jacob's biscuit factory, began to organise rent strikes. By Friday, several factory bosses came to the negotiating table, and more than 4,000 women had joined the National Federation of Women Workers. By the end of the following week the dispute was mostly over. Strikes had taken place at 21 factories and in 18 of them the women had made considerable gains in pay, achieved agreements to end piecework, and established a union in most of them.[15] In the three factories where no gains were made, Macarthur believed the women might have won if they had held out longer.

Alfred Salter and Mary Macarthur calculated that the pay increases, between one shilling and four shillings a week, would mean a redistribution of at least £7,000 from company profits to the pockets of local women workers over the coming year, probably considerably more. The women cherished that increase but just as importantly Macarthur believed they had acquired

---

15 Peek Frean (biscuits) and Southwell (jam) agreed pay rises but would not recognise a permanent union.

'a new sense of self-reliance, solidarity and comradeship ... making it certain that, whatever the difficulties and dangers of the future, they will never again be ... without hope'.[16]

The ILP gained prestige for its prominent role during the strike. Salter told the press, 'I shall not rest satisfied until every working man, woman and girl in Bermondsey is a member of a trade union.' The response was immediate. In early September a National Union of Barmen, Barmaids and Potmen was launched at the Labour Institute. Leaflets inviting barworkers to join this union described bar staff earning 14 shillings for a 100-hour week. Publicans said they provided many barworkers with free board and lodgings but barworkers retorted that accommodation was overcrowded and they shared poor quality food.

The August strikes inspired women workers beyond Bermondsey. In September, the ILP journal, *Labour Leader*, reported that women workers had formed unions in Clapton, Hoxton, Shadwell and Woolwich. Three hundred women among a 1,000-strong workforce at Murray's confectioners in Turnmill Street, Farringdon, came out on strike in late August. The women there were known locally as 'Murray's white mice', because of the powder that clung to them. Some of them earned just four shillings and eight pence a week for a 56-hour week, with few breaks. They were subject to petty fines, while any bonuses for increased productivity went to the foremen. The women had started to form a union and, inspired by the Bermondsey strikers, they decided to take action.

At the end of their first week on strike, they ambushed a convoy of food intended for 'loyal workers' who had not come

---

16 *Women's Trade Union Review*, October 1911.

out. The strikers celebrated this moment in a picket-line song (to the tune of 'Three Blind Mice'):[17]

> Murray's white mice
> See how they fight
> They collared the fish and the cheese and the bread
> 'Twas meant for the blacklegs, they ate it instead
> And the boss was so wild that he stood on his head
> Murray's white mice.

The following week, the employers offered to cease fining employees and start a profit-sharing scheme for women who had worked in the factory for at least twelve months. But they made the women's return to work conditional on them giving up their trade union membership. The women stayed out. A few days later a settlement was reached which left the Board of Trade to establish fair wage rates; all the strikers were reinstated.

During the 1911 strikes, Bermondsey ILP engaged directly with large numbers of local workers on a daily basis. One of its members – an employer rather than an employee – proposed an initiative which would increase regular contact and support the party materially. John Dhonau, whose mother Margaret had married a German immigrant from Sobernheim in the Rhineland, ran a successful bakery in Keetons Road, near Peek Frean's factory. He proposed to Alfred Salter that the ILP should take over his private bakery and turn it into a cooperative venture. The profits would support the ILP's political activities.

Political groups frequently raised funds through sales of groceries, tea and tobacco, or through jumble sales, but this was a

---

17 *Weekly Times and Echo*, 27 August 1911.

much bigger project. The ILP publicised the scheme and received a very enthusiastic response. They formed a bakery management committee, with Salter as secretary. Having acquired a number of loans through a friendly society connected with the party, they opened a new state-of-the-art bakery behind the Labour Institute in July 1914, and employed Dhonau as manager. In a trade notorious for long shifts at low pay, the ILP established exemplary trade union conditions. Customers joined the cooperative venture and shared its success, and the ILP became a regular feature in their lives.

The party's forward march in Bermondsey, which looked so promising, ran into the buffers that same year when Britain went to war. The war was enthusiastically supported in many working-class areas, including Bermondsey, as young men signed up. The ILP nationally had a proud record of anti-war activism in the Second Boer War,[18] and promoted pacifist politics. Its leader, Keir Hardie, said in 1913: 'All forms of militarism belong to the past ... Militarism and democracy cannot be blended. The workers of the world have nothing to fight each other about ... Patriotism is for them a term of no meaning.'

Fenner Brockway, the editor of *Labour Leader*, had launched the 'No Conscription Fellowship', which enrolled men of military age pledging to resist conscription. Alfred Salter was a staunch pacifist, as much from Quaker convictions as socialist beliefs. He helped to found a Bermondsey branch of the Fellowship. Charles Ammon, a Postal Sorters' Union activist, who was elected chair of the fledgling Bermondsey ILP at its initial meeting, was another outspoken pacifist.

---

18 The First Boer War, fought between December 1880 and March 1881, preceded the formation of the Independent Labour Party.

The ILP's work before the war had earned it respect, affection and support from the local community and practical involvement in campaigns. Suddenly, though, many members of that community were swept up in a wave of patriotic hysteria. Opponents of the war were portrayed as 'pro-German', or as 'traitors'. The Fort Road Institute, which epitomised unity and progress, became a place of conflict and violence. Anti-war meetings there were physically attacked. The cooperative bakery came under sustained vilification for giving donations to anti-war campaigns and hiring conscientious objectors as workers. When forced conscription legislation was passed in 1916, many ILP members locally resisted this measure. In July that year, 19 members of Bermondsey ILP were imprisoned for conscientious objection and anti-war campaigning, making it extremely difficult for the branch to function.

As the war dragged on, though, the initial zeal for it among Bermondsey's working class began to subside. But those who had supported the war were slow to restore their faith in the ILP. At the parliamentary election in December 1918, and with the franchise now extended to more working-class voters, Alfred Salter fought West Bermondsey for Labour. But, like other candidates associated with anti-war campaigning such as Charlotte Despard in Battersea, he lost. Graham Taylor, author of a biography of Ada Salter, remarks how 'Emmeline and Christabel Pankhurst, now openly supporting the Conservatives' sent activists to Bermondsey calling on 'the patriotic women of Bermondsey ... to fight the pacifists and pro-Germans in the district'.[19]

Gradually, though, war-supporting workers came to doubt the 'patriotic' parties' rhetoric about a 'peace dividend' and 'homes

---

19 Graham Taylor, *Ada Salter: Pioneeer of Ethical Socialism*, London: Lawrence & Wishart, 2016, p. 172.

fit for heroes' and started to return to the Labour fold, regardless of the ILP's war-time positioning. The 1919 local election results were more promising. Labour captured 24 of the 54 seats and 16 of those Labour councillors were from the ILP, including Jessie Stephen and Ada Broughton, who had both been very active in the suffragette movement.[20]

During 1919, the Labour Institute resumed its role as an organising centre for striking trade unionists, a support centre for strikers' families, and a base for campaigns to improve everyday lives. The most significant strike that year involved railworkers whose powerful local branch participated in a bitter national dispute. Lloyd George denounced the strikers as an 'anarchist conspiracy' but ultimately had to accede to most of their demands. The railworkers had strong support locally, and the community witnessed the anti-war ILP solidly supporting working people's struggles.

At the next local election, in 1922, Labour won 38 of the 54 seats. Ada Salter was elected Mayor – but, like Lansbury in Poplar, refused to wear the mayoral robes and chain. That same year her husband was elected to Parliament in West Bermondsey. Labour, with the ILP as its beating heart, could finally implement real and sustainable changes to the lives of Bermondsey's residents, starting to turn dreams they articulated 12 years earlier into reality. Their manifesto promised

> to make Bermondsey a fit place to live in . . . to promote health, to lower the death rate, and to increase the well-being . . . of the 120,000 people who live here. We will

---

20 Stephen had been active in the East London Federation of Suffragettes, and Broughton among suffragettes in Liverpool.

not allow our district to continue to be . . . vilified by the Daily Press as a horrible, evil-smelling, slum-ridden and unlovely place. We will . . . cleanse, repair, rebuild and beautify it, make it a city of which all citizens can be proud. Bermondsey is our home and your home.

During the Bermondsey Revolution the council embarked on a massive programme of slum clearance, developing model cottage-style council housing, improving residents' living structures and sanitation, and simultaneously rescuing many of them from the clutches of slum landlords. The Salters opposed high-rise flats, but the population density and the demand arising from slum clearance meant that new council housing necessarily included four- and five-storey blocks. Nevertheless, these were built to an excellent standard, and with adequate play spaces for children.

A promise to plant 10,000 trees in the first five years in power proved too ambitious, but they did plant more than 5,000. Disused green spaces, including graveyards, were reclaimed and redeveloped as gardens, and new spaces carved out where possible to make additional gardens and playgrounds. Flower-growing competitions were enthusiastically promoted and taken up by Bermondsey's families. In 1926, the council's Beautification Committee, initiated by Ada Salter, employed 36 workers.

Radical transformations in housing were accompanied by visionary investment in health provision, creating an 'NHS before the NHS'. A community health centre which still stands on Grange Road brought a range of surgeries under one roof – maternity welfare, dental surgeries, a foot clinic and Britain's first municipal solarium for treating the borough's many TB sufferers.

The council developed garden tuberculosis shelters in some parks and gardens, allowing sufferers to sleep in the fresh air, and sent some children for treatment in Switzerland.

The innovative approach to health that Bermondsey Labour pioneered also provided information so that people could confront health hazards themselves. The council customised a set of 'cinemotors' – vans with screens on the back – which stopped at housing estates, near community centres and next to parks, and used power from adapted lamp-posts to show health films to crowds that sometimes reached 1,000 people. They also showed films indoors in schools, youth clubs and workingmen's clubs, and at the Town Hall. Bermondsey's Labour Council presided over one of London's most impoverished boroughs but drastically reduced death rates, including infant mortality, achieving similar successes to Poplar's radical Labour Council where the ILP was also very prominent.

Radical Labour councils were able to lead a rebellion against destitution and hopelessness because they had the political legitimacy and some of the powers and resources to do so, though they constantly battled with the London County Council and central government for more resources. But the 1911 women's uprising had shown that people at the grassroots could also effect change themselves by acting collectively, in solidarity with each other, rather than waiting for politicians to take the lead. That spirit revealed itself once again on Bermondsey's streets during the 1926 General Strike. Bermondsey and its neighbouring districts, Southwark and Camberwell, were strategically important for the strike in London – Bermondsey because it included the docks and many unionised factories, Camberwell because a major bus company, Tillings, founded in 1897, was located there, and

Southwark because of the confluence of roads at Elephant and Castle, used by large numbers of buses and commercial vehicles.

Bermondsey's Trades Council, to which dozens of local unions were affiliated, formed a local Council of Action (COA). Bermondsey's radical Labour Council set up an emergency committee on the first day of the strike to liaise with that COA, and provided municipal facilities for meetings and rallies, and for the distribution of strike pay. It helped Bermondsey COA bring out a daily strike bulletin using Labour Party and council equipment and materials. Alfred Salter regularly phoned through information for this bulletin from Parliament or TUC headquarters. Seven bulletin distribution points were established, which handed out 6,000 copies a day throughout the strike.

Southwark COA did not have the same level of support from its local politicians, but one National Union of Railwaymen (NUR) activist and Communist Party member, Tommy Strudwick, had a typewriter and printer at his home in Swan Street near Old Kent Road. He produced a newssheet for Southwark district until police raided his home, arrested him and confiscated his equipment. He was sentenced to two months hard labour for 'spreading disaffection'. The authorities identified the NUR as a key player in the local COAs. On 6 May, police invaded an NUR meeting at the Bricklayers Arms pub on Old Kent Road, arresting many strike organisers.

At Bermondsey's Surrey Docks, which normally had a 2,000-strong workforce, just seven dockers came to work on the first strike day. The 'turbulent' scenes of 1911 on Tower Bridge Road were repeated as strikers attempted to block delivery vehicles. With government encouragement, dock companies recruited blackleg labour, including soldiers and several hundred students from Oxford and Cambridge universities, to unload ships. The *South London Press* reported that Guy's Hospital students also played a 'patriotic' role signing up as 'specials' to bolster police numbers. On Thursday 6 May, when police and strikers clashed near Hay's Wharf, there were 32 arrests. The most dramatic scenes were played out at Elephant and Castle, where mounted police fought large crowds blockading the streets leading to the roundabout and preventing goods traffic and buses from getting through. Some strikers climbed up buildings and rained missiles down on the police.

During the strike, Bermondsey Council twinned with the mining village of Blaenau in the South Wales valleys. Bermondsey continued making community collections and contributed over £7,000 to support the Welsh miners over the coming months, while they continued to strike.

In the early 1930s, the whole country was in the throes of a terrible economic depression and dramatically rising unemployment. Bermondsey was partly cushioned by the diversity of its industrial base, but unemployment was high enough locally to cause severe hardship to many families. The depression forced people to compete for scarce resources, and tested the resilience and bonds of solidarity between members of the community. It undermined ordinary people's faith that their local and national politicians could find a way out of the crisis. A fast-growing fascist movement, led by Sir Oswald Mosley, exploited the situation. Although his main focus in London was north of the Thames, in the East End, he established branches and supporters' groups south of the river in Battersea, Balham, Brixton, Camberwell, Lewisham, Peckham and Streatham. But he was never able to establish a branch in Bermondsey, where trade union organisation and identification with Labour's local achievements were strong. That did not stop Mosley from planning to march thousands of fascists through Bermondsey on 3 October 1937 in an attempt to establish a local base. The dramatic events of that day are described in the next chapter.

On Saturday 7 September 1940, the London Blitz began, and Bermondsey, whose docks and factories handled crucial supplies, suffered terrible bombing. The very next evening, a bomb destroyed the Labour Institute and the cooperative bakery, killing four bakery workers. Alfred Salter was philosophical about the fate of these two institutions that, for nearly three decades, had played such a pivotal role in advancing the struggles of Bermondsey's people for better lives, truly providing them with 'bread and roses'. He wrote to a pacifist socialist friend, 'It is a terrible tragedy but even greater is the loss of life in Bermondsey.'

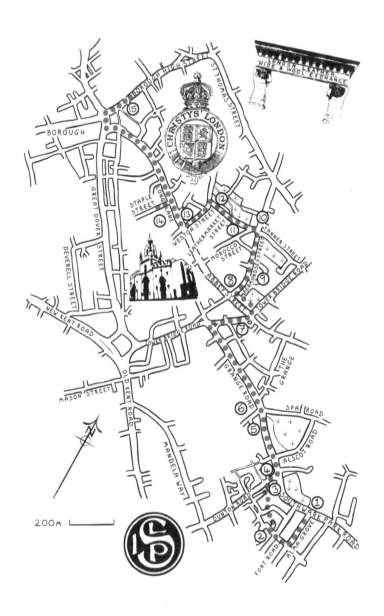

BOROUGH HIGH STREET
ST THOMAS STREET
CHRISTYS LONDON
BOROUGH
GREAT DOVER STREET
DEVERELL STREET
STAPLE STREET
LONG LANE
WESTON STREET
LEATHERMARKET STREET
MOROCCO STREET
TANNER STREET
ABBEY STREET
BERMONDSEY STREET
TOWER BRIDGE ROAD
NEW KENT ROAD
TOWER BRIDGE ROAD
GRANGE ROAD
THE GRANGE
SPA ROAD
OLD KENT ROAD
MASON STREET
ALSCOT ROAD
MANDELA WAY
SOUTHWARK PARK ROAD
DUNTON ROAD
FORT ROAD
ALMA GROVE ROAD

LONDON LEATHER
HIDE & WOOL EXCHANGE

200M

WALK

Start at the corner of Southwark Park Road and Alma Grove, opposite the Harris Academy, SE16 3T2.

1. Southwark Park Road

The roundel on the building that curves into Alma Grove indicates a former public house (the Rose and Crown), but no trace remains of the pub opposite, the General Garibaldi, where local socialists and trade unionists met in the 1890s. Regulars included Harry Quelch, an associate of Lenin, and editor of the socialist newspaper *Justice*. Walk down Alma Grove and turn right into Fort Road.

2. Fort Road

As you enter the estate at the end of the street, a sign on the left marks Alfred Salter House. The Labour Institute that stood near here was the hub of Bermondsey's progressive struggles until it was destroyed in the Blitz. Behind it stood Bermondsey Independent Labour Party's (ILP) cooperative bakery. Cross diagonally rightwards through the estate, towards Dunton Road.

3. Dunton Road

Exit the estate on to Dunton Road at Dhonau House, named after John Dhonau, a socialist baker of German heritage whose private bakery business was transformed into the ILP's cooperative bakery. Turn right then left into Southwark Park Road, which becomes Grange Road.

4. Grange Road (1)

The health centre on the corner with Alscott Road was the centrepiece of Bermondsey Labour Council's radical and pioneering healthcare initiatives. Notice the sculpture, by Allan Howes, of a mother and child, high above the entrance. Turn left into Alscott Road to see the physical depth of the building that was a one-stop health centre for the people of Bermondsey before the NHS. Return to Grange Road and turn left.

5. Grange Road (2)

At number 79, Bermondsey ILP established its first meeting hall, and published propaganda leaflets on a printer it installed here. Continue a short distance to the Alaska Factory, now converted into flats but retaining its distinctive typography.

6. Grange Road (3)

The Alaska Factory, which opened in 1869, made products from seal fur. Its exterior is still intact. An information board nearby describes the company's history. Opposite is Spa Road. The artist Thomas Keyse, whose house was at the spa entrance, established a pleasure garden here in the 1700s. Pearce Duff's Custard factory, whose workers joined the 'Women's Uprising' in 1911, was on Spa Road. Continue to Tower Bridge Road and turn right.

7. Tower Bridge Road

The scene of confrontations between police and striking transport workers during 'the great unrest' of 1911 and during the General Strike of 1926, as strikers sought to prevent delivery lorries from transporting goods to destinations across the river.

A busy Sunday morning street market was held at the southern end of Tower Bridge Road for many decades. Enter the garden/graveyard on the corner of Abbey Street.

8. Abbey Street

The garden behind the seventeenth-century St Mary Magdalene Church has ornate gravestones and tombs, including one for the Rolls family – later of Rolls-Royce cars. Walk through the gardens, exit on Bermondsey Street and turn right.

9. Bermondsey Street

Wealthy West End volunteers supporting girl and women workers established the charitable Time and Talents settlement just past the church, in the early 1900s. Christy's – the biggest hat factory in Europe – was established in the 1840s at number 175, and occupied two large buildings opposite each other. The factory used beaver, bear, marten, minx, hare and rabbit skins to make hats. Stop at the park on the corner with Tanner Street.

10. Tanner Street

Tanner Street's name reflects Bermondsey's leather industry, developed in the fourteenth century. The park was opened in 1929 on the site of the former Tanner Street workhouse and St Olave's Church, as part of the environmental improvement and beautification of the borough, led by Ada Salter. A plaque below the noticeboard credits Bermondsey's progressive Labour Council with the park's creation. Its fountain is made from a section of St Olave's tower. Cross Bermondsey Street into Morocco Street.

11. Morocco Street

There are further indications of the historical leather industry here and on Leathermarket Street, including the large Morocco Store sign on the left (Morocco leather is made from goatskin). This building was originally a spice warehouse. Continue into Leathermarket Street.

12. Leathermarket Street

The Leather, Hide and Wool Exchange was established here in the late 1870s, but has now been converted into a pub. A series of relief sculptures depict the different processes of leatherwork. Follow the road round into Weston Street, past the Leathermarket industrial estate, converted largely into studios. The Leather Market was established here in 1833. It suffered considerable bomb damage in the Blitz. Turn right into Long Lane.

13. Long Lane

Thousands of anti-fascists erected barricades here, to prevent Mosley's British Union of Fascists marching through Bermondsey. See Chapter 11.

14. Staple Street

Pink's jam factory was established here in the 1880s. Its workers were prominent in the women's strikes of 1911. The factory was closed in 1925 and demolished to make way for municipal housing in the 1930s. Continue on Long Lane and turn right into Borough High Street.

15. Borough High Street

The John Harvard Library celebrates a seventeenth-century

local clergyman who went to America and left a bequest, with money he had inherited, to help establish an education facility – Harvard University! The local history library at the back of the building is on the site that was once Marshalsea Prison, where Charles Dickens's father was held.

Bermondsey Labour Institute.

Middle section of Cable Street mural.

11

NO PASARAN!

Cable Street and Long Lane

Rebel movements of the 1830s, such as the Chartists, placed democracy at the heart of their agenda. But a hundred years later London's fastest-growing rebel movement condemned democracy as the greatest evil and aimed to replace it with dictatorship. The British Union of Fascists (BUF) commandeered the language of freedom and redemption but threatened every democratic gain and step towards equality achieved during decades of struggle. Leading this energetic new movement was a charismatic, young, aristocratic politician: Sir Oswald Mosley.

Mosley won a Conservative seat in Harrow, West London, at the age of 22, regaining the same seat twice as an Independent, after falling out with the Tories over Ireland.[1] He flirted with the Liberals but joined Labour (gaining a reputation for extra-parliamentary flirting, too), and won a by-election for Labour in the West Midlands seat of Smethwick in 1926.[2] His first wife, Cynthia 'Cimmie' Curzon, daughter of India's former Viceroy, joined him on the Labour benches when she won Stoke-on-Trent in 1929.

---

1   Mosley supported self-determination for the Irish people in a united Ireland and was a harsh critic of the Black and Tans.

2   In 1964 this safe Labour seat achieved national notoriety when it unexpectedly returned a Tory majority as voters were swayed by a campaign crudely exploiting racial tensions.

By February 1931, the economic crash was near its peak. Unemployment in Britain had almost doubled from an unprecedented 1.5 million in 1929. Mosley had proposed radical remedies influenced by his close associate, John Maynard Keynes, but a suspicious Labour hierarchy rejected them and thwarted Mosley's political ambitions.[3] That month, the Mosleys and several Labour activists, including a handful of MPs, left Labour to form the New Party. A party of 'action based on youth' mobilising 'energy, vitality and manhood to save and rebuild the nation', it combined left- and right-wing policies and unashamedly advocated dictatorship. It had a militaristic internal hierarchy, and its own physical defence force (the 'Biff Boys'), trained by Oxford-educated Peter Howard, who captained the English rugby union team, and the recently retired East End boxer, Ted 'Kid' Lewis, born Gershon Mendeloff to Jewish immigrant parents.

The New Party's trajectory became clearer after Mosley returned from a fact-finding mission to Europe in early 1932, centred on Mussolini's fascist Italy. In October 1932 the New Party rebranded itself as an insurrectionary movement called the British Union of Fascists and dressed its members in jackboots and militaristic black uniforms with lightning flash armbands. It launched a weekly newspaper, the *Blackshirt*, in February 1933, with the slogan 'Britain First'.[4] Issue 1 declared: 'On to Fascist Revolution!' Mosley's emphasis on young people featured powerfully in BUF propaganda. Other parties, he said, only called upon youth 'to immolate themselves on the battlefield';

---

3 Nationalisation of key industries, public works programmes, higher pensions and protectionist trade and industry policies.

4 In 2011, a fascist political organisation calling itself 'Britain First' was created by members who had splintered from the British National Party.

his party offered young people 'the chance . . . to serve the . . . country in times of peace'. A powerful message for all who had lived through the First World War.

The fascists recruited a mini-army of 200 Blackshirts – largely unemployed youth – to live in its Chelsea barracks. A pair of boots, three meals a day and daily wages from three shillings and sixpence to ten shillings and sixpence were attractive bait. Food tickets were issued at a 7.30 a.m. roll call. Blackshirts worked until 5 p.m., though some had evening duties supporting public meetings. They needed a signed pass to leave the barracks, and at 11.15 p.m. it was 'lights out'.

Beyond this mini-army, Mosley's movement in London did not initially pursue the young or hungry.[5] Under the name 'January Club', it hosted wining and dining soirees at the Ritz and the Savoy for well-heeled potential recruits. They dined on fine food while Mosley whined about broken Britain. His biggest catch, in late 1933, was press baron Lord Rothermere, whose *Daily Mail* outstripped all its competitors. He also published the *Daily Mirror*, the *Sunday Pictorial* and London's *Evening News*.

Outside London, Mosley wooed miners in the Northeast and Wales, cotton workers in Lancashire, farmers in Dorset, and small business owners and unemployed ex-military personnel in many towns. Having established 500 local branches, an unpredictable turn of events during 1934 forced the BUF leaders to drastically rethink, after which the movement focused primarily on east London, where it had members but no branches.

On 14 January 1934 Mosley's movement received an extraordinary boost. Britain's widest-read newspaper published a

---

5   Battersea was an exception – see Chapter 7.

double-page spread proclaiming 'Hurrah for the Blackshirts'. Rothermere's article rehashed Mosley's stock phrases: the 'tired old gang' of 'senile politicians'; the 'revival of national strength'; and the 'new age requires new methods'. Rothermere claimed that young people wanted Britain 'to develop that spirit of patriotic pride . . . which has transformed Germany and Italy'. He provided contact details so 'young men' could join up. Mosley, a supporter of the suffragettes in the 1920s, wanted women recruits too; Rothermere was more old-school.[6]

With Rothermere's backing, though, Mosley planned an ambitious set of indoor rallies in London. The first filled the Albert Hall on 22 April. Rothermere's rival, Lord Beaverbrook, gushed: 'The peroration was perfect . . . Suddenly Sir Oswald's voice ceased . . . the cheers and the handclapping rose to a storm.'[7] The *Manchester Guardian*, allergic to Mosley's hyper-nationalist doctrines, noted several occasions where the applause became 'almost rapturous', especially when Mosley told Britain's Jews to 'put Britain before Jewry'.

The second rally, at Olympia, attracted 15,000 people but was a public relations disaster for Mosley. Workers snapped up cheap tickets, while the most expensive ones were presented by captains of industry seeking decisive leadership in hazardous times, with couples arriving in Daimlers and Rolls-Royces. The political class was there too: 150 MPs searching for inspiration, while some peers wore black shirts – blending in with 2,000 others similarly attired, half of them stewards.

Two radical left-wing forces – the Communist Party (CP)

---

6 Three prominent suffragettes – Mary Richardson, Norah Elam and Mary Mien – became very active within the BUF.

7 *Daily Express*, 23 April 1934.

and the Independent Labour Party (ILP) – combined to confront Mosley's movement ideologically and on the streets. The CP, which launched the *Daily Worker* newspaper in 1930, had previously denounced more mainstream Labourites as 'social fascists', but it was jolted by events in Germany in January 1933, where the Nazis took power, while communists and socialists fought each other. In 1932 the ILP shed members when it freed itself from the discipline of a rightward-drifting Labour Party, but was committed to intensifying its grassroots campaigns.

The day before the rally, Mosley assured Police Commissioner Viscount Trenchard that the BUF would maintain order inside the hall since they had trained stewards, and proposed that the police focus on anti-fascist demonstrators outside the building. Trenchard complied. However, dozens of anti-fascists surreptitiously ensconced themselves *inside*. Rothermere's papers had offered £1 and a free rally ticket to authors of published letters beginning 'Why I like the Blackshirts'. Anti-fascists wrote convincing spoof letters, obtained tickets, and forged more.

In the hall a spotlight illuminated Mosley, who believed his hour had come, but three minutes into his speech a heckler shouted 'Down with Mosley, down with Mussolini, down with Hitler. Fascism means hunger and war!' Three minutes later a similar interjection emanated elsewhere. The outbursts continued like clockwork. One protester climbed the rafters for an aerial heckle. On the leader's signal, stewards, concealing knuckledusters under their gloves, viciously beat up further hecklers inside the hall; a 21-year-old student, Jack Miller, was thrown over a balcony and received serious head injuries. Stewards inflicted further beatings in the gallery surrounding the hall before dumping bloodied hecklers outside.

Doctors treated 80 protesters that night. If Mosley imagined this display would impress business magnates who might require a force to combat militant workers, he misjudged them. Most were repelled by these methods and soon withdrew their backing. His explicit antisemitism alienated others. At Olympia Mosley denounced Labour politicians 'inspired by the German Jew, Karl Marx', Tories who admired 'the Italian Jew Benjamin Disraeli', and Liberals led by that 'typical John Bull, Herbert Samuel'. Rothermere took several weeks to observe other people's reactions then distanced himself through a public letter exchange, hypocritically citing Mosley's antisemitism, while continuing to idolise Hitler.[8]

Mosley's party went into free fall. The White City rally pencilled in for August was replaced with a September gathering in Hyde Park, pre-empting the embarrassment of empty seats. The *Blackshirt* showed snapshots of saluting supporters; other newspapers, though, used panoramic images showing 5,000 fascists encircled by police and 100,000 anti-fascist protesters, who drowned out Mosley's speech.

The growing anti-fascist movement could not foresee the consequences of its success. After the Olympia and Hyde Park fiascos, they expected Mosley's movement to melt away. Instead it reinvented itself, focusing on east London – an area known for militant industrial struggles and home to London's largest Jewish community, many of whom came to Hyde Park in response to CP leaflets printed in Yiddish. Two young Jewish communists, Max Levitas and Jack Clifford, eager to mobilise others, were arrested at 4 a.m. near Nelson's Column. The plinth bore a slogan: 'All out

---

8   Rothermere continued avidly to support Adolf Hitler until just before the Second World War broke out.

on September 9 to fight fascism.' Levitas had a wet paintbrush in his pocket. He failed to convince Magistrate Barker that, although he intended to paint slogans, he hadn't actually done so. Levitas was fined £5.[9] The *Jewish Chronicle* urged Jews concerned about fascism to stay indoors and avoid adding to the police's troubles; the first of several times that East End Jews would ignore *meyvins* (self-appointed experts) commenting from a distance.

The BUF opened its first east London branch, in Bow, in October 1934, signalling its intention to build a populist, working-class, fascist movement, especially in Irish-Catholic areas bordering Jewish communities. Mosley thought he was pushing at an open door, encouraging antisemitism there. His emergent movement would have visible targets on which to vent their growing frustration about their own circumstances. One year later, *Blackshirt* writer Clement Bruning celebrated the movement's 'great popular support in East London'. The BUF, he said, had brought 'hope and sunlight into lives darkened by long years of hunger, squalor and despair', and shown how 'to cast off the foreign yoke of a domineering, all pervading Yiddish culture, which strives to make East London take on the character of Odessa or Warsaw'.[10]

Mosley still relished his central London showpieces. At the Albert Hall in late October 1934, he announced a 'new battle in British history', in which the 'great cleansing spirit of fascism' was pitted against the 'unclean, alien influence in our national and imperial life' – Jews. In March 1935, he returned to the

---

9   Report in the *Blackshirt*, 14 September 1934, entitled 'Jews desecrate Nelson's Column'. On Max Levitas's 99th birthday in June 2014 the author presented him with an enlarged copy of this report.

10   *Blackshirt*, 4 October 1935.

Albert Hall, to condemn the Jewish community as the 'nameless, homeless and all-powerful force which stretches its greedy fingers from the shelter of England . . . grasping the puppets of Westminster, dominating every party of the state'.[11] But East End Jews, too busy looking for work to grasp any puppets, were more worried by local speakers on soapboxes inciting their non-Jewish neighbours against them, than by Mosley's theatrical antics in glitzy venues. The fascists built vibrant branches in Bow, Bethnal Green, Limehouse and Shoreditch. At first they parachuted in experienced street orators but gradually developed a cadre of well-known local speakers, including Mick Clarke and Owen Burke, who drew support especially among Catholics.

The physical threat to East End Jews grew as the fascists introduced new strains of antisemitic propaganda. In February 1936, Mosley's movement renamed itself the British Union of Fascists *and National Socialists*, a shift from Mussolini's fascism towards Hitler's more racially obsessed brand. Until then, most BUF antisemitism targeted Jewish *behaviour*, alleging that Jews were price-cutters, sweating employers, slum landlords, pedlars of criminality and vice, and physically violent against fascists. In 1936 fascist street-orators began to describe Jews as 'rats and vermin from the gutters of Whitechapel' and 'hook-nosed, yellow skinned dirty Jewish swine'. Speakers declared: 'It is gentiles versus Jews, white man versus black man.' Jews were 'a species of sub-humanity'.[12] By declaring Jews less than human, they legitimised brutality. Physical attacks, death threats, daubings and smashed windows became daily occurrences. East

---

11   *Blackshirt*, 29 March 1935.

12   D. Rosenberg, *Battle for the East End*, Nottingham: Five Leaves, 2011, pp. 100–1.

End Jews complained that the police were failing to protect them.

Parliament debated antisemitic terror in east London in March and July that year. Local MPs detailed dozens of sickening incidents. The Home Secretary denied police partiality and asked, pathetically, for 'everyone on all sides' to 'behave reasonably'. Beleaguered East End Jews sought help from their West End-based community leaders, but the Anglo-Jewish Association and Board of Deputies trivialised or dismissed their claims, while the *Jewish Chronicle* generally downplayed the threat.[13] Local Jewish activists concluded that they had to find solutions within the East End by mobilising and empowering the local Jewish community and gaining support from local non-Jews.

The *Arbeter Ring* (Workers' Circle)[14] became the catalyst. Its Jewish Labour Council called a conference in July 1936 at ABSA House, 46 Commercial Road. Delegates came from 87 Jewish organisations and associations, including synagogues, youth groups, trade unions and friendly societies. This conference created the Jewish People's Council Against Fascism and Antisemitism (JPC), a united grassroots body ready to combat the fascists and make common cause with non-Jewish antifascists. The JPC took a sophisticated view of Mosley's endgame, understanding how he was using anti-Jewish violence and antisemitic rhetoric to gain power and overthrow democracy. The JPC argued that all who valued democracy had an interest in fighting both antisemitism and fascism. Mosley dismissed the JPC as a 'Communist front'. It was much broader, but several leading members were communists, and this contributed to its success.

13　The exception was a *Jewish Chronicle* special correspondent reporting from the East End in July/August 1936, who gave more realistic assessments of the problems Jews faced there.

14　See Chapter 4.

Mosley Speaks

IN

East London

Sunday, 4th October, 1936

● FOUR MARCHING COLUMNS
● FOUR GREAT MEETINGS

MOSLEY WILL SPEAK AT ALL MEETINGS
HER SPEAKERS:

JOYCE   **BECKETT**
THOMSON   **MORAN**

MEETINGS AT——
ASKE STREET, Shoreditch, at 6-30 p.m.
SALMON LANE, Limehouse, at 5 p.m.
STAFFORD ROAD, Bow, at 6 p.m.
VICTORIA PARK SQUARE, Bethnal Green, at 6 p.m.

FULL PARTICULARS from:—
BRITISH UNION OF FASCISTS &
NATIONAL SOCIALISTS

22a, GREEN STREET, Bethnal Green, E.2.
29, ESSIAN STREET, Limehouse, E.1.
1a, DANE PLACE, Rosebank Road, Old Ford, E.3.
46, NEWTON STREET, Hoxton, N.1.

British Union of Fascists mobilising leaflet.

Within CP branches, the Jewish and Irish communities that the fascists tried to set against each other began to build cooperation.

The JPC organised public meetings with joint Jewish/ non-Jewish platforms to attract mixed audiences. When Mosley announced plans to invade Jewish areas of the East End on 4 October, promising 'four marching columns and four great meetings' to celebrate the BUF's fourth anniversary, the JPC petitioned the Home Secretary to ban the march, collecting nearly 100,000 signatures of local Jews and Gentiles in two days. Home Secretary Sir John Simon said freedom of speech and movement was vital for democracy, and privileged the BUF's freedom over the local community's voice, so the JPC urged 'Citizens of London' to collectively ban the march themselves.

The ILP and CP both played crucial roles in the final mobilisations, as did the Labour League of Youth – a radical Labour Party segment. The CP, though, had to overcome a severe wobble in the week preceding the event. When Mosley chose to march on 4 October he was deliberately disrupting the CP's plans. Its Young Communist League had booked Trafalgar Square that day for an anti-Franco rally aiming to raise £100 towards Spanish Medical Aid. Faced with Mosley's spoiler, the CP proposed to go to Trafalgar Square to rally for Spain, then march to the East End to show opposition to Mosley, and hold an evening meeting in Shoreditch, a Blackshirt stronghold. But with the march to Trafalgar Square commencing as Mosley would be entering the East End, the march back east could only be a token gesture. Local CP branches rebelled, continuing their work to prevent Mosley's march. Halfway through the week the Party's London District Committee cancelled the Trafalgar Square rally and printed over its leaflets, 'Alteration: Rally to Aldgate 2 p.m.' Gardiners Corner clock tower at Aldgate overlooked the streets through which Mosley's troops intended to pass.

On Thursday morning, CP branch secretaries received a revised plan and embarked on 72 hours of non-stop activity to maximise the number of demonstrators and prepare tactics. They set up ad hoc medical points where anti-fascists could receive treatment arising from expected confrontations without lying in hospital waiting to be arrested; identified places where youngsters could roll marbles under police horses to halt charges; appointed a network of runners to carry information and direct crowds to maximum effect; and gathered materials to erect barricades in Cable Street and the surrounding streets (assuming correctly that fascists would be redirected there if Gardiners Corner was blockaded). Walls were whitewashed and pavements chalked with anti-fascist slogans and mobilising calls. The *Daily Worker*'s special London Supplement published on the Saturday directed protesters to strategic points.

Trade union militants mobilised sweatshop workers – mostly Jewish – and dock and railway workers, many of whom were of Irish heritage. The Irish community's role would be pivotal, since Mosley's project of cementing an East End base depended on exploiting antagonisms between them and the Jewish communities. Beyond the East End, the Printing and Allied Trades Anti-Fascist Movement[15] and other trade unionists with a record of anti-fascist activism, mobilised members too for 4 October.

While grassroots bodies prepared for defiance, the leaders of the main political parties, and the TUC, and editors of mainstream newspapers advised people to stay indoors. The *Jewish Chronicle* published an 'urgent warning', instructing Jews to 'keep away'. It declared: 'Jews who . . . become involved in . . . disorders, will be actively helping antisemitism and Jew-baiting.' Rabbis read similar messages from the Board of Deputies to their congregants 24 hours before the demonstration.

East End Jews voted with their feet. Tens of thousands, supported by local non-Jews, completely blockaded Gardiners Corner. Anti-fascist transport workers parked trams in front of Gardiners as a barricade. Mounted police swung long truncheons and broke heads but the wall of people stood firm.

Five-year-old Binnie Yankovitch had a bird's-eye view of the action from her Sunday morning dance class on the top floor of Gardiners. Binnie's parents knew that an anti-fascist

15 Several members of this union in London later fought in the International Brigades against Franco's fascists.

demonstration would take place that afternoon but assumed she would be safely home before then. However, Binnie and her friends were still dancing when the conflagration began:

> there was this incredible noise . . . [we] kids rushed to the window . . . The people were fighting the police . . . horses neighing and . . . rearing up . . . police hitting men with their truncheons . . . people shouting, running, throwing things, holding their heads with blood pouring down their faces. I never went back to dance class again.[16]

Unable to clear a path through Gardiners Corner the police considered an alternative march route further south, closer to Royal Mint Street where the fascists were waiting. Directly opposite them was Cable Street – a narrow artery leading from the city towards the docks lined with shops beneath tenement flats. The signs and name plates – Feldman's buttonholes, Feigenbaum's provisions, Wonofsky's boot repairers, Lefcovitch's stationers – typified Cable Street's first half mile.[17] Most of the shopkeepers and residents on this stretch were Jewish. There were fewer Jewish businesses at the Limehouse end where names such as Kelly, O'Brien, Higgins and Sullivan adorned the shop-fronts. Fascists and anti-fascists had battled for the allegiance of the Irish community: the barometer of this struggle was Cable Street.

At the City end, shopkeepers pulled down their shutters. Anti-fascists built barricades. An overturned lorry filled the width of the street, buttressed by bedding and furniture. Members of

---

16 Interview with Binnie Yeates (née Yankovitch) by the author, in 2011, for the film, *From Cable Street to Brick Lane*, by Hazuan Hashim and Phil Maxwell.

17 Olive Lefcovitch who ran the stationery shop was the cousin of the author's grandfather.

Cable Street's Irish community and their local friends came to the Jewish end to help repel fascist interlopers. Dockers and railway workers carried crowbars to lift paving stones and reinforce the barricades. Labour League of Youth activist, Aubrey Morris, whose grandmother owned a bagel bakery in Cable Street, recalled the first wave of mounted police attempting to clear Cable Street being 'pelted from ground level with broken paving and cobble stones and from every window with missiles ranging from filled piss-pots to lumps of wood, rotten fruit and old bedding'. Women kept up this aerial barrage. 'As more police entered the fray,' Morris recalls, 'a large number of dockworkers . . . helped sustain the resistance.'[18]

By late afternoon the police conceded defeat. They ordered Mosley to turn round and disperse his followers. Mosley accused the government of surrendering to 'red and Jewish terror', but complied. Exuberant anti-fascists marched to Victoria Park Square, occupying a platform that local fascists had been protecting for their leader. At a meeting to mark the 75th anniversary of the battle, Cable Street veteran, Ubby Cowan, commented, 'The Home Secretary had said there could be a march, so we gave him one!'[19]

The words, 'They shall not pass!' (borrowed from the Spanish Republicans, simultaneously resisting Franco's forces) were chalked on pavements and barricades, whitewashed on walls, and chanted by anti-fascist demonstrators. Twenty-one-year-old Charlie Goodman was one of 79 anti-fascists arrested on 4 October: he received a custodial sentence. One of his prison experiences highlighted the clash between the conservative

---

18 A. Morris, *Unfinished Journey*, London: Artery, 2006, pp. 54–5.

19 Talk by Ubby Cowan at a Cable Street commemorative meeting at the Jewish Museum, London, October 2011. Cowan died in 2016.

Jewish establishment and rebellious East End Jews. Goodman recalled:

> I was visited by a Mr Prince from the Jewish Discharged Prisoners Aid society . . . an arm of the Board of Deputies [who] called all the Jewish prisoners together and asked 'What are you here for?' . . . one chap said: ' . . . I've been out of work, things have been bad . . . I went and did a bust (robbery).' Prince replied, 'Don't worry, we'll look after you.' The next five or six received the same response and then he came to me. 'What are you here for?' he asked. 'Fighting fascism,' I said. 'You!' said Prince. 'You are the kind of Jew who gives us a bad name . . . it is people like you that are causing all the aggravation to the Jewish people.'

Goodman became one of approximately 200 Eastenders whose experience in Cable Street impelled them to volunteer for the International Brigades to fight Spanish fascism. He returned from Spain wounded. At least 36 Eastenders never returned. In 1939, as the Second World War started, Goodman enlisted in the British army, but like other *brigadistas*, who had actually used weapons against fascists, he was given a menial role. He confided that his first 'action' in the war was punching his own superior officer for making an antisemitic remark.[20]

Despite their massive setback at Cable Street, the fascists saw the local elections of March 1937 as the opportunity to make their east London political breakthrough. They concentrated on their

---

20 C. Goodman, 'The East End Battles On', *Jewish Socialist*, Spring 1985; and informal conversations with the author, mid-1980s to early 1990s.

three strongest areas, Bethnal Green, Limehouse and Shoreditch, standing two candidates in each. They paired high-profile party ideologues with well-known local activists. The BUF local paper confidently announced: 'The March to Victory Begins'. They failed to win any seats. In Bethnal Green they took 23 per cent of the vote but, on average, across the three areas, four out of five voters rejected the fascists. Mosley accused Jews of block-voting Labour to defeat his candidates. But Jewish voters were concentrated in Whitechapel, and were relatively insignificant in the districts the BUF contested. Certainly the Jewish People's Council campaigned vigorously and influenced voters during the election, but it was overwhelmingly non-Jewish Eastenders who defeated Mosley at the ballot box.

In July 1937 the BUF applied for permission to march through Limehouse, but the Home Office refused.[21] When the fascists sought permission to march through the East End in October 1937, exactly a year after the Battle of Cable Street, they were again stymied after local organisations lobbied the new Home Secretary, Samuel Hoare. Undeterred, the *Blackshirt*'s newly appointed editor, A.K. Chesterton (cousin of the writer G.K. Chesterton) promised to invade 'unconquered' areas with propaganda, insisting that 'On October 3rd we shall march again.'

Still smarting with disbelief that East End Irish dockers had supported the Jews the previous year, Mosley selected another dockers' area – this time south of the Thames. The fascists announced a route from Parliament Square to New Kent Road, then through Tooley Street and Dockhead to an open-air rally at

---

21 They were granted permission to march that day from Kentish Town in north London to Trafalgar Square.

Mill Pool in West Lane, Bermondsey. Bermondsey's Communist Party immediately proposed a counter-march and won instant support from the local ILP. Bermondsey and Rotherhithe Trades Council, representing 60 local trade union branches, came on board and issued a belligerent anti-fascist statement:

> Mosley has no branch in Bermondsey – he represents no mass movement . . . This spot . . . is surrounded by the new flats erected by the Labour Council . . . a monument to Labour's magnificent record of social progress in the borough. It was as if he came to demolish these buildings brick by brick before the very eyes of the people who put them up.

Local political figures lobbied the Home Office to ban the march but the Home Secretary argued that, since very few Jews lived there, the threat to individuals was negligible. Local radicals, including the Trades Council, favoured a militant response but there were divisions on tactics. London's Labour Party Executive proposed a boycott, allowing the march to pass, ignored, through empty streets. A respected local churchman, Revd Leslie Davidson, Rotherhithe Labour MP Ben Smith, and the left-leaning *News Chronicle* supported this strategy. Smith told a large public meeting that Mosley's procession would happen anyway, but 'If we leave the route empty we will have achieved our object. We can have unity for a boycott but not for force.' His audience rebelled. The majority favoured direct confrontation to block Mosley's march. Over the next few days, several local Labour Party branches defied the London Labour Party Executive, declaring their support for a militant counter-protest.

The day before the march, the *Blackshirt* reserved its front page for Mosley's florid anniversary message:

> ... five years of advance in the face of money power, press power, party power and Jewish power ... during which the flame of the faith has grown within us until the blaze of our belief and of our determination lights the dark places of our land and summons our people as a beacon of hope and of rebirth.

The bombshell was tucked away inside the paper. The march route had been altered: the starting and finishing points were unchanged, but it would now pass through Marshalsea Road, Long Lane and Abbey Street, taking it through the heart of working-class Bermondsey. This development gave added impetus to those planning physically to prevent the fascists entering the area.

Mosley's supporters assembled near Millbank. Banned by the 1937 Public Order Act from wearing a political uniform, Mosley wore a grey jacket over his black shirt. Some 3,000 marchers formed up three abreast, convoyed by 30 mounted police at the front, and busloads of foot police bringing up the rear; 'one policeman for every fascist marcher', the *Daily Mirror* remarked.

Just as at Cable Street, thousands of anti-fascists constructed their own barricades with locally available materials. In Long Lane, protesters 'borrowed' a huge water tank from a nearby factory, which became the centre of a 30-foot-wide barricade. The *News Chronicle* reported: 'Iron ovens, cisterns and wheelbarrows were chained together and strung across roads.' The *Daily Herald* described how

[b]arricades of costers' barrows, fences with barbed wire, with red flags flying at the top, were flung up at incredible speed; when police tore them down, others were erected a few yards further on ... Mounted and foot police, with lashing batons, swept ... into the crowds of anti-fascist demonstrators ... Missiles were hurled from roofs: eggs, stones and fireworks were flung at the marchers and at police horses.

The *News Chronicle* described how mounted police 'charged down Staple Street into the crowd in Long Lane ... One man who was being taken away by the police after being struck on the head with a baton was rescued by a crowd of about 40 dockers.'

Faced with angry crowds and improvised barricades, the police diverted Mosley's troops from their chosen route and led them instead around the rim of the borough. The *Daily Worker* reported that, when they finally returned to their planned path and reached Jamaica Road, they 'met another barricade ... of men, women and children from the great flats that Labour has built in Bermondsey'. Banners hanging from these blocks proclaimed: 'Socialism builds. Fascism destroys. Bermondsey against fascism.'

Mosley never reached Mill Pool, where he had planned to address local people at an open-air rally. The police funnelled his marchers into Southwark Park Road and cordoned off local side streets, leaving Mosley speaking only to his marchers. Meanwhile, anti-fascists occupied Mill Pool, where a Communist Party speaker, Ted Bramley, said: 'The 100 per cent cockney borough of Bermondsey has given the same answer to Mosley as the Jewish lads and girls did in Stepney just twelve months ago.'

Bermondsey's protest involved smaller numbers than the East End in 1936, but the authorities' response was harsher. Several East End Jews were among 111 people arrested. Magistrate Campion commented, 'It is extraordinary how many of the population of Whitechapel and the East End seemed to choose Bermondsey for a Sunday afternoon walk.' Campion condemned the anti-fascist demonstrators for causing disorder and threatened to punish them 'vigorously'. At least 23 custodial sentences were imposed. Former dock union secretary, Frederick Thompson, aged 60, received three months after being identified at the centre of a 'violent crowd'; John Morton received five months for assault and three months for insulting behaviour after he tried to rescue another man who had been arrested. Betsy Malone, 23, was treated more lightly – fined a pound for taking a running kick at a policeman and telling him to arrest someone his own size!

The *Blackshirt* put its best gloss on a frustrating day, insisting that their marchers *did* pass despite the 'violence of the apes'. But the defeat at Bermondsey represented the last major street confrontation between the two rival rebel movements of 1930s London. After Bermondsey, Mosley's Blackshirts struggled to maintain their working-class base or make further inroads in the capital's poorer districts.

It is tempting to attribute the BUF's defeat in London to the superior street tactics used by the anti-fascists. Each major public show of fascist strength had been countered, especially in Hyde Park, Cable Street and Bermondsey. Mosley himself made many errors, starting with the Olympia fiasco. But an additional strategy, cementing these street victories and preventing the fascists from dividing Londoners along ethnic lines, was enacted in the housing sphere, especially in the East End. Here people lived in overcrowded, damp, dilapidated accommodation. They were at the mercy of private slum landlords, who evaded demands for rent controls, put off making repairs, but moved swiftly to evict families in arrears. Mosley's movement tried to convince non-Jewish tenants, especially those living in compact Irish communities, that Jews monopolised the best housing and best jobs locally, when, in truth, both peoples suffered. But impoverished communities rarely encountering each other directly were vulnerable to messages harnessing fear and envy.

The Stepney Tenants Defence League (STDL) was a broad-based, grassroots organisation started by communist activists, which began working on estates where Jews and non-Jews lived side by side. The STDL drew tenants together in joint campaigns to reduce rents, improve their estates, and defend those at risk of evictions. The movement mushroomed between 1937 and 1939, spreading to other East End districts. Two people from different backgrounds but sharing common values, who played key roles in the STDL, were Father John Groser and Phil Piratin.

Groser came from Australia but studied theology in Yorkshire. He worked in a slum parish of Newcastle, and then as an army chaplain during the First World War, during which he expressed the view that the war was caused by capitalism. He then spent two years working in Cornwall before taking a post at St Michael's Church, Poplar, in 1922. By then he had familiarised himself with Conrad Noel's Catholic Crusade for Social Justice, which aimed to create heaven on earth rather than painting heaven as the reward for a good life.[22] Groser, a Labour Party supporter, moved to Christ Church, in Watney Street, Stepney in 1929,

---

22 Noel was known as the 'Red Vicar' of Thaxted, where he lived from 1910 until his death in 1942.

as the economic depression was rendering life hell on earth for the poorest Eastenders. He helped congregants with their daily problems and encouraged them to fight for their rights. In 1932 he organised a conference on unemployment locally, and spoke of how unemployment caused physical depression, ill health, 'frustration of personality, the loss of proper self-respect' and created 'an embittered and hopeless section of the community'. People devoid of hope were ripe for receiving fascist messages that promised to restore their self-esteem.

Phil Piratin was born on Coke Street, Whitechapel, to Ukrainian Jewish immigrants. As an atheist and materialist, he focused on the same pressing problems. Piratin demonstrated outside Mosley's Olympia meeting in 1934, joining the Communist Party a week later. He struggled to understand how an aristocratic interloper such as Mosley got a hearing among poor Eastenders, but was convinced it was not simply by pushing antisemitism. He surreptitiously attended local fascist meetings and observed:

> There were certain latent antisemitic prejudices . . . but above all these people . . . [lived] miserable squalid lives. Their homes were slums. Many were unemployed. Those at work were often in low-paid jobs. We urged that the Communist Party should help the people to improve their conditions of life [so] we could show them who was really responsible for their conditions and get them organised to fight their real exploiters.[23]

---

23 P. Piratin, *Our Flag Stays Red*, London: Thames, 1948.

Groser and Piratin encountered each other through the STDL. Groser was its president from 1938. The STDL's main strategy was to hold meetings enabling tenants to identify their problems – usually hygiene and health issues, vermin, lighting, urgently needed repairs – then encourage collective campaigning. Where landlords would not respond to reasonable demands, the STDL initiated rent strikes. Tenants placed their rent weekly in the hands of a third party. The STDL informed the landlord that the rent was available to be collected when the repairs were done, hygiene was improved and so on. Several slum landlords refused to negotiate and tried to enforce evictions, but they met united resistance from their tenants. The STDL won a spate of victories,

Barricades in Cable Street, 4 October 1936.

including a landmark case in June 1937 on Paragon Mansions estate near Stepney Green, where STDL action prevented the eviction of two large families of BUF members who had fallen behind with their rent.[24] In the aftermath, those families tore up their BUF membership cards and the STDL leafleted residents of other estates to show what unity across boundaries of hate could achieve. As Jewish and non-Jewish neighbours built friendship and solidarity in the course of fighting for housing rights, it made fascist messages scapegoating Jews much less credible.

Halfway along Cable Street there is a remarkable artwork covering one side of a large building. The Cable Street mural, commissioned in 1976 and completed in the early 1980s, depicts the dramatic events of 4 October 1936 when Eastenders united against Mosley's fascist invaders. The location is very apt. West of the mural was the Jewish section of Cable Street; the east leads to the Irish end. On the day of the battle, people walked past this building from the Irish end, not to attack the Jews but to support them. The building was St George's Town Hall. In March 1939, it hosted a large conference addressed by Michael Shapiro and Ella Donovan, leading STDL activists of Jewish and Irish heritage respectively. Communities that could have been at each other's throats were discussing 'Better Housing for the East End' and planning a common future.

Shortly before this conference, two East End estates began simultaneous rent strikes through the STDL. One was Brady Street Mansions, an overwhelmingly Jewish estate in Whitechapel;[25] the other, Langdale Mansions, a more mixed estate closer to Cable

---

24 In Hayfield Passage. A gated community stands on the site today.

25 Max Levitas, who led the Brady Street Mansions rent strike died in November 2018 aged 103.

Street. Hampstead-based landlords, rejoicing in the names Craps and Gold, owned both estates. This became the STDL's longest running dispute, eventually resolved on 30 June 1939 after 21 weeks, during which the estates were barricaded with barbed wire and a constant rota of pickets guarded against incursions by bailiffs or police. Only residents could enter. Regular tradesmen and milkmen carried a special pass. The tenants won rent reductions; £10,000 of arrears were written off; the landlords agreed to spend £2,500 on repairs immediately and £1,500 annually in subsequent years.[26]

By then the BUF had become irrelevant in the East End. The 'people's victories' in Cable Street and Bermondsey in 1937 and the crucial work of the STDL had stopped Mosley from consolidating the populist movement he had tried to build among London's disadvantaged and disempowered. But he gradually recovered his middle-class following. Six weeks before war broke out, the BUF held an anti-war rally in Earls Court attended by 20,000 supporters. When an audience member asked Mosley what his party would do if Britain was attacked by fascist Germany, Mosley replied that if Britain was attacked by *anyone*, every BUF member would defend Britain, but, he added, 'a million Britons shall not die in your Jews' quarrel'. During the war Mosley was among nearly 1,800 individuals imprisoned as potential fifth columnists. His nemesis, the communist movement, continued to grow, despite wartime restrictions. A radical, reforming, Labour government elected in 1945 brought real material gains for working-class Londoners, proving, as Bermondsey's banners proclaimed, that while fascism destroys, socialism builds.

---

26 £2,500 was equivalent to nearly £150,000 today.

ALDGATE EAST

① WHITECHAPEL HIGH STREET

ALIE STREET

LEMAN STREET

② ALTAB ALI PARK

MULBERRY STREET

ADLER STREET

COMMERCIAL ROAD

③

COKE STREET

PLUMBERS ROW

FIELDGATE STREET

④

⑤

GREENFIELD ROAD

⑥

TOWER HAMLETS INTERNATIONAL BRIGADE

in honour of the volunteers and the Tower Hamlets
to fight in the International Brigade Spain 1936 - 1938
They fought alongside the Spanish people to
stop Fascism and save world democracy for all
They went because their hurt ached for no other way
No Pasaran !

CHRISTIAN STREET

BURSLEM STREET

HESSEL ST E1

PONLER STREET

CABLE STREET

⑦

HESSEL STREET

COMMERCIAL ROAD

⑧

LANGDALE STREET

CANNON STREET ROAD

⑨

CABLE STREET

⑩ ST GEORGE'S GARDENS

100M

354

WALK

Start at Whitechapel Art Gallery (Aldgate East station), E1 7QX.

1. Whitechapel High Street/Gardiners Corner

The Aldgate Place development (across the road and to your right at the corner with Leman Street) with luxury penthouses and an onsite fitness suite stands roughly on the site of Gardiners department store, which closed in 1971 and collapsed in a fire a year later. Here the City and East End thoroughfares meet. This was completely blockaded on 4 October 1936, preventing the police from clearing a path for Mosley's fascists. Turn left and cross over to Altab Ali Park.

2. Altab Ali Park

St Mary's Gardens was renamed Altab Ali Park in 1998, to commemorate a 24-year-old Bengali clothing worker killed in a racist attack in May 1978 by youths influenced by the National Front, political descendants of Mosley's Blackshirts. The 80th anniversary commemoration of the Battle of Cable Street began with a rally in this park before marching to Cable Street. Walk through the park and turn right to St Boniface's Church.

3. Mulberry Street

The original German church standing here was bombed by the Nazis and rebuilt in the 1960s. Germans were one of several minorities living in the East End. Walk down Mulberry Street, turn left, then right into Fieldgate Street.

4. Fieldgate Street

The lettering of a former synagogue opened in 1899, closed in 2013, is visible on the left. It began as a *shtibel* (prayer room in a house), one of dozens in the area through which Mosley wanted to march. Three Ashkenazi Synagogues still function in the East End plus one Sephardi synagogue on the East End/ City Border.[27] At 15 Fieldgate Street, the Communist Party had local headquarters. Rowton House on the left (now luxury apartments) was a former doss-house in which Stalin and Maxim Litvinov stayed during part of the 1907 Congress of the Russian revolutionary movement. Turn into Greenfield Street. Walk to the junction with Coke Street.

5. Greenfield Street

Phil Piratin, who joined the Communist Party after demonstrating outside the fascists' Olympia meeting, grew up on Coke Street then Greenfield Road (Street). Chief architect of the communists' anti-fascist strategy, he was a key figure in the Stepney Tenants Defence League. Turn left at Commercial Road.

6. Commercial Road

The Jewish People's Council Against Fascism and Antisemitism (JPC) was created at a conference in July 1936 at 46 Commercial Road. The JPC opened an office at 164 Commercial Road. The building with a decorative arch above the door at 133 was formerly the Grand Palais Yiddish Theatre, which closed in 1961. Turn right into Hessel Street.

---

27 *Ashkenazi* refers to Jewish communities from western, central and eastern Europe; *Sephardi*, to communities that were established over several centuries in Spain and Portugal before being expelled in 1492.

7. Hessel Street

Named after Phoebe Hessel, born Phoebe Smith in Stepney in 1713. She disguised herself as a man to serve in the army. She is also commemorated by a turning off Hessel Street called Amazon Street. Hessel Street was one of the main Jewish market streets of the East End in the 1920s and 1930s. Cross Burslem Street into Langdale Street.

8. Langdale Street

Just to the right was Langdale Mansions where Jewish and non-Jewish tenants united in a successful rent strike lasting 21 weeks in 1939. That unity was typified by the family of rent-strike leader Frank Whipple, born into a Catholic family in Cork and married to a Jewish banjo player and tap dancer, Lily Kosky. The photographer and artist Hester Mallin, who died in 2018, grew up on this estate. Continue to the junction with Ponler Street. Turn left along Ponler Street then right into Cannon Street Road. Continue to the crossroad with Cable Street.

9. Cable Street

Look rightwards. Between these traffic lights on Cable Street and those at Leman Street, three sets of barricades blocked the fascists from marching through Cable Street. Turn left and cross to the Cable Street mural, depicting the events of 4 October 1936, on the side of St George's Town Hall. The mural, designed by Dave Binnington, was adapted and completed by three artists including Paul Butler, who restored it in 2011. The gardens behind the Town Hall hosted the closing rally of the 80th anniversary commemoration of the Battle of Cable Street. The speakers included a battle veteran, Max Levitas, then 101.

10. St George's Town Hall

This building hosted the Better Housing for Stepney conference in March 1939. A small plaque on the right-hand side of the building commemorates East End volunteers who went to fight against fascism in Spain. The text of the plaque ends with a quote: 'They went because their open eyes could see no other way', which is taken from Cecil Day Lewis's poem 'The Volunteer – an ode to the International Brigade'.

Detail from Cable Street mural.

CONCLUSION

In March 2011, I stood in front of the Cable Street mural interviewing Paul Butler, one of the three artists who completed it in 1983. He was looking forward to spending the summer restoring the mural in time for the Battle's 75th anniversary celebrations in October that year.

The mural is a startling, disturbing and exciting piece of work which shows missiles, bottles and fists flying, truncheons drawn, marbles ready to be rolled under the hooves of police horses, while the fascists wait for their opportunity to march. Butler assured me 'it is not a celebration of violence'. It 'celebrates the barricade, the slogan from the Spanish civil war, "they shall not pass" . . . [and] the left's solidarity – the mix of Irish dockers and Jewish workers and all the other groups involved in the Battle . . . it was painted for the local community to celebrate this place', but it was also 'a monument that transcended . . . [the] local aspect'. Anti-fascists from far and wide continue to visit it.

Compared with several of the rebellious campaigns recorded in this book, the community uprising against the police, who were facilitating Mosley's fascists that day, is privileged by having a large, permanent, public reminder of what took place, as well as a local committee which organises commemorative events every five or 10 years, including meetings, marches and community festivals. In 2016, the eightieth anniversary, more than 2,000 people marched from Altab Ali Park on Whitechapel Road, a park named after a Bengali victim of a racist murder in 1978, to St George's Gardens, which houses the Cable Street mural. Just behind the banner of Cable Street 80, made for this occasion, the banners of Jewish and Irish socialists and the Communist Party were held proudly aloft, reflecting and recreating the alliance of 1936. They were followed by the banners of Bengali organisations recalling their role in fighting the racists and fascists who re-emerged in the area in the 1970s.

Murals celebrating London's radical history are few and far between. The walk accompanying Chapter 7 includes the 'Battersea in Perspective' mural, which celebrates local heroes, of whom four are intimately connected with its radical history. In Copenhagen Street, Islington, a mural alongside the former Mitre pub (converted since for residential use) commemorates the huge 1834 march that started nearby, demanding freedom for the Tolpuddle Martyrs. A striking new mural celebrating Sylvia Pankhurst and east London suffragettes was unveiled in early 2018. Two Poplar radicals, George Lansbury and the suffragette activist and rebel councillor Minnie Lansbury (Glassman), are commemorated through large rectangular plaques at separate locations on Bow Road, which detail their political involvements. Other rebels featured in this book, though, are remembered with small circular plaques which in most cases obscure or dilute their political radicalism.

Several local authorities in London now have plaques commemorating events. At the Highbury Barn pub in Islington in 2011, the late Tony Benn unveiled a plaque marking the Peasants' Revolt of 1381, during which they burnt down Highbury Manor House. It would seem fitting to mount a plaque at the former site of Gardiners Corner in Aldgate, where a mass blockade prevented the fascists from entering the East End in 1936 and forced the police to try, unsuccessfully, to reroute the march via

Cable Street. But where could such a plaque be meaningfully mounted when the corner itself is monopolised by glass towers providing luxury flats and plush City offices?

Those who seek to illuminate the city's rebellious past and put it into a conversation with the present, so that the rebels of today and tomorrow can draw encouragement and inspiration from earlier struggles on these streets, are challenged by the speed with which areas of London are being transformed, made more exclusive, and severed from their past. I hope that this book will help that conversation to take place.

The campaigns this book highlights reflect rebellions in London between the 1790s and the 1930s against different targets: political and economic elites ring-fencing democratic rights; traditional sources of authority and moral leadership such as the churches; large employers of labour in gasworks and on the docks, as well as smaller employers exploiting sweatshop labour; and those who have sought to divide workers on racist lines. We can detect similarities in the tactics adopted to wage these struggles, recognise how one struggle influenced another, and attempt to identify common qualities among those outstanding individuals so prominent within these campaigns.

Several of these individuals had to struggle to overcome personal challenges before thrusting themselves into radical politics. Will Thorne and Ben Tillett, leading figures in industrial struggles of the1880s, both knew the hardship of long hours of work when they were six and seven years old respectively. Their colleague Tom Mann at least had the benefit of three years of education from the age of six, but was down a pit at ten. Rudolf Rocker, the anarchist/libertarian agitator and champion of the East End's immigrant sweatshop workers, had fought against an authoritarian regime that pervaded the orphanage in which he was confined after his parents died young. The suffragette Rosa May Billinghurst and the Chartist William Cuffay both fought against disability from their earliest years. George Lansbury endured a torrid time in his early twenties in Australia where he had been lured with promises of economic advancement. Long stretches of unemployment were interrupted by periods of work on the land where he compared his treatment to that of a serf.

Each of these individuals displayed great personal resilience that supported their efforts to effect change for the many among whom they organised. They were 'dreadnoughts' in the sense that the East London Federation of Suffragettes identified – people who feared nothing. They were prepared to take risks for what they considered to be right, and face the consequences, including imprisonment. And some paid the ultimate price for their activism. Minnie Lansbury died at 32, within months of having endured harsh conditions in prison. Emily Wilding Davison was just 40 in 1913, when she never regained consciousness after her Derby Day protest. Mary Macarthur, a hugely energetic organiser of women workers who, according to her colleagues, had 'the heart of a lion', died at 40, two years after her husband and eight years after her stillborn son.

Several individuals featured in this book supported multiple struggles during years of campaigning. Charlotte Despard fought against poverty in Battersea, supported women strikers, and led campaigns for women's votes and equal opportunities through the Women's Freedom League. George Lansbury helped mobilise support for the dock strike, promoted the suffragette cause, and fought as a councillor against discriminatory rates policies imposed by the London County Council. Nellie

Cressall and Minnie Lansbury were both active campaigners in the east London suffragettes before they ended up imprisoned as rebel Poplar councillors. Ben Tillett was a key organiser in the dock strike and later played an active role in establishing the *Daily Herald* newspaper. Israel Zangwill was active in the Men's League for Women's Suffrage and later in the pacifist Union of Democratic Control. However, that probably tells us as much about the linked nature of the struggles themselves as it does about the individuals who participated in them.

Campaigns linked thematically over gaps of several decades honoured the influences of previous generations of fighters. The Chartists of the 1830s, the Reform League of the 1860s and 1870s and the suffragettes in the first two decades of the twentieth century led London's assault on the exclusive access to institutions of political power maintained by elites. When the suffragettes adopted the purple, green and white tricolour, they consciously adopted a symbol previously used by the Chartists.[1] At the gigantic suffragette rally in Hyde Park in 1908, speakers recalled the dramatic Reform League demonstrations of the 1860s in the very same park.

Peter Kropotkin, a Russian political exile who settled in London in 1886, argued that, 'Without mutual confidence no struggle is possible.'[2] His observation was borne out by the rebellious campaigns that have been recorded in this book. Although grassroots movements threw up extraordinary leaders, it was these movements' shared sense that change could be won, and their ability to engage in united collective actions, based on mutual confidence, especially in workplace struggles, that

---

1   Chartists also carried red, green and white flags.

2   P. Kropotkin, *Anarchist Morality*, Edmonton: Black Cat Press, 2005 (1897).

enabled them to sustain their campaigns and win important victories. The methods they shared – leaflets, petitions, newspapers, strikes, mass demonstrations and rallies and, where it was felt necessary, physical force – were geared towards collective rather than individual actions.

The suffragettes were one of London's most successful rebel movements but pose the biggest challenge to our understanding of how change is brought about. Their movement did not pass Kropotkin's 'mutual confidence' test. It was far from united. The Women's Freedom League (WFL) split from the dominant Women's Social and Political Union (WSPU), and the East London Federation of Suffragettes (ELFS) were forced out. The more long-standing campaigners of the National Union of Women's Suffrage Societies (NUWSS) disagreed with WSPU tactics and remained aloof from them, as did many leading women who were trade union activists, suspicious of the WSPU's willingness to accept partial suffrage that would maintain class distinctions.

The WSPU can claim to be fearless and courageous tactical innovators – adding hunger strikes, stone-throwing and arson attacks to the range of militant activities adopted by London's rebel campaigns – although these tactics also symbolised a move away from collective action. Other sectors of the suffrage movement maintained collective approaches and introduced their own non-violent forms of civil disobedience such as the refusal to pay taxes, the deliberate disruption of the census, and rallies on the doorsteps of government ministers' homes. Paradoxically, the divided and devolved nature of the movement meant that the suffragettes' opponents were continually challenged from many different angles. But, more pertinently, dominant suffragette histories need to give more credit to those who adopted less flamboyant, less sensational, but more sustained collective actions.

The poet and writer Anthony Anaxagorou, born in north London in 1983, has said: 'Rebellion is when you look society in the face and say I understand who you want me to be, but I'm going to show you who I actually am.' He captures the spirit of defiance, the refusal to accept second-class status, and the drive for change that has animated movements for better lives in London over the last 200 years. Throughout that period, London has continued to nurture rebels and agitators, visionaries and dreamers. Their impact has been felt in every decade. Dreams have been crushed, hopes have been dashed, campaigns were won and lost and fought for all over again, and new activists have emerged.

But Anaxagorou, as the son of Cypriot migrants to London, also embodies a crucial element that dominant narratives have pushed to the margins. Migrants have played a key role in several of the movements that have shaped London's rebel history, from freed black slave Catharine Despard, who campaigned for prisoners' rights, and William Cuffay, the black leader of London's Chartist movement in the 1840s, son of a Caribbean slave, to the women and men of Irish heritage whose strikes at Bryant & May's match factory and on the docks ignited the new unionism. From the early Indian MPs, Dadabhai Naoroji and Shapurji Saklatvala, and Battersea's first black mayor, John Archer, who overcame entrenched racist attitudes to win popular support across communities, to the Jewish workers who fought for their rights in sweatshops and battled against Mosley's fascists, immigrants have been vital in the struggle to improve conditions for all Londoners.

A vignette in Chapter 2 described those sweatshop workers marching from the East End to Hyde Park singing a Yiddish anthem, 'In Kamf'. Its closing stanza includes the line: '*Nayer kemfer vet brengen di tsayt*', which means 'new fighters/activists will be brought by the [new] times'. In 1983 and 1984, activity in London's financial district was brought to a halt by Stop the City blockades. In 1991, Trafalgar Square, location of the Bloody Sunday protests and of many political rallies since, was filled with gay and lesbian activists who staged a mass queer wedding ceremony. A few years later the authorities, who kept a tight rein on protests around government buildings, were outwitted by guerrilla gardeners who mounted Winston Churchill's statue and gave him a bright green mohican. In June 2011, as the Occupy movement made its presence felt in cities around the world, activists pitched a tent city outside St Paul's Cathedral. It was finally evicted in February 2012. That same connection with global politics saw nearly 100,000 women brave the cold to march from the American Embassy in Grosvenor Square to Trafalgar Square in January 2017, the day after Donald Trump's presidential inauguration, in a glorious carnival of protest where home-made placards bearing slogans such as 'Feminism: back by popular demand', 'Girls just want to have FUN-damental human rights' and 'Disobedient women of the world unite' heavily outnumbered the branded placards of organisations hoping to stamp their leadership on the protest.

Away from the centre, young people in black communities led uprisings against the police and set shops and cars on fire in Brixton and Broadwater Farm, Tottenham in the 1980s, and again in Tottenham in 2011, following the police shooting of Mark Duggan. The participants in 2011 were a more ethnically diverse group of impoverished lower classes in the locality, including white people. Back in the heart of the City, in 2013, migrant cleaners at the Barbican, Guildhall and across Corporation of London buildings won the living wage after a two-year battle involving strike action organised through the radical Independent Workers Union of Great Britain (IWGB).

London remains a vibrant and rebellious city, and we should honour those who had the courage, conviction and determination to blaze the trail.

BIBLIOGRAPHY

Ahmed, R. and S. Mukherjee (eds), *South Asian Resistances in Britain*, London: Continuum, 2012

Beames, T., *The Rookeries of London*, London: Thomas Bosworth, 1850

Besant, A., *Annie Besant: An Autobiography*, London: Theosophical Society, 1893

Booth, J., *Guilty and Proud of It*, London: Merlin, 2009

Branson, N., *Poplarism 1919–1925*, London: Lawrence & Wishart, 1979

Briggs, J., *A woman of Passion: the life of E. Nesbit*, London: Penguin, 1989

Brockway, F., *Bermondsey Story: The Life of Alfred Salter*, London: ILP, 1995 (1949)

Brust, H., *I Guarded Kings: Memoirs of a Political Police Officer*, New York: Hillman-Curl, 1936

Charlton, J., *It Went Just Like Tinder*, London: Redwords, 1999

Connelly, K., *Sylvia Pankhurst*, London: Pluto Press, 2013

Davis, M., *Sylvia Pankhurst: A Life in Radical Politics*, London: Pluto Press, 1999

Despard, C., *Women in the New Era*, London: Suffrage Shop, 1910

Fishman, W., *East End Jewish Radicals 1875–1914*, London: Duckworth, 1975

—— *East End 1888*, London: Duckworth, 1988

Fryer, P., *Staying Power: The History of Black People in Britain*, London: Pluto Press, 1984

German, L. and J. Rees, *A People's History of London*, London: Verso, 2012

Gissing, G., *The Nether World*, London: Smith, Elder & Co., 1889

Goldman, E., *Living My Life, Vol. 1*, London: Pluto Press, 1988 (1931)

Goodway, D., *London Chartism 1838–1848*, Cambridge: Cambridge University Press, 1982

Gorgut, O., *Strange Confused Tumults of the Minde: Wanderings in the past, present and future of radical pamphleteering*, London, Past Tense, 2014

Jacobs, J., *Out of the Ghetto*, London: J. Simon, 1978

James, C.L.R., *Letters from London*, Oxford: Signal Books, 2006

Kapp, Y., *Eleanor Marx: The Crowded Years 1884–1898*, London: Virago, 1979 (1976)

Kitz, F., *Recollections and Reflections*, London: Freedom Press, 1912

Kropotkin, P., *Anarchist Morality*, Edmonton: Black Cat Press , 2005 (1897)

Laity, P., *The British Peace Movement 1870–1914*, Oxford: Clarendon Press, 2002

Lansbury, G., *My Life*, London: Constable and Co., 1928

—— *Looking Backwards and Forwards*, London: Blackie, 1935

Lapides, K., (ed) *Marx and Engels on the Trade Unions*, New York: Praeger, 1987

Linehan, T., *East London for Mosley*, London: Frank Cass, 1996

Lovett, W., *Life and Struggles of William Lovett in His Pursuit of Bread, Knowledge, and Freedom*, New York: A. A. Knopf, 1920 (1877)

Mackay, J. H., *The Anarchists*, Boston: Benj R. Tucker, 1891

Mayhew, H., London Labour and the London Poor, Vol 3, Oxford: OUP, 2010 (1861-62)

Marcus, J., *Suffrage and the Pankhursts*, London: Routledge & Kegan Paul, 2005

McCarthy, T., *The Great Dock Strike 1889*, London: Weidenfeld and Nicholson, 1988

Montefiore, D., *From a Victorian to a Modern*, London: Archer, 1927

Morris, A., *Unfinished Journey*, London: Artery, 2006

Mulvihill, M., *Charlotte Despard: A Biography*, London: Pandora, 1989

Pankhurst, S., *The Suffragette Movement*, London: Virago, 1977 (1931)

Paine, T., *The Rights of Man*, London: 1791 (part 1), 1792 (part 2)

Piratin, P., *Our Flag Stays Red*, London: Thames, 1948

Pugh, M., *The Pankhursts*, London: Penguin, 2002

Radice, E.A. and G.H. Radice, *Will Thorne: Constructive Militant*, London: Allen & Unwin, 1974

Raw, L., *Striking a Light: The Bryant and May Matchwomen and Their Place in History*, London: Continuum, 2009

Rocker, R., *The London Years*, Nottingham: Five Leaves/AK Press, 2005 (1956)

Rosen, A., *Rise Up Women!*, London: Routledge & Kegan Paul, 1974

Rosenberg, D., *Battle for the East End*, Nottingham: Five Leaves, 2011

Rudder, B., *Builders of the Borough*, London: Battersea & Wandsworth TUC, 1994

Russell, D. and M. Tichelar, *Class Struggles in South London 1850–1950*, London: Southwark-Lambeth History Workshop, 1981

Saklatvala, S. (Sehri), *The Fifth Commandment*, Manchester: Miranda Press, 1991

Srebrnik, H., *London Jews and British Communism 1935–45*, London: Vallentine Mitchell, 1995

Sugden, K. (ed.), *Criminal Islington*, London: Islington Archaeology & History Society, 1989

Taylor, G., *Ada Salter: Pioneer of Ethical Socialism*, London: Lawrence and Wishart, 2016

Taylor, R., *In Letters of Gold*, London: Stepney Books, 1993

Thale , M. (ed)., *Selections from the Papers of the London Corresponding Society*, London: 1983

Thompson, D., *The Early Chartists*, London: Macmillan, 1971

Thornbury, W., *Old and New London*, Vol ll, London: Cassell & Co, 1879

Thorne, W., *My Life's Battles*, London: G. Newnes, 1925

Visram, R., *Ayahs, Lascars and Princes*, London: Pluto Press, 1986

Wadsworth, M., *Comrade Sak: A Political Biography*, Leeds: Peepal Tree, 1998

Wayne, L., *Union Bread*, London: Jewish Socialists' Group and Socialist History Society, 2009

White, J., *The Rothschild Buildings*, London: Routledge & Kegan Paul, 1980

—— *London in the Nineteenth Century*, London: Jonathan Cape, 2007

Wise, S., *The Blackest Streets*, London: Bodley Head, 2008

Wohl, A., *The Eternal Slum*, Cambridge: CUP, 1977

Wollstonecraft, M., *A Vindication of the Rights of Woman*, London, 1792

INDEX

ABOUT THE AUTHOR

David Rosenberg is an educator, writer and tour guide, and author of *Battle for the East End* (2011). He has written on history and current affairs for several online and print publications, including the *Guardian*, *TES*, *Morning Star*, *New Statesman*, *Red Pepper*, *Third Sector*, and the Channel 4 website. Since 2007, he has led tours of key sites in London's social and political history, especially in London's East End, and teaches about London's radical history through the City Lit, the Bishopsgate Institute and Conway Hall. He is a founder member of History from Below, an informal international network of activists, artists, archivists and political archaeologists.